P9-DBM-744

Learning Perl

Commands

Exit Expression, when Expression is omitted, exits
  with 0 status.
    0 for success ⎤ only *recognized values for
    1 for error   ⎦   Expression.
                     universally

BSC

Learning Perl

Third Edition

Randal L. Schwartz and Tom Phoenix

O'REILLY®

Beijing · Cambridge · Farnham · Köln · Paris · Sebastopol · Taipei · Tokyo

Learning Perl, Third Edition

by Randal L. Schwartz and Tom Phoenix

Copyright © 2001, 1997, 1993 O'Reilly & Associates, Inc. All rights reserved.
Printed in the United States of America.

Published by O'Reilly & Associates, Inc., 101 Morris Street, Sebastopol, CA 95472.

Editor: Linda Mui

Production Editors: Sarah Jane Shangraw and Ann Schirmer

Cover Designer: Edie Freedman

Printing History:

November 1993:	First Edition.
July 1997:	Second Edition.
July 2001:	Third Edition.

Nutshell Handbook, the Nutshell Handbook logo, and the O'Reilly logo are registered
trademarks of O'Reilly & Associates, Inc. Many of the designations used by manufacturers and
sellers to distinguish their products are claimed as trademarks. Where those designations
appear in this book, and O'Reilly & Associates, Inc. was aware of a trademark claim, the
designations have been printed in caps or initial caps. The association between the image of
a llama and Perl is a trademark of O'Reilly & Associates, Inc.

While every precaution has been taken in the preparation of this book, the publisher assumes
no responsibility for errors or omissions, or for damages resulting from the use of the
information contained herein.

Library of Congress Cataloging-in-Publication Data

Schwartz, Randal L.
    Learning Perl / Randal L. Schwartz and Tom Phoenix.—3rd ed.
        p. cm.
    Includes index.
    ISBN 0-596-00132-0
    1. Perl (Computer program language) I. Phoenix, Tom. II. Title.

QA76.73.P22 S37 2001
005.13'3—dc21   2001033909

[M]

Table of Contents

Preface

Welcome to the third edition of *Learning Perl*.

If you're looking for the best way to spend your first 30 to 45 hours with the Perl programming language, look no further. In the pages that follow, you'll find a carefully paced introduction to the language that remains the workhorse of the Internet, as well as the language of choice for system administrators, web hackers, and casual programmers around the world.

We can't give you all of Perl in just a few hours. The books that promise that are probably fibbing a bit. Instead, we've carefully selected a complete and useful subset of Perl for you to learn, good for programs from one to 128 lines long, which end up being about 90% of the programs in use out there. And when you're ready to go on, we've included a number of pointers for further education.

Each chapter is small enough to be read in an hour or two. Each chapter ends with a series of exercises to help you practice what you've just learned, with the answers in Appendix A for your reference. Thus, this book is ideally suited for a classroom "introduction to Perl" course. We know this directly, because the material for this book was lifted almost word-for-word from our flagship "Learning Perl" course, delivered to thousands of students around the world. However, we've designed the book for self-study as well.

Although Perl lives as the "toolbox for Unix," you don't have to be a Unix guru, or even a Unix user, to use this book. Unless otherwise noted, everything we're saying applies equally well to Windows ActivePerl from ActiveState, as well as to the later releases of MacPerl for the Macintosh and pretty much every other modern implementation of Perl.

Although you don't need to know a single bit about Perl to begin reading this book, we do recommend that you already have familiarity with basic programming concepts such as variables, loops, subroutines, and arrays, and the all-important "editing a source code file with your favorite text editor." We won't spend any time trying to explain those concepts. Although we're pleased that we've had many reports of people successfully picking up *Learning Perl* and grasping Perl as their first programming language, of course we can't promise the same results for everyone.

Typographical Conventions

The following font conventions are used in this book:

`Constant width`
> is used for method names, function names, variables, and attributes. It is also used for code examples.

`Constant width bold`
> is used to indicate user input.

`Constant width italic`
> is used to indicate a replaceable item in code (e.g., `filename`, where you are supposed to substitute an actual filename).

Italic
> is used for filenames, URLs, hostnames, commands in text, important words on first mention, and emphasis.

Footnotes
> are used to attach parenthetical notes that you *should not* read on your first (or perhaps second or third) reading of this book. Sometimes lies are spoken to simplify the presentation, and the footnotes restore the lie to truth. Often the material in the footnote will be advanced material not even discussed anywhere else in the book.

How to Contact Us

We have tested and verified all the information in this book to the best of our abilities, but you may find that features have changed or that we have let errors slip through the production of the book. Please let us know of any errors that you find, as well as suggestions for future editions, by writing to:

O'Reilly & Associates, Inc.
101 Morris St.
Sebastopol, CA 95472
1-800-998-9938 (in the U.S. or Canada)
1-707-829-0515 (international/local)
1-707-829-0104 (fax)

You can also send messages electronically. To be put on our mailing list or to request a catalog, send email to:

> *info@oreilly.com*

To ask technical questions or to comment on the book, send email to:

> *bookquestions@oreilly.com*

We have a web site for the book, where we'll list examples, errata, and any plans for future editions. It also offers a downloadable set of text files (and a couple of Perl programs) which are useful, but not required, when doing some of the exercises. You can access this page at:

> *http://www.oreilly.com/catalog/lperl/*

For more information about this book and others, see the O'Reilly web site:

> *http://www.oreilly.com*

Code Examples

You are invited to copy the code in the book and adapt it for your own needs. Rather than copying by hand, however, we encourage you to download the code from *http://www.oreilly.com/catalog/lperl/*.

History of This Book

For the curious, here's how Randal tells the story of how this book came about:

After I had finished the first *Programming Perl* book with Larry Wall (in 1991), I was approached by Taos Mountain Software in Silicon Valley to produce a training course. This included having me deliver the first dozen or so courses and train their staff to continue offering the course. I wrote the course for them* and delivered it for them as promised.

On the third or fourth delivery of that course (in late 1991), someone came up to me and said, "you know, I really like *Programming Perl*, but the way the material is presented in this course is so much easier to follow—you oughta write a book like this course." It sounded like an opportunity to me, so I started thinking about it.

I wrote to Tim O'Reilly with a proposal based on an outline that was similar to the course I was presenting for Taos—although I had rearranged and modified a few

---

* In the contract, I retained the rights to the exercises, hoping someday to reuse them in some other way, like in the magazine columns I was writing at the time. The exercises are the only things that lept from the Taos course to the book.

of the chapters based on observations in the classroom. I think that was my fastest proposal acceptance in history—I got a message from Tim within fifteen minutes saying "we've been waiting for you to pitch a second book—*Programming Perl* is selling like gangbusters." That started the effort over the next eighteen months to finish the first edition of *Learning Perl*.

During that time, I was starting to see an opportunity to teach Perl classes outside Silicon Valley*, so I created a class based on the text I was writing for *Learning Perl*. I gave a dozen classes for various clients (including my primary contractor, Intel Oregon), and used the feedback to fine-tune the book draft even further.

The first edition hit the streets on the first day of November, 1993† and became a smashing success, frequently even outpacing *Programming Perl* book sales.

The back-cover jacket of the first book said "written by a leading Perl trainer." Well, that became a self-fulfilling prophesy. Within a few months, I was starting to get email from all over the United States from people asking to have me teach at their site. In the following seven years, my company became the leading world-wide on-site Perl training company, and I had personally racked up (literally) a million frequent-flier miles. It didn't hurt that the Web started taking off about then, and the webmasters and webmistresses picked Perl as the language of choice for content management, interaction through CGI, and maintenance.

For the past two years, I've been working closely with Tom Phoenix in his role as lead trainer and content manager for Stonehenge, giving him charter to experiment with the "Llama" course by moving things around and breaking things up. When we had come up with what we thought was the best major revision of the course, I contacted O'Reilly and said "it's time for a new book!" And now you're reading it.

Some of the differences you may notice from prior editions:

- The text is completely new. Rather than simply copy-and-paste from previous editions, we have derived the text from our Stonehenge "Learning Perl" courseware and the instructor notes we've created and road-tested. (Some of the exercises are similar to the originals simply because we were using the prior editions as our textbook until recently. But even those have mutated during the rewrites.)

- We've broken the hard-to-swallow-all-at-once regular expressions section into three easily digestible sections.

---

* My Taos contract had a no-compete clause, so I had to stay out of Silicon Valley with any similar courses, which I respected for many years.

† I remember that date very well, because it was also the day I was arrested at my home for computer-related-activities around my Intel contract, a series of felony charges for which I was later convicted. The appeals battle continues—see *http://www.lightlink.com/fors/* for details.

- We've created exercises with both Unix and Windows in mind.

- We got rid of the artificial "control structures" chapter, moving the `while` and `if` statement earlier, and the `foreach` and `for` loops later. This gives us more useful examples and exercises for the scalars chapter, for example.

- We moved subroutines much earlier to permit subsequent exercises to use subroutines for the questions and answers.

- We now teach element syntax before the aggregate syntax for both arrays and hashes. This has worked a bit of a miracle in the classrooms, since it nearly always keeps beginners from the all-too-common mistake of writing a slice where they mean an element. At the risk of hubris, we'll admit that we expect other Perl instructors and books to follow our lead here.

- The exercises are more real-world and better paced.

- We've included information on `use strict`, warnings, and modules, although mostly as pointers for further information.

- We've made the book much less addressed to the Unix system administrator, and much more to the general programmer. The phrase "like C" has been nearly completely eliminated.

- The jokes are better. (We're constantly improvising jokes in the classroom, and some of these end up as part of the standard Stonehenge script. The best of *those* ended up here. You should see what didn't make the cut!)

- We deeply regret that this edition lacks the wonderfully witty Foreword, written by Larry Wall, who was busy defining Perl 6 as we went to press. Larry is always supportive of our efforts, and we know that he's still part of the book in spirit, if not in word, to wish you the best as you start your holiday in the lustrous land of Perl.

Acknowledgments

From Randal. I want to thank the Stonehenge trainers past and present (Joseph Hall, Tom Phoenix, Chip Salzenberg, brian d foy, and Tad McClellan) for their willingness to go out and teach in front of classrooms week after week and to come back with their notes about what's working (and what's not) so we could fine-tune the material for this book. I especially want to single out my co-author and business associate, Tom Phoenix, for having spent many, many hours working to improve Stonehenge's Llama course and to provide the wonderful core text for most of this book.

I also want to thank everyone at O'Reilly, especially our very encouraging and patient editor, Linda Mui, and Tim O'Reilly himself for taking a chance on me in the first place with the Camel and Llama books.

I am also absolutely indebted to the thousands of people who have purchased the past editions of the Llama so that I could use the money to stay "off the streets and out of jail," and to those students in my classrooms who have trained me to be a better trainer, and to the stunning array of Fortune 1000 clients who have purchased our classes in the past and will continue to do so into the future.

As always, a special thanks to Lyle and Jack, for teaching me nearly everything I know about writing. I won't ever forget you guys.

From Tom. I've got to echo Randal's thanks to our editor, Linda Mui, for her patience in pointing out which jokes and footnotes were most excessive, while pointing out that she is in no way to blame for the ones that remain. Both she and Randal have guided me through the process of writing, and I am grateful.

And another echo with regard to Randal and the other Stonehenge trainers, who hardly ever complained when I unexpectedly updated the course materials to try out a new teaching technique. You folks have contributed many different viewpoints on teaching methods that I would never have seen.

For many years, I worked at the Oregon Museum of Science and Industry (OMSI), and I'd like to thank the folks there for letting me hone my teaching skills as I learned to build a joke or two into every activity, explosion, or dissection.

To the many folks on Usenet who have given me your appreciation and encouragement for my contributions there, thanks. As always, I hope this helps.

Of course, deep thanks are due especially to my co-author, Randal, for giving me the freedom to try various ways of presenting the material both in the classroom and here in the book, as well as for the push to make this material into a book in the first place. And without fail, I must say that I am indeed inspired by your ongoing work to ensure that no one else becomes ensnared by the legal troubles that have stolen so much of your time and energy; you're a fine example.

From Both of Us. Thanks to our reviewers (Elaine Ashton, Kevin Bingham, Jarkko Hietaniemi, Joe Johnston, and Ben Tilly) for providing comments on the draft of this book.

Thanks also to our many students who have let us know what parts of the course material have needed improvement over the years. It's because of you that we're both so proud of it today.

Thanks to the many Perl Mongers who have made us feel at home as we've visited your cities. Let's do it again sometime.

And finally, our sincerest thanks to our friend Larry Wall, for having the wisdom to share his really cool and powerful toys with the rest of the world so that we can all get our work done just a little bit faster, easier, and with more fun.

1

Introduction

Welcome to the Llama book!

This is the third edition of a book that has been enjoyed by half a million readers since 1993. At least, we hope they've enjoyed it. It's a sure thing that we've enjoyed writing it.[*]

Questions and Answers

You probably have some questions about Perl, and maybe even some about this book; especially if you've already flipped through the book to see what's coming. So we'll use this chapter to answer them.

Is This the Right Book for You?

If you're anything like us, you're probably standing in a bookstore right now,[†] wondering whether you should get this Llama book and learn Perl, or maybe that book over there and learn some language named after a snake, or a beverage, or a letter of the alphabet.[‡] You've got about two minutes before the bookstore manager comes over to tell you that this isn't a library,[§] and you need to buy something or

---

[*] To be sure, the first edition was written by Randal L. Schwartz, the second by Randal L. Schwartz and Tom Christiansen, and this one by Randal L. Schwartz and Tom Phoenix. So, whenever we say "we" in this edition, we mean those last two. Now, if you're wondering how we can say that we've *enjoyed* writing it (in the past tense) when we're still on the first page, that's easy: we started at the end, and worked our way backwards. It sounds like a strange way to do it, we know. But, honestly, once we finished writing the index, the rest was hardly any trouble at all.

[†] Actually, if you're like us, you're standing in a *library*, not a bookstore. But we're tightwads.

[‡] Before you write to tell us that it's a comedy troupe, not a snake, we should really explain that we're dyslexically thinking of CORBA.

[§] Unless it *is*.

get out. Maybe you want to use these two minutes to see a quick Perl program, so you'll know something about how powerful Perl is and what it can do. In that case, you should check out the whirlwind tour of Perl, later in this chapter.

Why Are There So Many Footnotes?

Thank you for noticing. There *are* a lot of footnotes in this book. Ignore them. They're needed because Perl is chock-full of exceptions to its rules. This is a good thing, as real life is chock-full of exceptions to rules.

But it means that we can't honestly say, "The fizzbin operator frobnicates the hoozistatic variables" without a footnote giving the exceptions.* We're pretty honest, so we have to write the footnotes. But you can be honest without reading them. (It's funny how that works out.)

Many of the exceptions have to do with portability. Perl began on Unix systems, and it still has deep roots in Unix. But wherever possible, we've tried to show when something may behave unexpectedly, whether that's because it's running on a non-Unix system, or for another reason. We hope that readers who know nothing about Unix will nevertheless find this book a good introduction to Perl. (And they'll learn a little about Unix along the way, at no extra charge.)

And many of the other exceptions have to do with the old "80/20" rule. By that we mean that 80% of the behavior of Perl can be described in 20% of the documentation, and the other 20 percent of the behavior takes up the other 80% of the documentation. So to keep this book small, we'll talk about the most common, easy-to-talk-about behavior in the main text, and hint in the direction of the other stuff in the footnotes (which are in a smaller font, so we can say more in the same space).†

Once you've read the book all the way through without reading the footnotes, you'll probably want to look back at some sections for reference. At that point, or if you become unbearably curious along the way, go ahead and read the notes. A lot of them are just computer jokes anyway.

What About the Exercises and Their Answers?

The exercises are at the end of each chapter because, between the two of us, we've presented this same course material to several thousand students.‡ We have carefully crafted these exercises to give you the chance to make mistakes as well.

---

* Except on Tuesdays, during a power outage, when you hold your elbow at a funny angle during the equinox, or when use `integer` is in effect inside a loop block being called by a prototyped subroutine prior to Perl version 5.6.

† We even discussed doing the entire book as a footnote to save the pagecount, but footnotes on footnotes started to get a bit crazy.

‡ Not all at once.

It's not that we *want* you to make mistakes, but you need to have the *chance*. That's because you are going to make most of these mistakes during your Perl programming career, and it may as well be now. Any mistake that you make while reading this book you won't make again when you're writing a program on a deadline. And we're always here to help you out if something goes wrong, in the form of Appendix A, *Exercise Answers*, which has our answer for each exercise and a little text to go with it, explaining the mistakes you made and a few you didn't. Check out the answers when you're done with the exercises.

Try not to peek at the answer until you've given the problem a good try, though. You'll learn better if you figure it out rather than if you read about it.

Even if you never make any mistakes, you should look at the answers when you're done; the accompanying text will point out some details of the program that might not be obvious at first.

What Do Those Numbers Mean at the Start of the Exercise?

Each exercise has a number in square brackets in front of the exercise text, looking something like this:

1. [2] What does the number 2 inside square brackets mean, when it appears at the start of an exercise's text?

That number is our (very rough) estimate of how many minutes you can expect to spend on that particular exercise. It's rough, so don't be too surprised if you're all done (with writing, testing, and debugging) in half that time, or not done in twice that long. On the other hand, if you're really stuck, we won't tell anyone that you peeked at Appendix A to see what our answer looked like.

What If I'm a Perl Course Instructor?

If you're a Perl instructor who has decided to use this as your textbook (as many have over the years), you should know that we've tried to make each set of exercises short enough that most students could do the whole set in 45 minutes to an hour, with a little time left over for a break. Some chapters' exercises should be quicker, and some may take longer. That's because, once we had written all of those little numbers in square brackets, we discovered that we don't know how to add.

What Does "Perl" Stand For?

Perl is short for "Practical Extraction and Report Language," although it has also been called a "Pathologically Eclectic Rubbish Lister," among other expansions.* There's no point in arguing which expansion is correct, because both of those are endorsed by Larry Wall, Perl's creator and chief architect, implementor, and maintainer. He created Perl in the mid-1980s when he was trying to produce some reports from a Usenet-news-like hierarchy of files for a bug-reporting system, and *awk* ran out of steam. Larry, being the lazy programmer that he is,† decided to overkill the problem with a general-purpose tool that he could use in at least one other place. The result was Perl version zero.

Why Didn't Larry Just Use Some Other Language?

There's no shortage of computer languages, is there? But, at the time, Larry didn't see anything that really met his needs. If one of the other languages of today had been available back then, perhaps Larry would have used one of those. He needed something with the quickness of coding available in shell or *awk* programming, and with some of the power of more advanced tools like *grep, cut, sort,* and *sed*,‡ without having to resort to a language like C.

Perl tries to fill the gap between low-level programming (such as in C or C++ or assembly) and high-level programming (such as "shell" programming). Low-level programming is usually hard to write and ugly, but fast and unlimited; it's hard to beat the speed of a well-written low-level program on a given machine. And there's not much you can't do there. High-level programming, at the other extreme, tends to be slow, hard, ugly, and limited; there are many things you can't do at all with the shell, if there's no command on your system that provides the needed functionality. Perl is easy, nearly unlimited, mostly fast, and kind of ugly.

Let's take another look at those four claims we just made about Perl:

First, Perl is easy. As you'll see, though, this means it's easy to *use*. It's not especially easy to *learn*. If you drive a car, you spent many weeks or months learning

---

* It's actually a retronym, not an acronym. That is, Larry came up with the name first, and the expansion later. That's why "Perl" isn't in all caps.

† We're not insulting Larry by saying he's lazy; laziness is a virtue. The wheelbarrow was invented by someone who was too lazy to carry things; writing was invented by someone who was too lazy to memorize; Perl was invented by someone who was too lazy to get the job done without inventing a whole new computer language.

‡ Don't worry if you don't know what these are. All that matters is that they were the programs Larry had in his Unix toolbox, but they weren't up to the tasks at hand.

that, and now it's easy to drive. When you've been programming Perl for about as many hours as it took you to learn to drive, Perl will be easy for you.*

Perl is nearly unlimited. There are very few things you can't do with Perl. You wouldn't want to write a interrupt-microkernel-level device driver in Perl (even though that's been done), but most things that ordinary folks need most of the time are good tasks for Perl, from quick little one-off programs to major industrial-strength applications.

Perl is mostly fast. That's because nobody is developing Perl who doesn't also use it—so we all want it to be fast. If someone wants to add a feature that would be really cool, but which would slow down other programs, Larry is almost certain to refuse the new feature until we find a way to make it quick enough.

Perl is kind of ugly. This is true. The symbol of Perl has become the camel, from the cover of the venerable Camel book (also known as *Programming Perl*), a sister to this one. Camels are kind of ugly, too. But they work hard, even in tough conditions. Camels are there to get the job done despite all difficulties, even when they look bad and smell worse and sometimes spit at you. Perl is a little like that.

Is Perl Easy or Hard?

It's easy to use, but sometimes hard to learn. This is a generalization, of course. But in designing Perl, Larry has had to make many trade-offs. When he's had the chance to make something easier for the programmer at the expense of being more difficult for the student, he's decided in the programmer's favor nearly every time. That's because you'll learn Perl only once, but you'll use it again and again.†

Perl has any number of conveniences that let the programmer save time. For example, most functions will have a default; frequently, the default is the way that you'll want to use the function. So you'll see lines of Perl code like these:‡

```
while (<>) {
    chomp;
    print join("\t", (split /:/)[0, 2, 1, 5] ), "\n";
}
```

Written out in full, without using Perl's defaults and shortcuts, that snippet would be roughly ten or twelve times longer, so it would take much longer to read and write. It would be harder to maintain and debug, too, with more variables. If you already know some Perl, and you don't see the variables in that code, that's part of

---

* But we hope you'll crash less often with the car.

† If you're going to use a programming language for only a few minutes each week or month, you'd prefer one that is easier to learn, since you'll have forgotten nearly all of it from one use to the next. Perl is for people who are programmers for at least twenty minutes per day, and probably most of that in Perl.

‡ We won't explain it all here, but this example pulls some data from an input file or files in one format and writes some of it out in another format. All of its features are covered in this book.

the point. They're all being used by default. But to have this ease at the programmer's tasks means paying the price when you're learning; you have to learn those defaults and shortcuts.

Once you become familiar with Perl, you may find yourself spending less time trying to get shell quoting (or C declarations) right, and more time surfing the Web, because Perl is a great tool for leverage. Perl's concise constructs allow you to create (with minimal fuss) some very cool one-up solutions or general tools. Also, you can drag those tools along to your next job, because Perl is highly portable and readily available, so you'll have even more time to surf.

Perl is a very high-level language. That means that the code is quite dense; a Perl program may be around 30% to 70% as long as the corresponding program in C. This makes Perl faster to write, faster to read, faster to debug, and faster to maintain. It doesn't take much programming before you realize that, when the entire subroutine is small enough to fit onscreen all at once, you don't have to keep scrolling back and forth to see what's going on. Also, since the number of bugs in a program is roughly proportional to the length of the source code[*] (rather than being proportional to the program's functionality), the shorter source in Perl will mean fewer bugs on average.

Like any language, Perl can be "write-only"—it's possible to write programs that are impossible to read. But with proper care, you can avoid this common accusation. Yes, sometimes Perl looks like line-noise to the uninitiated, but to the seasoned Perl programmer, it looks like checksummed line-noise with a mission in life. If you follow the guidelines of this book, your programs should be easy to read and easy to maintain, and they probably won't win The Obfuscated Perl Contest.[†]

How Did Perl Get to Be So Popular?

After playing with Perl a bit, adding stuff here and there, Larry released it to the community of Usenet readers, commonly known as "the Net." The users on this ragtag fugitive fleet of systems around the world (tens of thousands of them) gave him feedback, asking for ways to do this, that, or the other thing, many of which Larry had never envisioned his little Perl handling.

But as a result, Perl grew, and grew, and grew. It grew in features. It grew in portability. What was once a little language available on only a couple of Unix systems has now grown to have thousands of pages of free online documentation, dozens of books, several mainstream Usenet newsgroups (and a dozen

---

[*] With a sharp jump when any one section of the program exceeds the size of your screen.

[†] An actual annual event sponsored by the *Perl Journal* (at *http://www.tpj.com/*).

newsgroups and mailing lists outside the mainstream) with an uncountable number of readers, and implementations on nearly every system in use today—and don't forget this Llama book as well.

What's Happening with Perl Now?

Larry is still in charge of Perl, although the Perl development team is now made up of approximately thirty key people and a few hundred others from around the world. And Perl is still growing.

These days, Perl is still free for you to use. In fact, Larry promises that it will *always* be free. (He's a really nice guy; you'd like him.) So go ahead and write code in Perl today, without worrying that there will be a licensing fee on your program tomorrow.

So, if Perl is free, who pays Larry and the other Perl developers? Well, the majority of us contribute to Perl as a labor of love; Perl helps us, and we help Perl. (If you ever see some way in which you could improve Perl, we encourage you to send in your contributions, too.) In some cases, though, a person or firm has paid someone to do some development work. This may be because they needed some new functionality badly enough to pay for it, or because they wanted to make the world a better place.

Larry doesn't write all of the code these days, but he still guides the development and makes the big decisions. One of the most important rules he's given us is this one: "Common things should be easy; advanced things should at least be possible."

Because of that rule, you can be sure that anything that you need to do frequently will have a shortcut in Perl. In fact, by the end of this book, you'll probably be using at least ten shortcuts in a typical ten-line program. That is the sort of thing that makes Perl easier to use, at the price of being harder to learn.

What's Perl Really Good For?

Perl is good for quick-and-dirty programs that you whip up in three minutes. Perl is also good for long-and-extensive programs that will take a dozen programmers three years to finish. Of course, you'll probably find yourself writing many programs that take you less than an hour to complete, from the initial plan to the fully tested code.

Perl is optimized for problems which are about 90% working with text and about 10% everything else. That description seems to fit most programming tasks that pop up these days. In a perfect world, every programmer could know every language; you'd always be able to choose the best language for each project. Most of the time, you'd choose Perl.*

Although the Web wasn't even a twinkle in Tim Berners-Lee's eye when Larry created Perl, it was a marriage made on the Net. Some claim that the deployment of Perl in the early 1990s permitted lots of content to be moved into HTML format very rapidly, and the Web couldn't exist without content. Of course, Perl is the darling language for small CGI scripting (programs run by a web server) as well— so much so that many of the uninformed still make statements like "Isn't CGI just Perl?" or "Why would you use Perl other than for CGI?" We find those statements amusing.

What Is Perl Not Good For?

So, if it's good for so many things, what is Perl *not* good for? Well, you shouldn't choose Perl if you're trying to make an *opaque binary*. That's a program that you could give away or sell to someone who then can't see your secret algorithms in the source, and thus can't help you to maintain or debug your code either. When you give someone your Perl program, you'll normally be giving them the source, not an opaque binary.

If you're wishing for an opaque binary, though, we have to tell you that they don't exist. If someone can install and run your program, they can turn it back into source code. Granted, this won't necessarily be the same source that you started with, but it will be some kind of source code. The real way to keep your secret algorithm a secret is, alas, to apply the proper number of attorneys; they can write a license that says "you can do *this* with the code, but you can't do *that*. And if you break our rules, we've got the proper number of attorneys to ensure that you'll regret it."

If you think you really want to compile your Perl code to make a binary, though, see "But How Do I Compile Perl?" later in this chapter.

How Can I Get Perl?

You probably already have it. At least, we find Perl wherever *we* go. It ships with many systems, and system administrators often install it on every machine at their site.† But if you can't find it already on your system, you can still get it for free.

---

* Don't just take our word for it, though. If you want to know whether Perl is better than language X, learn them both and try them both, then see which one you use most often. That's the one that's best for you. In the end, you'll understand Perl better because of your study of language X, and vice versa, so it will be time well spent.

† Well, each machine that is made for programming, at least.

Perl is distributed under two different licenses. For most people, since you'll merely be *using* it, either license is as good as the other. If you'll be modifying Perl, however, you'll want to read the licenses more closely, because they put some small restrictions on distributing the modified code. For people who won't modify Perl, the licenses essentially say "it's free—have fun with it."

In fact, it's not only free, but it runs rather nicely on nearly everything that calls itself Unix and has a C compiler. You download it, type a command or two, and it starts configuring and building itself. Or, better yet, you get your system administrator to type those two commands and install it for you.[*]

Besides Unix and Unix-like systems, people have also been addicted enough to Perl to port it to other systems, like the Macintosh,[†] VMS, OS/2, even MS/DOS and every modern species of Windows—and probably even more by the time you read this.[‡] Many of these *ports* of Perl come with an installation program that's even easier to use than the process for installing Perl on Unix. Check for links in the "ports" section on CPAN.

What Is CPAN?

CPAN is the Comprehensive Perl Archive Network, your one-stop shopping for Perl. It has the source code for Perl itself, ready-to-install ports of Perl to all sorts of non-Unix systems,[§] examples, documentation, extensions to Perl, and archives of messages about Perl. In short, CPAN is comprehensive.

CPAN is replicated on hundreds of mirror machines around the world; start at *http://www.cpan.org/* to find one near you. Most of the time, you can also simply visit *http://*COUNTRYCODE*.cpan.org/* where COUNTRYCODE is your two-letter official country code (like on the end of your national domain names). Or, if you don't have access to the Net, you might find a CD-ROM or DVD-ROM with all of the useful parts of CPAN on it; check with your local technical bookstore. Look for a recently minted archive, though; since CPAN changes daily, an archive from two years ago is an antique. (Better yet, get a kind friend with Net access to burn you one with today's CPAN.)

---

[*] If system administrators can't install software, what good are they? If you have trouble convincing your admin to install Perl, offer to buy a pizza. We've never met a sys admin who could say no to a free pizza, or at least counter-offer with something just as easy to get.

[†] MacPerl runs under the "classic" Mac OS. If you have Mac OS X, which is a Unix-based system, you have mainstream Perl.

[‡] And no, as we write this, it won't fit in your Palm handheld—it's just too darn big, even stripped down.

[§] It's nearly always better to compile Perl from the source on Unix systems. Other systems may not have a C compiler and other tools needed for compilation, so CPAN has binaries for these.

CPAN is pretty-well organized; most of the time, you should find what you want with just a few clicks of the mouse. But there's also a couple of nice search interfaces on the Web at *http://search.cpan.org/* and *http://kobesearch.cpan.org/,* which are especially helpful when you're looking for an extension to Perl.

How Can I Get Support for Perl?

Well, you get the complete source—so you get to fix the bugs yourself!

That doesn't sound so good, does it? But it really is a good thing. Since there's no "source code escrow" on Perl, anyone can fix a bug—in fact, by the time you've found and verified a bug, someone else has probably already got a fix for it. There are thousands of people around the world who help to maintain Perl.

Now, we're not saying that Perl has a lot of bugs. But it's a program, and every program has at least one bug.*

To see why it's so useful to have the source to Perl, imagine that instead of using Perl, you licensed a programming language called Forehead from a giant, powerful corporation owned by a zillionaire with a bad haircut. (This is all hypothetical. Everyone knows there's no such programming language as Forehead.) Now think of what you can do when you find a bug in Forehead. First, you can report it; second, you can hope—hope that they fix the bug, hope that they fix it *soon,* hope that they won't charge too much for the new version. You can hope that the new version doesn't add new features with new bugs, and hope that the giant company doesn't get broken up in an anti-trust lawsuit.

But with Perl, you've got the source. In the rare and unlikely event that you can't get a bug fixed any other way, you can hire a programmer or ten and get to work. For that matter, if you buy a new machine that Perl doesn't yet run on, you can port it yourself. Or if you need a feature that doesn't yet exist, well, you know what to do.

Are There Any Other Kinds of Support?

Sure; one of our favorites is the Perl Mongers. This is a worldwide association of Perl users' groups; see *http://www.pm.org/* for more information. There's probably a group near you with an expert or someone who knows an expert. If there's no group, you can easily start one.

---

* Programmers also know that every program has at least one line of unnecessary source code. By combining these two rules and using logical induction, it's a simple matter to prove that any program could be reduced to a single line of code with a bug.

Of course, for the first line of support, you shouldn't neglect the documentation. Besides the manpages* themselves, Perl's documentation includes the voluminous FAQ (Frequently Asked Questions) and many tutorials.

Another authoritative source is the book *Programming Perl*, commonly known as "the Camel book" because of its cover animal (just as this book has come to be known as "the Llama book"). The Camel book contains the complete reference information, some tutorial stuff, and a bunch of miscellaneous information about Perl. There's also a separate pocket-sized quick reference to Perl (by Johan Vromans) that's handy to keep at hand (or in your pocket).

If you need to ask a question of someone, there are newsgroups on Usenet and any number of mailing lists.† At any hour of the day or night, there's a Perl expert awake in some timezone answering questions on Usenet's Perl newsgroups—the sun never sets on the Perl empire. This means that if you ask a question, you'll often get an answer within minutes. If you didn't check the documentation and FAQ first, you'll get flamed within minutes.

We generally recommend the newsgroup *comp.lang.perl.moderated*, where (as the name implies) a moderator will check over your question before posting it. If there's something wrong with your question, you'll still get flamed of course, but it's a small, private flame in email rather than a big public one in a newsgroup.‡ But for most questions, you'll get an answer back within the hour. Just try getting that level of support from your favorite software vendor for free!

The official Perl newsgroups on Usenet are located in the *comp.lang.perl.** part of the hierarchy. As of this writing, there are five of them, but they change from time to time. You (or whoever is in charge of Perl at your site) should generally subscribe to *comp.lang.perl.announce,* which is a low-volume newsgroup just for important announcements about Perl, including especially any security-related announcements. Ask your local expert if you need help with Usenet.

Also, a few web communities have sprung up around Perl discussions. One very popular one, known as The Perl Monastery (*http://www.perlmonks.org*) has seen quite a bit of participation from many Perl book and column authors, including at least one of the authors of this book.

---

* The term *manpages* is a Unix-ism meaning documentation. If you're not on a Unix system, the manpages for Perl should be available via your system's native documentation system. If you can't find them anywhere else, the manpages are available directly on CPAN.

† Many mailing lists are listed at *http://lists.perl.org*.

‡ Of course, we're joking here. Unless you've done something amazingly boneheaded, the moderators are all kind, polite, helpful folks, who will gently point you in the direction of the information you need, with just enough flame to remind you to be more careful next time. Don't be afraid to ask.

If you find yourself needing a support contract for Perl, there are a number of firms who are willing to charge as much as you'd like. In most cases, these other support avenues will take care of you for free.

What If I Find a Bug in Perl?

The first thing to do when you find a bug is to check the documentation* again.†
Perl has so many special features and exceptions to rules that you may have discovered a feature, not a bug. Also, check that you don't have an older version of Perl; maybe you found something that's been fixed in a more recent version.

Once you're 99% certain that you've found a real bug, ask around. Ask someone at work, at your local Perl Mongers' meeting, or at a Perl conference. Chances are, it's *still* a feature, not a bug.

Once you're 100% certain that you've found a real bug, cook up a test case (if you haven't done so already). The ideal test case is a tiny self-contained program that any Perl user could run to see the same (mis-)behavior as you've found. Once you've got a test case that clearly shows the bug, use the *perlbug* utility (which comes with Perl) to report the bug. That will normally send email from you to the Perl developers, so don't use *perlbug* until you've got your test case ready.

Once you've sent off your bug report, if you've done everything right, it's not unusual to get a response within minutes. Typically, you can apply a simple patch and get right back to work. Of course, you may (at worst) get no response at all; the Perl developers are under no obligation to even read your bug reports. But all of us love Perl, so nobody likes to let a bug escape our notice.

How Do I Make a Perl Program?

It's about time you asked (even if you didn't). Perl programs are text files; you can create and edit them with your favorite text editor. (You don't need any special development environment, although there are some commercial ones available from various vendors. We've never used any of these enough to recommend them.)

You should generally use a programmers' text editor, rather than an ordinary editor. What's the difference? Well, a programmers' text editor will let you do things that programmers need, like to indent or unindent a block of code, or to find the matching closing curly brace for a given opening curly brace. On Unix systems, the two most popular programmers' editors are *emacs* and *vi* (and their

---

* Even Larry admits to consulting the documentation from time to time.

† Maybe even twice or three times. Many times, we've gone into the documentation looking to explain a particular unexpected behavior and found some new little nuance that ends up on a slide or in a column.

variants and clones). Both of these have been ported to several non-Unix systems, and many systems today offer a graphical editor (which uses a pointing device like a mouse). In fact, there are even versions of *vi* and *emacs* that offer a graphical interface. Ask your local expert about text editors on your system.

For the simple programs you'll be writing for the exercises in this book, none of which will need to be more than about twenty or thirty lines of code, any text editor will be fine.

A few beginners try to use a word processor instead of a text editor. We recommend against this—it's inconvenient at best and impossible at worst. But we won't try to stop you. Be sure to tell the word processor to save your file as "text only"; the word processor's own format will almost certainly be unusable.

In some cases, you may need to compose the program on one machine, then transfer it to another to be run. If you do this, be sure that the transfer uses "text" or "ASCII" mode, and not "binary" mode. This step is needed because of the different text formats on different machines. Without that, you may get inconsistent results—some versions of Perl actually abort when they detect a mismatch in the line endings.

A Simple Program

According to the oldest rule in the book, any book about a computer language that has Unix-like roots has to start with showing the "Hello, world" program. So, here it is in Perl:

```
#!/usr/bin/perl
print "Hello, world!\n";
```

Let's imagine that you've typed that into your text editor. (Don't worry yet about what the parts mean and how it works. We'll see about those in a moment.) You can generally save that program under any name you wish. Perl doesn't require any special kind of filename or extension, and it's better to use no extension at all.* But some non-Unix systems may require an extension like *.plx* (meaning PerL eXecutable); see your system's release notes for more information.

You will also need to do something so that your system knows that it's an executable program (that is, a command). What you'll do depends upon your system; maybe you won't have to do anything more than to save the program in a certain

---

* Why is it better to have no extension? Imagine that you've written a program to calculate bowling scores and you've told all of your friends that it's called *bowling.plx*. One day you decide to rewrite it in C. Do you still call it by the same name, implying that it's still written in Perl? Or do you tell everyone that it has a new name? (And don't call it *bowling.c*, please!) The answer is that it's none of their business what language it's written in, if they're merely *using* it. So it should have simply been called *bowling* in the first place.

place. (Your current directory will generally be fine.) On Unix systems, you mark a program as being executable by using the *chmod* command, perhaps like this:

```
$ chmod a+x my_program
```

The dollar sign (and space) at the start of the line represents the shell prompt, which will probably look different on your system. If you're used to using *chmod* with a number like 755 instead of a symbolic parameter like a+x, that's fine too, of course. Either way, it tells the system that this file is now a program.

Now you're ready to run it:

```
$ ./my_program
```

The dot and slash at the start of this command mean to find the program in the current working directory. That's not needed in all cases, but you should use it at the start of each command invocation until you fully understand what it's doing.*

If everything worked, it's a miracle. More often, you'll find that your program has a bug. Edit and try again—but you don't need to use *chmod* each time, since that should "stick" to the file. (Of course, if the bug is that you didn't use *chmod* correctly, you'll probably get a "permission denied" message from your shell.)

What's Inside That Program?

Like other "free-form" languages, Perl generally lets you use insignificant whitespace (like spaces, tabs, and newlines) at will to make your program easier to read. Most Perl programs use a fairly standard format, though, much like most of what we show here. We strongly encourage you to properly indent your programs, since that makes your program easier to read; a good text editor will do most of the work for you. Good comments also make a program easier to read. In Perl, comments run from a pound sign (#) to the end of the line. (There are no "block comments" in Perl.†) We don't use many comments in the programs in this book, because the surrounding text explains their workings, but you should use comments as needed in your own programs.

So another way (a very strange way, it must be said) to write that same "Hello, world" program might be like this:

```
#!/usr/bin/perl
    print    # This is a comment
"Hello, world!\n"
  ;     # Don't write your Perl code like this!
```

---

* In short, it's preventing your shell from running another program (or shell builtin) of the same name. A common mistake among beginners is to name their first program test. Many systems already have a program (or shell builtin) with that name; that's what the beginners run instead of their program.

† But there are a number of ways to fake them. See the FAQ (accessible with *perldoc perlfaq* on most installations).

That first line is actually a very special comment. On Unix systems,* if the very first two characters on the first line of a text file are "#!", then what follows is the name of the program that actually executes the rest of the file. In this case, the program is stored in the file */usr/bin/perl.*

This #! line is actually the least portable part of a Perl program, because you'll need to find out what goes there for each machine. Fortunately, it's almost always either */usr/bin/perl* or */usr/local/bin/perl.* If you find that it's not, you can cast a magic spell on your system administrator to fix things. Just say "You know, I read in a book that both */usr/bin/perl* and */usr/local/bin/perl* should be symbolic links to the true Perl binary," and under the influence of your spell the admin will make everything work. All of the example programs you're likely to find on the Net and elsewhere will begin with one of those two forms.

On non-Unix systems, it's traditional (and even useful) to make the first line say #!perl. If nothing else, it tells your maintenance programmer as soon as he or she gets ready to fix it that it's a Perl program.

If that #! line is wrong, you'll generally get an error from your shell. This may be something unexpected, like "file not found." It's not your program that's not found, though; it's */usr/bin/perl* that wasn't where it should have been. We'd make the message clearer, but it's not coming from Perl; it's the shell that's complaining. (By the way, you should be careful to spell it *usr* and not *user*—the folks who invented Unix were lazy typists, so they omitted a lot of letters.)

Another problem you could have is if your system doesn't support the #! line at all. In that case, your shell (or whatever your system uses) will probably try to run your program all by itself, with results that may disappoint or astonish you. If you can't figure out what some strange error message is telling you, search for it in the *perldiag* manpage.

The "main" program consists of all of the ordinary Perl statements (not including anything in subroutines, which we'll see later). There's no "main" routine, as there is in languages like C or Java. In fact, many programs don't even have routines (in the form of subroutines).

There's also no required variable declaration section, as there is in some other languages. If you've always had to declare your variables, you may be startled or unsettled by this at first. But it allows us to write "quick-and-dirty" Perl programs. If your program is only two lines long, you don't want to have to use one of those lines just to declare your variables. If you really want to declare your variables, that's a good thing; we'll see how to do that in Chapter 4, *Subroutines.*

---

* Most modern ones, anyway. The "sh-bang" mechanism was introduced somewhere in the mid-1980s, and that's pretty ancient, even on the extensively long Unix timeline.

Most statements are an expression followed by a semicolon. Here's the one we've seen a few times so far:

```
print "Hello, world!\n";
```

As you may have guessed by now, this line prints the message `Hello, world!` At the end of that message is the shortcut `\n`, which is probably familiar to you if you've used another language like C, C++, or Java; it means a newline character. When that's printed after the message, the print position drops down to the start of the next line, allowing the following shell prompt to appear on a line of its own, rather than being attached to the message. Every line of output should end with a newline character. We'll see more about the newline shortcut and other so-called backslash escapes in the next chapter.

But How Do I Compile Perl?

You may be surprised to learn that all you have to do to compile Perl is to run it. When you run your program, Perl's internal compiler first runs through your entire source, turning it into internal *bytecodes* (an internal data structure representing the program); then Perl's bytecode engine actually runs them.*

So, if there's a syntax error on line 200, you'll get that error message before you start running line two.† If you have a loop that runs 5000 times, it's compiled just once; the actual loop can then run at top speed. And there's no runtime penalty for using as many comments and as much whitespace as you need to make your program easy to understand. You can even use calculations involving only constants, and the result is a constant computed once as the program is beginning—not each time through a loop.

To be sure, this compilation does take time—it's inefficient to have a voluminous Perl program that does one small quick task (out of many potential tasks, say) and then exits, because the runtime for the program will be dwarfed by the compile time. But the compiler is very fast; normally the compilation will be a tiny percentage of the runtime.

An exception might be if you were writing a program to be run over the Web, where it may be called hundreds or thousands of times every minute. (This is a very high usage rate. If it were called a few hundreds or thousands of times per *day*, like most programs on the Web, we probably wouldn't worry too much about it.) Many of these programs have very short runtimes, so the issue of recompilation may become significant. If this is an issue for you, you'll want to find a

---

* As usual, there's more to the story than what we say here. But this should be close enough for all but the technically advanced folks, and they already know about this.

† Unless line two happens to be a compile-time operation, like a `BEGIN` block or a `use` invocation.

way to keep your program resident in memory between invocations (whether it's written in Perl or not); see the documentation for your web server and ask your local expert for help with this.*

What if you could save the compiled bytecodes to avoid the overhead of compilation? Or, even better, what if you could turn the bytecodes into another language, like C, and then compile that? Well, both of these things are possible (although beyond the scope of this book), although they won't make most programs any easier to use, maintain, debug, or install, and they may (for somewhat technical reasons) make your program even slower.† We don't know anyone who has ever needed to compile a Perl program (except for experimental purposes), and we doubt you ever will ever meet one, either.

A Whirlwind Tour of Perl

So, you want to see a real Perl program with some meat? (If you don't, just play along for now.) Here you are:

```
#!/usr/bin/perl
@lines = `perldoc -u -f atan2`;
foreach (@lines) {
  s/\w<([^>]+)>/\U$1/g;
  print;
}
```

Now, the first time you see Perl code like this, it can seem pretty strange. (In fact, every time you see Perl code like this, it can seem pretty strange.) But let's take it line by line, and see what this example does. (These explanations are very brief; this is a whirlwind tour, after all. We'll see all of this program's features in more detail during the rest of this book. You're not really supposed to understand the whole thing until later.)

The first line is the #! line, as we saw before. You might need to change that line for your system, as we discussed earlier.

The second line runs an external command, named within backquotes (" ` ` "). (The backquote key is often found next to the number 1 on full-sized American keyboards. Be sure not to confuse the backquote with the single quote, " ' ".) The command we're using is *perldoc -u -f atan2*; try typing that at your command line to see what its output looks like. The *perldoc* command is used on most systems

---

* Point your local expert to *http://perl.apache.org* for one possible solution.

† On many (perhaps most) systems where you might want to compile a Perl program, the perl binary (the program that executes your Perl programs) is always in use by some process, so it's always resident in memory. A "compiled Perl" program will take time to load into memory. If it's a small program, it would probably compile at least as fast as it takes to load a compiled executable. If it's a large one, compilation is probably an insignificant part of its runtime anyway.

to read and display the documentation for Perl and its associated extensions and utilities, so it should normally be available.* This command tells you something about the trigonometric function `atan2`; we're using it here just as an example of an external command whose output we wish to process.

The output of that command in the backticks is saved in an array variable called `@lines`. The next line of code starts a loop that will process each one of those lines. Inside the loop, the statements are indented. Although Perl doesn't require this, good programmers do.

The first line inside the loop body is the scariest one; it says `s/\w<([^>]+)>/\U$1/g;`. Without going into too much detail, we'll just say that this can change any line that has a special marker made with angle brackets (`< >`), and there should be at least one of those in the output of the *perldoc* command.

The next line, in a surprise move, prints out each (possibly modified) line. The resulting output should be similar to what *perldoc -u -f atan2* would do on its own, but there will be a change where any of those markers appears.

Thus, in the span of a few lines, we've run another program, saved its output in memory, updated the memory items, and printed them out. This kind of program is a fairly common use of Perl, where one type of data is converted to another.

Exercises

Normally, each chapter will end with some exercises, with the answers in Appendix A. But in this chapter, the answers were already provided.

If you can't get these exercises to work on your machine, double-check your work and then consult your local expert. Remember that you may need to change each program a little, as described in the text.

1. [7] Type in the "Hello, world" program and get it to work! (You may name it anything you wish, but a good name might be `ex1-1`, for simplicity, since it's exercise 1 in Chapter 1.)

2. [5] Type the command *perldoc -u -f atan2* at a command prompt and note its output. If you can't get that to work, then find out from a local administrator or the documentation for your version of Perl about how to invoke *perldoc* or its equivalent. (You'll need this for the next exercise anyway.)

3. [6] Type in the second example program (from the previous section) and see what it prints. (Hint: Be careful to type those punctuation marks exactly as shown!) Do you see how it changed the output of the command?

---

* If *perldoc* is not available, that probably means that your system doesn't have a command-line interface, and your Perl can't run commands (like *perldoc*) in backticks or via the piped-open, which we'll see in Chapter 14, *Process Management*. In that case, you should simply skip the exercises that use *perldoc*.

2

Scalar Data

What Is Scalar Data?

In English, as in many other spoken languages, we're used to distinguishing between singular and plural. As a computer language designed by a human linguist, Perl is similar. As a general rule, when Perl has just one of something, that's a *scalar.**

A *scalar* is the simplest kind of data that Perl manipulates. Most scalars are either a number (like 255 or 3.25e20) or a string of characters (like `hello`† or the Gettysburg Address). Although you may think of numbers and strings as very different things, Perl uses them nearly interchangeably.

A scalar value can be acted upon with operators (like addition or concatenate), generally yielding a scalar result. A scalar value can be stored into a scalar variable. Scalars can be read from files and devices, and can be written out as well.

Numbers

Although a scalar is most often either a number or a string, it's useful to look at numbers and strings separately for the moment. We'll cover numbers first, and then move on to strings.

---

* This has little to do with the similar term from mathematics or physics in that a scalar is a single thing; there are no "vectors" in Perl.

† If you have been using other programming languages, you may think of `hello` as a collection of five characters, rather than as a single thing. But in Perl, a string is a single scalar value. Of course, we can access the individual characters when we need to; we'll see how to do that in later chapters.

All Numbers Are the Same Format Internally

As you'll see in the next few paragraphs, you can specify both integers (whole numbers, like 255 or 2001) and floating-point numbers (real numbers with decimal points, like 3.14159, or 1.35 × 10^{25}). But internally, Perl computes with double-precision floating-point values.* This means that there are no integer values internal to Perl—an integer constant in the program is treated as the equivalent floating-point value.† You probably won't notice the conversion (or care much), but you should stop looking for distinct integer operations (as opposed to *floating-point* operations), because there aren't any.‡

Floating-Point Literals

A literal is the way a value is represented in the source code of the Perl program. A literal is not the result of a calculation or an I/O operation; it's data written directly into the source code.

Perl's floating-point literals should look familiar to you. Numbers with and without decimal points are allowed (including an optional plus or minus prefix), as well as tacking on a power-of-10 indicator (exponential notation) with E notation. For example:

```
1.25
255.000
255.0
7.25e45   # 7.25 times 10 to the 45th power (a big number)
-6.5e24   # negative 6.5 times 10 to the 24th
          # (a big negative number)
-12e-24   # negative 12 times 10 to the -24th
          # (a very small negative number)
-1.2E-23  # another way to say that - the E may be uppercase
```

---

* A double-precision floating-point value is whatever the C compiler that compiled Perl used for a `double` declaration. While the size may vary from machine to machine, most modern systems use IEEE floating-point formats, which suggest 15 digits of precision and a range of at least `1e-100` to `1e100`.

† Well, Perl will sometimes use internal integers in ways that are not visible to the programmer. That is, the only difference you should generally be able to see is that your program runs faster. And who could complain about that?

‡ Okay, there is the `integer` pragma. But using that is beyond the scope of this book. And yes, some operations force an integer to be computed from a given floating-point number, as we'll see later. But that's not what we're talking about here.

Integer Literals

Integer literals are also straightforward, as in:

```
0
2001
-40
255
61298040283768
```

That last one is a little hard to read. Perl allows underscores for clarity within integer literals, so we can also write that number like this:

```
61_298_040_283_768
```

It's the same value; it merely looks different to us human beings. You might have thought that commas should be used for this purpose, but commas are already used for a more-important purpose in Perl (as we'll see in the next chapter).

Nondecimal Integer Literals

Like many other programming languages, Perl allows you to specify numbers in other than base 10 (decimal). Octal (base 8) literals start with a leading 0, hexadecimal (base 16) literals start with a leading 0x, and binary (base 2) literals start with a leading 0b.* The hex digits A through F (or a through f) represent the conventional digit values of ten through fifteen. For example:

```
0377       # 377 octal, same as 255 decimal
0xff       # FF hex, also 255 decimal
0b11111111 # also 255 decimal (available in version 5.6 and later)
```

Although these values look different to us humans, they're all three the same number to Perl. It makes no difference to Perl whether you write 0xFF or 255. 000, so choose the representation that makes the most sense to you and your maintenance programmer (by which we mean the poor chap who gets stuck trying to figure out what you meant when you wrote your code. Most often, this poor chap is you, and you can't recall whay you did what you did three months ago).

When a non-decimal literal is more than about four characters long, it may be hard to read. For this reason, starting in version 5.6, Perl allows underscores for clarity within these literals:

```
0x1377_0b77
0x50_65_72_7C
```

---

* The "leading zero" indicator works only for literals—not for automatic string-to-number conversion, which we'll see later in this chapter. You can convert a data string that looks like an octal or hex value into a number with oct() or hex(). Although there's no "bin" function for converting binary values, oct() can do that for strings beginning with 0b.

Numeric Operators

Perl provides the typical ordinary addition, subtraction, multiplication, and division operators, and so on. For example:

```
2 + 3      # 2 plus 3, or 5
5.1 - 2.4  # 5.1 minus 2.4, or 2.7
3 * 12     # 3 times 12 = 36
14 / 2     # 14 divided by 2, or 7
10.2 / 0.3 # 10.2 divided by 0.3, or 34
10 / 3     # always floating-point divide, so 3.3333333...
```

Perl also supports a *modulus* operator (%). The value of the expression 10 % 3 is the remainder when ten is divided by three, which is one. Both values are first reduced to their integer values, so 10.5 % 3.2 is computed as 10 % 3.[*]

Additionally, Perl provides the FORTRAN-like *exponentiation* operator, which many have yearned for in Pascal and C. The operator is represented by the double asterisk, such as 2**3, which is two to the third power, or eight.[†]

In addition, there are other numeric operators, which we'll introduce as we need them.

Strings

Strings are sequences of characters (like hello). Strings may contain any combination of any characters.[‡]

The shortest possible string has no characters. The longest string fills all of your available memory (although you wouldn't be able to do much with that). This is in accordance with the principle of "no built-in limits" that Perl follows at every opportunity. Typical strings are printable sequences of letters and digits and punctuation in the ASCII 32 to ASCII 126 range. However, the ability to have any character in a string means you can create, scan, and manipulate raw binary data as strings—something with which many other utilities would have great difficulty. For example, you could update a graphical image or compiled program by reading it into a Perl string, making the change, and writing the result back out.

---

[*] The result of a modulus operator when a negative number (or two) is involved can vary between Perl implementations. Beware.

[†] You can't normally raise a negative number to a noninteger exponent. Math geeks know that the result would be a complex number. To make that possible, you'll need the help of the Math::Complex module.

[‡] Unlike C or C++, there's nothing special about the NUL character in Perl, because Perl uses length counting, not a null byte, to determine the end of the string.

Like numbers, strings have a literal representation, which is the way you represent the string in a Perl program. Literal strings come in two different flavors: *single-quoted string literals* and *double-quoted string literals.*[*]

Single-Quoted String Literals

A *single-quoted string literal* is a sequence of characters enclosed in single quotes. The single quotes are not part of the string itself—they're just there to let Perl identify the beginning and the ending of the string. Any character other than a single quote or a backslash between the quote marks (including newline characters, if the string continues onto successive lines) stands for itself inside a string. To get a backslash, put two backslashes in a row, and to get a single quote, put a backslash followed by a single quote. In other words:

```
'fred'      # those four characters: f, r, e, and d
'barney'    # those six characters
''          # the null string (no characters)
'Don\'t let an apostrophe end this string prematurely!'
'the last character of this string is a backslash: \\'
'hello\n'   # hello followed by backslash followed by n
'hello
there'      # hello, newline, there (11 characters total)
'\'\\'      # single quote followed by backslash
```

Note that the \n within a single-quoted string is not interpreted as a newline, but as the two characters backslash and n. Only when the backslash is followed by another backslash or a single quote does it have special meaning.

Double-Quoted String Literals

A *double-quoted string literal* is similar to the strings you may have seen in other languages. Once again, it's a sequence of characters, although this time enclosed in double quotes. But now the backslash takes on its full power to specify certain control characters, or even any character at all through octal and hex representations. Here are some double-quoted strings:

```
"barney"        # just the same as 'barney'
"hello world\n" # hello world, and a newline
"The last character of this string is a quote mark: \""
"coke\tsprite"  # coke, a tab, and sprite
```

Note that the double-quoted literal string **"barney"** means the same six-character string to Perl as does the single-quoted literal string **'barney'**. It's like what we saw with numeric literals, where we saw that 0377 was another way to write 255.0. Perl

---

[*] There are also the *here* strings, similar to the shell's *here* documents, which are documented in the *perldata* manpage.

lets you write the literal in the way that makes more sense to you. Of course, if you wish to use a backslash escape (like \n to mean a newline character), you'll need to use the double quotes.

The backslash can precede many different characters to mean different things (generally called a *backslash escape*). The nearly complete* list of double-quoted string escapes is given in Table 2-1.

Table 2-1. Double-quoted string backslash escapes

Construct	Meaning
\n	Newline
\r	Return
\t	Tab
\f	Formfeed
\b	Backspace
\a	Bell
\e	Escape (ASCII escape character)
\007	Any octal ASCII value (here, 007 = bell)
\x7f	Any hex ASCII value (here, 7f = delete)
\cC	A "control" character (here, Ctrl-C)
\\	Backslash
\"	Double quote
\l	Lowercase next letter
\L	Lowercase all following letters until \E
\u	Uppercase next letter
\U	Uppercase all following letters until \E
\Q	Quote non-word characters by adding a backslash until \E
\E	Terminate \L, \U, or \Q

Another feature of double-quoted strings is that they are *variable interpolated,* meaning that some variable names within the string are replaced with their current values when the strings are used. We haven't formally been introduced to what a variable looks like yet, so we'll get back to this later in this chapter.

String Operators

String values can be concatenated with the . operator. (Yes, that's a single period.) This does not alter either string, any more than 2+3 alters either 2 or 3. The

---

* Recent versions of Perl have introduced "Unicode" escapes, which we aren't going to be talking about here.

resulting (longer) string is then available for further computation or to be stored into a variable. For example:

```
"hello" . "world"        # same as "helloworld"
"hello" . ' ' . "world"  # same as 'hello world'
'hello world' . "\n"     # same as "hello world\n"
```

Note that the concatenation must be explicitly requested with the . operator, unlike in some other languages where you merely have to stick the two values next to each other.

A special string operator is the *string repetition* operator, consisting of the single lowercase letter **x**. This operator takes its left operand (a string) and makes as many concatenated copies of that string as indicated by its right operand (a number). For example:

```
"fred" x 3         # is "fredfredfred"
"barney" x (4+1)   # is "barney" x 5, or "barneybarneybarneybarneybarney"
5 x 4              # is really "5" x 4, which is "5555"
```

That last example is worth spelling out slowly. The string repetition operator wants a string for a left operand, so the number 5 is converted to the string "5" (using rules described in detail later), giving a one-character string. This new string is then copied four times, yielding the four-character string 5555. Note that if we had reversed the order of the operands, as **4 x 5**, we would have made five copies of the string 4, yielding 44444. This shows that string repetition is not commutative.

The copy count (the right operand) is first truncated to an integer value (4.8 becomes 4) before being used. A copy count of less than one results in an empty (zero-length) string.

Automatic Conversion Between Numbers and Strings

For the most part, Perl automatically converts between numbers to strings as needed. How does it know whether a number or a string is needed? It all depends upon the operator being used on the scalar value. If an operator expects a number (like + does), Perl will see the value as a number. If an operator expects a string (like . does), Perl will see the value as a string. So you don't need to worry about the difference between numbers and strings; just use the proper operators, and Perl will make it all work.

When a string value is used where an operator needs a number (say, for multiplication), Perl automatically converts the string to its equivalent numeric value, as if it had been entered as a decimal floating-point value.* So `"12"` `*` `"3"` gives the value 36. Trailing nonnumber stuff and leading whitespace are discarded, so `"12fred34"` `*` `"   3"` will also give 36 without any complaints.† At the extreme end of this, something that isn't a number at all converts to zero. This would happen if you used the string `"fred"` as a number.

Likewise, if a numeric value is given when a string value is needed (say, for string concatenation), the numeric value is expanded into whatever string would have been printed for that number. For example, if you want to concatenate the string Z followed by the result of 5 multiplied by 7,‡ you can say this simply as:

```
"Z" . 5 * 7 # same as "Z" . 35, or "Z35"
```

In other words, you don't really have to worry about whether you have a number or a string (most of the time). Perl performs all the conversions for you.§ And if you're worried about efficiency, don't be. Perl generally remembers the result of a conversion so that it's done only once.

Perl's Built-in Warnings

Perl can be told to warn you when it sees something suspicious going on in your program. To run your program with warnings turned on, use the -w option on the command line:

```
$ perl -w my_program
```

Or, if you always want warnings, you may request them on the #! line:

```
#!/usr/bin/perl -w
```

That works even on non-Unix systems, where it's traditional to write something like this, since the path to Perl doesn't generally matter:

```
#!perl -w
```

Now, Perl will warn you if you use `'12fred34'` as if it were a number:

```
Argument "12fred34" isn't numeric
```

Of course, warnings are generally meant for programmers, not for end-users. If the warning won't be seen by a programmer, it probably won't do any good. And

---

* The trick of using a leading zero to mean a nondecimal value works for literals, but never for automatic conversion. Use `hex()` or `oct()` to convert those kinds of strings.

† Unless you request warnings, which we'll discuss in a moment.

‡ We'll see about precedence and parentheses shortly.

§ It's usually not an issue, but these conversions can cause small round-off errors. That is, if you start with a number, convert it to a string, then convert that string back to a number, the result may not be the same number as you started with. It's not just Perl that does this; it's a consequence of the conversion process, so it happens to any powerful programming language.

warnings won't change the behavior of your program, except that now it will emit gripes once in a while. If you get a warning message you don't understand, look for its explanation in the *perldiag* manpage.

Warnings change from one version of Perl to the next. This may mean that your well-tuned program runs silently when warnings are on today, but not when it's used with a newer (or older) version of Perl. To help with this situation, version 5.6 of Perl introduces *lexical warnings*. These are warnings that may be turned on or off in different sections of code, providing more detailed control than the single -w switch could. See the *perllexwarn* manpage for more information on these warnings.

As we run across situations in which Perl will usually be able to warn you about a mistake in your code, we'll point them out. But you shouldn't count on the text or behavior of any warning staying exactly the same in future Perl releases.

Scalar Variables

A *variable* is a name for a container that holds one or more values.* The name of the variable stays the same throughout the program, but the value or values contained in that variable typically change over and over again throughout the execution of the program.

A scalar variable holds a single scalar value, as you'd expect. Scalar variable names begin with a dollar sign followed by what we'll call a *Perl identifier*: a letter or underscore, and then possibly more letters, or digits, or underscores. Another way to think of it is that it's made up of alphanumerics and underscores, but can't start with a digit. Uppercase and lowercase letters are distinct: the variable `$Fred` is a different variable from `$fred`. And all of the letters, digits, and underscores are significant, so:

```
$a_very_long_variable_that_ends_in_1
```

is different from:

```
$a_very_long_variable_that_ends_in_2
```

Scalar variables in Perl are always referenced with the leading $. In the shell, you use $ to get the value, but leave the $ off to assign a new value. In *awk* or C, you leave the $ off entirely. If you bounce back and forth a lot, you'll find yourself typing the wrong things occasionally. This is expected. (Most Perl programmers would recommend that you stop writing shell, *awk*, and C programs, but that may not work for you.)

---

* As we'll see, a scalar variable can hold only one value. But other types of variables, such as arrays and hashes, may hold many values.

Choosing Good Variable Names

You should generally select variable names that mean something regarding the purpose of the variable. For example, $r is probably not very descriptive but $line_length is. A variable used for only two or three lines close together may be called something simple, like $n, but a variable used throughout a program should probably have a more descriptive name.

Similarly, properly placed underscores can make a name easier to read and understand, especially if your maintenance programmer has a different spoken language background than you have. For example, $super_bowl is a better name than $superbowl, since that last one might look like $superb_owl. Does $stopid mean $sto_pid (storing a process-ID of some kind?) or $s_to_pid (converting something to a process-ID?) or $stop_id (the ID for some kind of "stop" object?) or is it just a stopid mispelling?

Most variable names in our Perl programs are all lowercase, like most of the ones we'll see in this book. In a few special cases, capitalization is used. Using all-caps (like $ARGV) generally indicates that there's something special about that variable. (But you can get into an all-out brawl if you choose sides on the $underscores_are_cool versus the $giveMeInitialCaps argument. So be careful.)

Of course, choosing good or poor names makes no difference to Perl. You *could* name your program's three most-important variables $OOO00O0O0, $00O00OO0, and $O00000O00 and Perl wouldn't be bothered—but in that case, please, don't ask us to maintain your code.

Scalar Assignment

The most common operation on a scalar variable is *assignment*, which is the way to give a value to a variable. The Perl assignment operator is the equals sign (much like other languages), which takes a variable name on the left side, and gives it the value of the expression on the right. For example:

```
$fred = 17;              # give $fred the value of 17
$barney = 'hello';       # give $barney the five-character string 'hello'
$barney = $fred + 3;     # give $barney the current value of $fred plus 3 (20)
$barney = $barney * 2;   # $barney is now $barney multiplied by 2 (40)
```

Notice that last line uses the $barney variable twice: once to get its value (on the right side of the equals sign), and once to define where to put the computed expression (on the left side of the equals sign). This is legal, safe, and in fact, rather common. In fact, it's so common that we can write it using a convenient shorthand, as we'll see in the next section.

Binary Assignment Operators

Expressions like `$fred = $fred + 5` (where the same variable appears on both sides of an assignment) occur frequently enough that Perl (like C and Java) has a shorthand for the operation of altering a variable—the *binary assignment operator*. Nearly all binary[*] operators that compute a value have a corresponding binary assignment form with an appended equals sign. For example, the following two lines are equivalent:

```
$fred = $fred + 5; # without the binary assignment operator
$fred += 5;        # with the binary assignment operator
```

These are also equivalent:

```
$barney = $barney * 3;
$barney *= 3;
```

In each case, the operator causes the existing value of the variable to be altered in some way, rather than simply overwriting the value with the result of some new expression.

Another common assignment operator is the string concatenate operator (.); this gives us an append operator (.=):

```
$str = $str . " "; # append a space to $str
$str .= " ";       # same thing with assignment operator
```

Nearly all binary operators are valid this way. For example, a *raise to the power of operator* is written as `**=`. So, `$fred **= 3` means "raise the number in `$fred` to the third power, placing the result back in `$fred`".

Output with print

It's generally a good idea to have your program produce some output; otherwise, someone may think it didn't do anything. The `print()` operator makes this possible. It takes a scalar argument and puts it out without any embellishment onto standard output. Unless you've done something odd, this will be your terminal display. For example:

```
print "hello world\n"; # say hello world, followed by a newline

print "The answer is ";
print 6 * 7;
print ".\n";
```

---

[*] The term "binary" here doesn't have anything to do with binary numbers. It merely means that these are operators that take two operands; for example, subtraction is a binary operation. There are also "unary" operators, which take just one operand. For example, the hyphen in `$barney = - $fred;` is a unary negation operator. And Perl even has one trinary operator (the wonderful `?:` operator), but we'll let you guess how many operands that takes.

You can actually give `print` a series of values, separated by commas.

```
print "The answer is ", 6 * 7, ".\n";
```

This is actually a *list*, but we haven't talked about lists yet, so we'll put that off for later.

Interpolation of Scalar Variables into Strings

When a string literal is double-quoted, it is subject to *variable interpolation*[*] (besides being checked for backslash escapes). This means that any scalar variable[†] name in the string is replaced with its current value. For example:

```
$meal = "brontosaurus steak";
$barney = "fred ate a $meal";    # $barney is now "fred ate a brontosaurus steak"
$barney = 'fred ate a ' . $meal; # another way to write that
```

As you see on the last line above, you can get the same results without the double quotes. But the double-quoted string is often the more convenient way to write it.

If the scalar variable has never been given a value,[‡] the empty string is used instead:

```
$barney = "fred ate a $meat"; # $barney is now "fred ate a "
```

Don't bother with interpolating if you have just the one lone variable:

```
print "$fred"; # unneeded quote marks
print $fred;   # better style
```

There's nothing really *wrong* with putting quote marks around a lone variable, but the other programmers will laugh at you behind your back.[§]

Variable interpolation is also known as *double-quote interpolation*, because it happens when double-quote marks (but not single quotes) are used. It happens for some other strings in Perl, which we'll mention as we get to them.

To put a real dollar sign into a double-quoted string, precede the dollar sign with a backslash, which turns off the dollar sign's special significance:

```
$fred = 'hello';
print "The name is \$fred.\n";    # prints a dollar sign
print 'The name is $fred' . "\n"; # so does this
```

---

[*] This has nothing to do with mathematical or statistical interpolation.

[†] And some other variable types, but we won't see those until later.

[‡] This is actually the special undefined value, `undef`, which we'll see a little later in this chapter. If warnings are turned on, Perl will complain about interpolating the undefined value.

[§] Well, it may force a value to be interpreted as a string, rather than a number. In a few rare cases that may be needed, but nearly always it's just a waste of typing.

The variable name will be the longest possible variable name that makes sense at that part of the string. This can be a problem if you want to follow the replaced value immediately with some constant text that begins with a letter, digit, or underscore.* As Perl scans for variable names, it would consider those characters to be additional name characters, which is not what you want. Perl provides a delimiter for the variable name in a manner similar to the shell. Simply enclose the *name* of the variable in a pair of curly braces. Or, you can end that part of the string and start another part of the string with a concatenation operator:

```
$what = "brontosaurus steak";
$n = 3;
print "fred ate $n $whats.\n";          # not the steaks, but the value of $whats
print "fred ate $n ${what}s.\n";        # now uses $what
print "fred ate $n $what" . "s.\n";     # another way to do it
print 'fred ate ' . $n . ' ' . $what . "s.\n"; # an especially difficult way
```

Operator Precedence and Associativity

Operator precedence determines which operations in a complex group of operations happen first. For example, in the expression 2+3*4, do we perform the addition first or the multiplication first? If we did the addition first, we'd get 5*4, or 20. But if we did the multiplication first (as we were taught in math class), we'd get 2+12, or 14. Fortunately, Perl chooses the common mathematical definition, performing the multiplication first. Because of this, we say multiplication has a *higher precedence* than addition.

You can override the default precedence order by using parentheses. Anything in parentheses is completely computed before the operator outside of the parentheses is applied (just like you learned in math class). So if I really want the addition before the multiplication, I can say (2+3)*4, yielding 20. Also, if I wanted to demonstrate that multiplication is performed before addition, I could add a decorative but unnecessary set of parentheses, as in 2+(3*4).

While precedence is simple for addition and multiplication, we start running into problems when faced with, say, string concatenation compared with exponentiation. The proper way to resolve this is to consult the official, accept-no-substitutes Perl operator precedence chart, shown in Table 2-2.† (Note that some of the

---

* There are some other characters that may be a problem as well. If you need a left square bracket or a left curly brace just after a scalar variable's name, precede it with a backslash. You may also do that if the variable's name is followed by an apostrophe or a pair of colons, or you could use the curly-brace method described in the main text

† C programmers: Rejoice! The operators that are available in both Perl and C have the same precedence and associativity in both.

operators have not yet been described, and in fact, may not even appear anywhere in this book, but don't let that scare you from reading about them in the *perlop* manpage.)

Table 2-2. Associativity and precedence of operators (highest to lowest)

Associativity	Operators
left	parentheses and arguments to list operators
left	->
	++ -- (autoincrement and autodecrement)
right	**
right	\ ! ~ + - (unary operators)
left	=~ !~
left	* / % x
left	+ - . (binary operators)
left	<< >>
	named unary operators (-X filetests, rand)
	< <= > >= lt le gt ge (the "unequal" ones)
	== != <=> eq ne cmp (the "equal" ones)
left	&
left	| ^
left	&&
left	||
	.. ...
right	?: (ternary)
right	= += -= .= (and similar assignment operators)
left	, =>
	list operators (rightward)
right	not
left	and
left	or xor

In the chart, any given operator has higher precedence than all of the operators listed below it, and lower precedence than all of the operators listed above it. Operators at the same precedence level resolve according to rules of *associativity* instead.

Just like precedence, associativity resolves the order of operations when two operators of the same precedence compete for three operands:

```
4 ** 3 ** 2 # 4 ** (3 ** 2), or 4 ** 9 (right associative)
72 / 12 / 3 # (72 / 12) / 3, or 6/3, or 2 (left associative)
36 / 6 * 3  # (36/6)*3, or 18
```

In the first case, the ** operator has right associativity, so the parentheses are implied on the right. Comparatively, the * and / operators have left associativity, yielding a set of implied parentheses on the left.

So should you just memorize the precedence chart? No! Nobody actually does that. Instead, just use parentheses when you don't remember the order of operations, or when you're too busy to look in the chart. After all, if you can't remember it without the parentheses, your maintenance programmer is going to have the same trouble. So be nice to your maintenance programmer.

Comparison Operators

For comparing numbers, Perl has the logical comparison operators that remind you of algebra: < <= == >= > !=. Each of these returns a *true* or *false* value. We'll find out more about those return values in the next section. Some of these may be different than you'd use in other languages. For example, == is used for equality, not a single = sign, because that's used for another purpose in Perl. And != is used for inequality testing, because <> is used for another purpose in Perl. And you'll need >= and not => for "greater than or equal to", because the latter is used for another purpose in Perl. In fact, nearly every sequence of punctuation is used for something in Perl.

For comparing strings, Perl has an equivalent set of string comparison operators which look like funny little words: lt le eq ge gt ne. These compare two strings character by character to see whether they're the same, or whether one comes first in standard string sorting order. (In ASCII, the capital letters come before the lowercase letters, so beware.)

The comparison operators (for both numbers and strings) are given in Table 2-3.

Table 2-3. Numeric and string comparison operators

Comparison	Numeric	String
Equal	==	eq
Not equal	!=	ne
Less than	<	lt
Greater than	>	gt
Less than or equal to	<=	le
Greater than or equal to	>=	ge

Here are some example expressions using these comparison operators:

```
35 != 30 + 5        # false
35 == 35.0          # true
'35' eq '35.0'      # false (comparing as strings)
```

```
'fred' lt 'barney'    # false
'fred' lt 'free'      # true
'fred' eq "fred"      # true
'fred' eq 'Fred'      # false
' ' gt ''             # true
```

The if Control Structure

Once you can compare two values, you'll probably want your program to make decisions based upon that comparison. Like all similar languages, Perl has an `if` control structure:

```
if ($name gt 'fred') {
  print "'$name' comes after 'fred' in sorted order.\n";
}
```

If you need an alternative choice, the `else` keyword provides that as well:

```
if ($name gt 'fred') {
  print "'$name' comes after 'fred' in sorted order.\n";
} else {
  print "'$name' does not come after 'fred'.\n";
  print "Maybe it's the same string, in fact.\n";
}
```

Unlike in C, those block curly braces are required around the conditional code. It's a good idea to indent the contents of the blocks of code as we show here; that makes it easier to see what's going on. If you're using a programmers' text editor (as discussed in Chapter 1), it'll do most of the work for you.

Boolean Values

You may actually use any scalar value as the conditional of the `if` control structure. That's handy if you want to store a true or false value into a variable, like this:

```
$is_bigger = $name gt 'fred';
if ($is_bigger) { ... }
```

But how does Perl decide whether a given value is true or false? Perl doesn't have a separate Boolean data type, like some languages have. Instead, it uses a few simple rules:

1. The special value **undef** is false. (We'll see this a little later in this section.)

2. Zero is false; all other numbers are true.

3. The empty string (`' '`) is false; all other strings are normally true.

4. The one exception: since numbers and strings are equivalent, the string form of zero, `'0'`, has the same value as its numeric form: false.

So, if your scalar value is **undef**, 0, ' ', or ' 0', it's false. All other scalars are true—including all of the types of scalars that we haven't told you about yet.

If you need to get the opposite of any Boolean value, use the unary *not* operator, !. If what follows it is a true value, it returns false; if what follows is false, it returns true:

```
if (! $is_bigger) {
  # Do something when $is_bigger is not true
}
```

Getting User Input

At this point, you're probably wondering how to get a value from the keyboard into a Perl program. Here's the simplest way: use the line-input operator, <STDIN>.* Each time you use <STDIN> in a place where a scalar value is expected, Perl reads the next complete text line from *standard input* (up to the first newline), and uses that string as the value of <STDIN>. Standard input can mean many things, but unless you do something uncommon, it means the keyboard of the user who invoked your program (probably you). If there's nothing waiting to be read (typically the case, unless you type ahead a complete line), the Perl program will stop and wait for you to enter some characters followed by a newline (return).†

The string value of <STDIN> typically has a newline character on the end of it.‡ So you *could* do something like this:

```
$line = <STDIN>;
if ($line eq "\n") {
  print "That was just a blank line!\n";
} else {
  print "That line of input was: $line";
}
```

But in practice, you don't often want to keep the newline, so you need the **chomp** operator.

---

* This is actually a line-input operator working on the filehandle STDIN, but we can't tell you about that until we get to filehandles (in Chapter 11, *Filehandles and File Tests*).

† To be honest, it's normally your system that waits for the input; Perl waits for your system. Although the details depend upon your system and its configuration, you can generally correct your mistyping with a backspace key before you press return—your system handles that, not Perl itself. If you need more control over the input, get the **Term::ReadLine** module from CPAN.

‡ The exception is if the standard input stream somehow runs out in the middle of a line. But that's not a proper text file, of course!

The chomp Operator

The first time you read about the **chomp** operator, it seems terribly overspecialized. It works on a variable. The variable has to hold a string. And if the string ends in a newline character, **chomp** can get rid of the newline. That's (nearly) all it does. For example:

```
$text = "a line of text\n"; # Or the same thing from <STDIN>
chomp($text);               # Gets rid of the newline character
```

But it turns out to be so useful, you'll put it into nearly every program you write. As you see, it's the best way to remove a trailing newline from a string in a variable. In fact, there's an easier way to use **chomp**, because of a simple rule: any time that you need a variable in Perl, you can use an assignment instead. First, Perl does the assignment. Then it uses the variable in whatever way you requested. So the most common use of **chomp** looks like this:

```
chomp($text = <STDIN>); # Read the text, without the newline character

$text = <STDIN>;        # Do the same thing...
chomp($text);           # ...but in two steps
```

At first glance, the combined **chomp** may not seem to be the easy way, especially if it seems more complex! If you think of it as two operations—read a line, then **chomp** it—then it's more natural to write it as two statements. But if you think of it as one operation—read just the text, not the newline—it's more natural to write the one statement. And since most other Perl programmers are going to write it that way, you may as well get used to it now.

chomp is actually a function. As a function, it has a return value, which is the number of characters removed. This number is hardly ever useful:

```
$food = <STDIN>;
$betty = chomp $food; # gets the value 1 - but we knew that!
```

As you see, you may write **chomp** with or without the parentheses. This is another general rule in Perl: except in cases where it changes the meaning to remove them, parentheses are always optional.

If a line ends with two or more newlines,* **chomp** removes only one. If there's no newline, it does nothing, and returns zero.

If you work with older Perl programs, you may run across the **chop** operator. It's similar, but removes *any* trailing character, not just a trailing newline. Since that could accidentally turn **pebbles** into **pebble**, it's usually not what you want.

---

* This situation can't arise if we're reading a line at a time, but it certainly can when we have set the input separator ($/) to something other than newline, or use the **read** function, or perhaps have glued some strings together ourselves.

The while Control Structure

Like most algorithmic programming languages, Perl has a number of looping structures.* The while loop repeats a block of code as long as a condition is true:

```
$count = 0;
while ($count < 10) {
  $count += 1;
  print "count is now $count\n"; # Gives values from 1 to 10
}
```

As always in Perl, the truth value here works like the truth value in the if test. Also like the if control structure, the block curly braces are required. The conditional expression is evaluated before the first iteration, so the loop may be skipped completely, if the condition is initially false.

The undef Value

What happens if you use a scalar variable before you give it a value? Nothing serious, and definitely nothing fatal. Variables have the special undef value before they are first assigned, which is just Perl's way of saying "nothing here to look at—move along, move along." If you try to use this "nothing" as a "numeric something," it acts like 0. If you try to use it as a "string something," it acts like the empty string. But undef is neither a number nor a string; it's an entirely separate kind of scalar value.

Because undef automatically acts like zero when used as a number, it's easy to make an numeric accumulator that starts out empty:

```
# Add up some odd numbers
$n = 1;
while ($n < 10) {
  $sum += $n;
  $n += 2; # On to the next odd number
}
print "The total was $sum.\n";
```

This works properly when $sum was undef before the loop started. The first time through the loop, $n is one, so the first line inside the loop adds one to $sum. That's like adding one to a variable that already holds zero (because we're using undef as if it were a number). So now it has the value 1. After that, since it's been initialized, adding works in the traditional way.

---

* Every programmer eventually creates an infinite loop by accident. If your program keeps running and running, though, you can generally stop it in the same way you'd stop any other program on your system. Often, typing Control-C will stop a runaway program; check with your system's documentation to be sure.

Similarly, you could have a string accumulator that starts out empty:

```
$string .= "more text\n";
```

If `$string` is undef, this will act as if it already held the empty string, putting `"more text\n"` into that variable. But if it already holds a string, the new text is simply appended.

Perl programmers frequently use a new variable in this way, letting it act as either zero or the empty string as needed.

Many operators return undef when the arguments are out of range or don't make sense. If you don't do anything special, you'll get a zero or a null string without major consequences. In practice, this is hardly a problem. In fact, most programmers will rely upon this behavior. But you should know that when warnings are turned on, Perl will typically warn about unusual uses of the undefined value, since that may indicate a bug. For example, simply copying undef from one variable into another isn't a problem, but trying to `print` it would generally cause a warning.

The defined Function

One operator that can return undef is the line-input operator, `<STDIN>`. Normally, it will return a line of text. But if there is no more input, such as at end-of-file, it returns undef to signal this.* To tell whether a value is undef and not the empty string, use the **defined** function, which returns false for undef, and true for everything else:

```
$madonna = <STDIN>;
if ( defined($madonna) ) {
  print "The input was $madonna";
} else {
  print "No input available!\n";
}
```

If you'd like to make your own undef values, you can use the obscurely named undef operator:

```
$madonna = undef; # As if it had never been touched
```

---

* Normally, there's no "end-of-file" when the input comes from the keyboard, but input may have been redirected to come from a file. Or the user may have pressed the key that the system recognizes to indicate end-of-file.

Exercises

See Appendix A for answers to the following exercises:

1. [5] Write a program that computes the circumference of a circle with a radius of 12.5. Circumference is 2π times the radius (approximately 2 times 3. 141592654). The answer you get should be about 78.5. bk 2-1.pl

2. [4] Modify the program from the previous exercise to prompt for and accept a radius from the person running the program. So, if the user enters 12.5 for the radius, she should get the same number as in the previous exercise. bk2-1.pl

3. [4] Modify the program from the previous exercise so that, if the user enters a number less than zero, the reported circumference will be zero, rather than negative. bk2-1.pl

4. [8] Write a program that prompts for and reads two numbers (on separate lines of input) and prints out the product of the two numbers multiplied together. bk2-4.pl

5. [8] Write a program that prompts for and reads a string and a number (on separate lines of input) and prints out the string the number of times indicated by the number on separate lines. (Hint: Use the "x" operator.) If the user enters "fred" and "3," the output should be three lines, each saying "fred". If the user enters "fred" and "299792," there may be a lot of output. bk2-5.pl

3

Lists and Arrays

If a scalar was the "singular" in Perl, as we described them at the beginning of Chapter two, the "plural" in Perl is represented by lists and arrays.

A *list* is an ordered collection of scalars. An *array* is a variable that contains a list. In Perl, the two terms are often used as if they're interchangeable. But, to be accurate, the list is the data, and the array is the variable. You can have a list value that isn't in an array, but every array variable holds a list (although that list may be empty). Figure 3-1 represents a list, whether it's stored in an array or not.

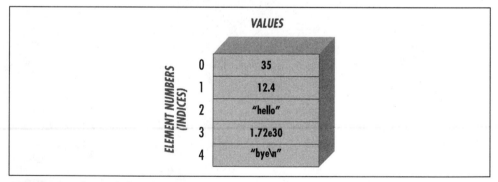

Figure 3-1. A list with five elements

Each *element* of an array or list is a separate scalar variable with an independent scalar value. These values are ordered—that is, they have a particular sequence from the first to the last element. The elements of an array or list are *indexed* by small integers starting at zero* and counting by ones, so the first element of any array or list is always element zero.

Since each element is an independent scalar value, a list or array may hold numbers, strings, undef values, or any mixture of different scalar values. Nevertheless, it's most common to have all elements of the same type, such as a list of book titles (all strings) or a list of cosines (all numbers).

Arrays and lists can have any number of elements. The smallest one has no elements, while the largest can fill all of available memory. Once again, this is in keeping with Perl's philosophy of "no unnecessary limits."

Accessing Elements of an Array

If you've used arrays in another language, you won't be surprised to find that Perl provides a way to subscript an array in order to refer to an element by a numeric index.

The array elements are numbered using sequential integers, beginning at zero and increasing by one for each element, like this:

```
$fred[0] = "yabba";
$fred[1] = "dabba";
$fred[2] = "doo";
```

The array name itself (in this case, "fred") is from a completely separate namespace than scalars use; you could have a scalar variable named $fred in the same program, and Perl will treat them as different things, and wouldn't be confused.† (Your maintenance programmer might be confused, though, so don't capriciously make all of your variable names the same!)

You can use an array element like $fred[2] in every place‡ where you could use any other scalar variable like $fred. For example, you can get the value from an array element or change that value by the same sorts of expressions we used in the previous chapter:

---

* Array and list indices always start at zero in Perl, unlike in some other languages. In early Perl, it was possible to change the starting number of array and list indexing (not for just one array or list, but for all of them at once!). Larry later realized that this was a misfeature, and its (ab)use is now strongly discouraged. But, if you're terminally curious, look up the $[variable in the *perlvar* manpage.

† The syntax is always unambiguous—tricky perhaps, but unambiguous.

‡ Well, almost. The most notable exception is that the control variable of a foreach loop, which we'll see later in this chapter, must be a simple scalar. And there are others, like the "indirect object slot" and "indirect filehandle slot" for print and printf.

```
print $fred[0];
$fred[2] = "diddley";
$fred[1] .= "whatsis";
```

Of course, the subscript may be any expression that gives a numeric value. If it's not an integer already, it'll automatically be truncated to the next lower integer:

```
$number = 2.71828;
print $fred[$number - 1]; # Same as printing $fred[1]
```

If the subscript indicates an element that would be beyond the end of the array, the corresponding value will be **undef**. This is just as with ordinary scalars; if you've never stored a value into the variable, it's **undef**.

```
$blank = $fred[ 142_857 ]; # unused array element gives undef
$blanc = $mel;             # unused scalar $mel also gives undef
```

Special Array Indices

If you store into an array element that is beyond the end of the array, the array is automatically extended as needed—there's no limit on its length, as long as there's available memory for Perl to use. If intervening elements need to be created, they'll be created as **undef** values.

```
$rocks[0] = 'bedrock';     # One element...
$rocks[1] = 'slate';       # another...
$rocks[2] = 'lava';        # and another...
$rocks[3] = 'crushed rock'; # and another...
$rocks[99] = 'schist';     # now there are 95 undef elements
```

Sometimes, you need to find out the last element index in an array. For the array of **rocks** that we've just been using, the last element index is **$#rocks**.* That's not the same as the number of elements, though, because there's an element number zero. As seen in the code snippet below, it's actually possible to assign to this value to change the size of the array, although this is rare in practice.†

```
$end = $#rocks;            # 99, which is the last element's index
$number_of_rocks = $end + 1; # okay, but we'll see a better way later
$#rocks = 2;               # Forget all rocks after 'lava'
$#rocks = 99;              # add 97 undef elements (the forgotten rocks are
                           # gone forever)
$rocks[ $#rocks ] = 'hard rock'; # the last rock
```

Using the **$#name** value as an index, like that last example, happens often enough that Larry has provided a shortcut: negative array indices count from the end of the array. But don't get the idea that these indices "wrap around." If you've got

---

* Blame this ugly syntax on the C shell. Fortunately, we don't have to look at this very often in the real world.

† This is very infrequently done to "pre-size" an array, so that Perl won't need to allocate memory in many small chunks as an array grows. See the Perl documentation for more information, in the unlikely case that you need this.

three elements in the array, the valid negative indices are -1 (the last element), -2 (the middle element), and -3 (the first element). In the real world, nobody seems to use any of these except -1, though.

```
$rocks[ -1 ] = 'hard rock'; # easier way to do that last example above
$dead_rock = $rocks[-100];  # gets 'bedrock'
$rocks[ -200 ] = 'crystal'; # fatal error!
```

List Literals

A *list literal* (the way you represent a list value within your program) is a list of comma-separated values enclosed in parentheses. These values form the elements of the list. For example:

```
(1, 2, 3)       # list of three values 1, 2, and 3
(1, 2, 3,)      # the same three values (the trailing comma is ignored)
("fred", 4.5)   # two values, "fred" and 4.5
()              # empty list - zero elements
(1..100)        # list of 100 integers
```

That last one uses the .. *range operator*, which is seen here for the first time. That operator creates a list of values by counting from the left scalar up to the right scalar by ones. For example:

```
(1..5)            # same as (1, 2, 3, 4, 5)
(1.7..5.7)        # same thing - both values are truncated
(5..1)            # empty list - .. only counts "uphill"
(0, 2..6, 10, 12) # same as (0, 2, 3, 4, 5, 6, 10, 12)
($a..$b)          # range determined by current values of $a and $b
(0..$#rocks)      # the indices of the rocks array from the previous section
```

As you can see from those last two items, the elements of an array are not necessarily constants—they can be expressions that will be newly evaluated each time the literal is used. For example:

```
($a, 17)        # two values: the current value of $a, and 17
($b+$c, $d+$e)  # two values
```

Of course, a list may have any scalar values, like this typical list of strings:

```
("fred", "barney", "betty", "wilma", "dino")
```

The qw Shortcut

It turns out that lists of simple words (like the previous example) are frequently needed in Perl programs. The **qw** shortcut makes it easy to generate them without typing a lot of extra quote marks:

```
qw/ fred barney betty wilma dino / # same as above, but less typing
```

qw stands for "quoted words" or "quoted by whitespace," depending upon whom you ask. Either way, Perl treats it like a single-quoted string (so, you can't use \n or `$fred` inside a qw list as you would in a double-quoted string). The whitespace (characters like spaces, tabs, and newlines) will be discarded, and whatever is left becomes the list of items. Since whitespace is discarded, here's another (but unusual) way to write that same list:

```
qw/fred
   barney     betty
wilma dino/    # same as above, but pretty strange whitespace
```

Since qw is a form of quoting, though, you can't put comments inside a qw list.

The previous two examples have used forward slashes as the delimiter, but Perl actually lets you choose any punctuation character as the delimiter. Here are some of the common ones:

```
qw! fred barney betty wilma dino !
qw# fred barney betty wilma dino #    # like in a comment!
qw( fred barney betty wilma dino )
qw{ fred barney betty wilma dino }
qw[ fred barney betty wilma dino ]
qw< fred barney betty wilma dino >
```

As those last four show, sometimes the two delimiters can be different. If the opening delimiter is one of those "left" characters, the corresponding "right" character is the proper closing delimiter. Other delimiters use the same character for start and finish.

If you need to include the closing delimiter *within* the string as one of the characters, you probably picked the wrong delimeter. But even if you can't or don't want to change the delimiter, you can still include the character using the backslash:

```
qw! yahoo\! google excite lycos ! # include yahoo! as an element
```

As in single-quoted strings, two consecutive backslashes contribute one single backslash to the item.

Now, although the Perl motto is "There's More Than One Way To Do It," you may well wonder why anyone would need all of those different ways! Well, we'll see later that there are other kinds of quoting where Perl uses this same rule, and it can come in handy in many of those. But even here, it could be useful if you were to need a list of Unix filenames:

```
qw{
   /usr/dict/words
   /home/rootbeer/.ispell_english
}
```

That list would be quite inconvenient to read, write, and maintain if the slash were the only delimiter available.

List Assignment

In much the same way as scalar values may be assigned to variables, list values may also be assigned to variables:

```
($fred, $barney, $dino) = ("flintstone", "rubble", undef);
```

All three variables in the list on the left get new values, just as if we did three separate assignments. Since the list is built up before the assignment starts, this makes it easy to swap two variables' values in Perl:*

```
($fred, $barney) = ($barney, $fred); # swap those values
($betty[0], $betty[1]) = ($betty[1], $betty[0]);
```

But what happens if the number of variables (on the left side of the equals sign) isn't the same as the number of values (from the right side)? In a list assignment, extra values are silently ignored—Perl figures that if you wanted those values stored somewhere, you would have told it where to store them. Alternatively, if you have too many variables, the extras get the value **undef**.†

```
($fred, $barney) = qw< flintstone rubble slate granite >; # two ignored items
($wilma, $dino) = qw[flintstone];                          # $dino gets undef
```

Now that we can assign lists, you *could* build up an array of strings with a line of code like this:‡

```
($rocks[0], $rocks[1], $rocks[2], $rocks[3]) = qw/talc mica feldspar quartz/;
```

But when you wish to refer to an entire array, Perl has a simpler notation. Just use the at-sign (**@**) before the name of the array (and no index brackets after it) to refer to the entire array at once. You can read this as "all of the," so **@rocks** is "all of the rocks."§ This works on either side of the assignment operator:

```
@rocks = qw/ bedrock slate lava /;
@tiny = ();                        # the empty list
@giant = 1..1e5;                   # a list with 100,000 elements
@stuff = (@giant, undef, @giant);  # a list with 200,001 elements
$dino = "granite";
@quarry = (@rocks, "crushed rock", @tiny, $dino);
```

---

* As opposed to in languages like C, which has no easy way to do this in general. C programmers usually resort to some kind of macro to do this, or use a variable to temporarily hold the value.

† Well, that's true for scalar variables. Array variables get an empty list, as we'll see in a moment.

‡ We're cheating by assuming that the rocks array is empty before this statement. If there were a value in $rocks[7], say, this assignment wouldn't affect that element.

§ Larry claims that he chose the dollar and at-sign because they can be read as $calar (scalar) and @rray (array). If you don't get that, or remember it that way, no big deal.

That last assignment gives @quarry the five-element list (bedrock, slate, lava, crushed rock, granite), since @tiny contributes zero elements to the list. (In particular, it doesn't put an undef item into the list—but we could do that explicitly, as we did with @stuff earlier.) It's also worth noting that an array name is replaced by the list it contains. An array doesn't become an element in the list, because these arrays can contain only scalars, not other arrays.*

The value of an array variable that has not yet been assigned is (), the empty list. Just as new, empty scalars start out with undef, new, empty arrays start out with the empty list.

It's worth noting that when an array is copied to another array, it's still a list assignment. The lists are simply stored in arrays. For example:

```
@copy = @quarry; # copy a list from one array to another
```

The pop and push Operators

You *could* add new items to the end of an array by simply storing them into elements with new, larger indices. But real Perl programmers don't use indices.† So in the next few sections, we'll present some ways to work with an array without using indices.

One common use of an array is as a stack of information, where new values are added to and removed from the right-hand side of the list. (This is the end with the "last" items in the array, the end with the highest index values.) These operations occur often enough to have their own special functions.

The pop operator takes the last element off of an array, and returns it:

```
@array = 5..9;
$fred = pop(@array);  # $fred gets 9, @array now has (5, 6, 7, 8)
$barney = pop @array; # $barney gets 8, @array now has (5, 6, 7)
pop @array;           # @array now has (5, 6). (The 7 is discarded.)
```

That last example uses pop "in a void context," which is merely a fancy way of saying the return value isn't going anywhere. There's nothing wrong with using pop in this way, if that's what you want.

---

* But when you get into more advanced Perl, you'll learn about a special kind of scalar called a reference. That lets us make what are informally called "lists of lists", among other interesting and useful structures. But in that case, you're still not really storing a list into a list; you're storing a reference to an array.

† Of course, we're joking. But there's a kernel of truth in this joke. Indexing into arrays is not using Perl's strengths. If you use the pop, push, and similar operators that avoid using indexing, your code will generally be faster than if you use many indices, as well as being more likely to avoid "off-by-one" errors, often called "fencepost" errors. Occasionally, a beginning Perl programmer (wanting to see how Perl's speed compares to C's) will take, say, a sorting algorithm optimized for C (with many array index operations), rewrite it straightforward in Perl (again, with many index operations) and wonder why it's so slow. The answer is that using a Stradivarius violin to pound nails should not be considered a sound construction technique.

If the array is empty, pop will leave it alone (since there is no element to remove), and it will return undef.

You may have noticed that pop may be used with or without parentheses. This is a general rule in Perl: as long as the meaning isn't changed by removing the parentheses, they're optional.[*]

The converse operation is push, which adds an element (or a list of elements) to the end of an array:

```
push(@array, 0);       # @array now has (5, 6, 0)
push @array, 8;        # @array now has (5, 6, 0, 8)
push @array, 1..10;    # @array now has those ten new elements
@others = qw/ 9 0 2 1 0 /;
push @array, @others;  # @array now has those five new elements (19 total)
```

Note that the first argument to push or the only argument for pop must be an array variable—pushing and popping would not make sense on a literal list.

The shift and unshift Operators

The push and pop operators do things to the end of an array (or the right side of an array, or the portion with the highest subscripts, depending upon how you like to think of it). Similarly, the unshift and shift operators perform the corresponding actions on the "start" of the array (or the "left" side of an array, or the portion with the lowest subscripts). Here are a few examples:

```
@array = qw# dino fred barney #;
$a = shift(@array);    # $a gets "dino", @array now has ("fred", "barney")
$b = shift @array;     # $b gets "fred", @array now has ("barney")
shift @array;          # @array is now empty
$c = shift @array;     # $c gets undef, @array is still empty
unshift(@array, 5);    # @array now has the one-element list (5)
unshift @array, 4;     # @array now has (4, 5);
@others = 1..3;
unshift @array, @others; # @array now has (1, 2, 3, 4, 5)
```

Analogous to pop, shift returns undef if given an empty array variable.

Interpolating Arrays into Strings

Like scalars, array values may be interpolated into a double-quoted string. Elements of an array are automatically separated by spaces[†] upon interpolation:

```
@rocks = qw{ flintstone slate rubble };
print "quartz @rocks limestone\n";  # prints five rocks separated by spaces
```

---

[*] A reader from the educated class will recognize that this is a tautology.

[†] Actually, the separator is the value of the special $" variable, which is a space by default.

There are no extra spaces added before or after an interpolated array; if you want those, you'll have to put them in yourself:

```
print "Three rocks are: @rocks.\n";
print "There's nothing in the parens (@empty) here.\n";
```

If you forget that arrays interpolate like this, you'll be surprised when you put an email address into a double-quoted string. For historical reasons,* this is a fatal error at compile time:

```
$email = "fred@bedrock.edu";  # WRONG! Tries to interpolate @bedrock
$email = "fred\@bedrock.edu"; # Correct
$email = 'fred@bedrock.edu';  # Another way to do that
```

A single element of an array will be replaced by its value, just as you'd expect:

```
@fred = qw(hello dolly);
$y = 2;
$x = "This is $fred[1]'s place";    # "This is dolly's place"
$x = "This is $fred[$y-1]'s place"; # same thing
```

Note that the index expression is evaluated as an ordinary expression, as if it were outside a string. It is *not* variable-interpolated first. In other words, if $y contains the string "2*4", we're still talking about element 1, not element 7, because "2*4" as a number (the value of $y used in a numeric expression) is just plain 2.†

If you want to follow a simple scalar variable with a left square bracket, you need to delimit the square bracket so that it isn't considered part of an array reference, as follows:

```
@fred = qw(eating rocks is wrong);
$fred = "right";                   # we are trying to say "this is right[3]"
print "this is $fred[3]\n";        # prints "wrong" using $fred[3]
print "this is ${fred}[3]\n";      # prints "right" (protected by braces)
print "this is $fred"."[3]\n";     # right again (different string)
print "this is $fred\[3]\n";       # right again (backslash hides it)
```

The foreach Control Structure

It's handy to be able to process an entire array or list, so Perl provides a control structure to do just that. The **foreach** loop steps through a list of values, executing one iteration (time through the loop) for each value:

```
foreach $rock (qw/ bedrock slate lava /) {
  print "One rock is $rock.\n";  # Prints names of three rocks
}
```

---

* Since you asked: Before version 5, Perl would silently leave uninterpolated an unused array's name in a double-quoted string. So, "fred@bedrock.edu" might be a string containing an email address. This attempt to Do What I Mean will backfire when someone adds a variable named @bedrock to the program—now the string becomes "fred.edu" or worse.

† Of course, if you've got warnings turned on, Perl is likely to remind you that "2*4" is a pretty funny-looking number.

The control variable ($rock in that example) takes on a new value from the list for each iteration. The first time through the loop, it's "bedrock"; the third time, it's "lava".

The control variable is not a copy of the list element—it actually *is* the list element. That is, if you modify the control variable inside the loop, you'll be modifying the element itself, as shown in the following code snippet. This is useful, and supported, but it would surprise you if you weren't expecting it.

```
@rocks = qw/ bedrock slate lava /;
foreach $rock (@rocks) {
  $rock = "\t$rock";          # put a tab in front of each element of @rocks
  $rock .= "\n";              # put a newline on the end of each
}
print "The rocks are:\n", @rocks; # Each one is indented, on its own line
```

What is the value of the control variable after the loop has finished? It's the same as it was before the loop started. The value of the control variable of a **foreach** loop is automatically saved and restored by Perl. While the loop is running, there's no way to access or alter that saved value. So after the loop is done, the variable has the value it had before the loop, or **undef** if it hadn't had a value. That means that if you want to name your loop control variable "$rock", you don't have to worry that maybe you've already used that name for another variable.*

Perl's Favorite Default: $_

If you omit the control variable from the beginning of the **foreach** loop, Perl uses its favorite default variable, $_. This is (mostly) just like any other scalar variable, except for its unusual name. For example:

```
foreach (1..10) {  # Uses $_ by default
  print "I can count to $_!\n";
}
```

Although this isn't Perl's only default by a long shot, it's Perl's most common default. We'll see many other cases in which Perl will automatically use $_ when you don't tell it to use some other variable or value, thereby saving the programmer from the heavy labor of having to think up and type a new variable name. So as not to keep you in suspense, one of those cases is **print**, which will print $_ if given no other argument:

```
$_ = "Yabba dabba doo\n";
print;  # prints $_ by default
```

---

* Unless the variable name has been declared as a lexical in the current scope, in which case you get a lexically local variable instead of a package local variable—more on this in Chapter 4.

The reverse Operator

The **reverse** operator takes a list of values (which may come from an array) and returns the list in the opposite order. So if you were disappointed that the range operator, . . , only counts upwards, this is the way to fix it:

```
@fred = 6..10;
@barney = reverse(@fred); # gets 10, 9, 8, 7, 6
@wilma = reverse 6..10;    # gets the same thing, without the other array
@fred = reverse @fred;     # puts the result back into the original array
```

The last line is noteworthy because it uses **@fred** twice. Perl always calculates the value being assigned (on the right) before it begins the actual assignment.

Remember that **reverse** returns the reversed list; it doesn't affect its arguments. If the return value isn't assigned anywhere, it's useless:

```
reverse @fred;       # WRONG - doesn't change @fred
@fred = reverse @fred; # that's better
```

The sort Operator

The **sort** operator takes a list of values (which may come from an array) and sorts them in the internal character ordering. For ASCII strings, that would be ASCIIbetical order. Of course, ASCII is a strange place where all of the capital letters come before all of the lowercase letters, where the numbers come before the letters, and the punctuation marks—well, those are here, there, and everywhere. But sorting in ASCII order is just the *default* behavior; we'll see in Chapter 15, *Strings and Sorting*, how to sort in whatever order you'd like:

```
@rocks = qw/ bedrock slate rubble granite /;
@sorted = sort(@rocks);      # gets bedrock, granite, rubble, slate
@back = reverse sort @rocks; # these go from slate to bedrock
@rocks = sort @rocks;        # puts sorted result back into @rocks
@numbers = sort 97..102;     # gets 100, 101, 102, 97, 98, 99
```

As you can see from that last example, sorting numbers as if they were strings may not give useful results. But, of course, any string that starts with 1 has to sort before any string that starts with 9, according to the default sorting rules. And like what happened with **reverse**, the arguments themselves aren't affected. If you want to sort an array, you must store the result back into that array:

```
sort @rocks;         # WRONG, doesn't modify @rocks
@rocks = sort @rocks; # Now the rock collection is in order
```

Scalar and List Context

This is the most important section in this chapter. In fact, it's the most important section in the entire book. In fact, it wouldn't be an exaggeration to say that your entire career in using Perl will depend upon understanding this section. So if you've gotten away with skimming the text up to this point, this is where you should really pay attention.

That's not to say that this section is in any way difficult to understand. It's actually a simple idea: a given expression may mean different things depending upon where it appears. This is nothing new to you; it happens all the time in natural languages. For example, in English,[*] suppose someone asked you what the word "read"[†] means. It has different meanings depending on how it's used. You can't identify the meaning, until you know the *context*.

The *context* refers to where an expression is found. As Perl is parsing your expressions, it always expects either a scalar value or a list value.[‡] What Perl expects is called the context of the expression.[§]

```
5 + something  # The something must be a scalar
sort something # The something must be a list
```

Even if *something* is the exact same sequence of characters, in one case it may give a single, scalar value, while in the other, it may give a list.[**]

Expressions in Perl always return the appropriate value for their context. For example, how about the "name"[††] of an array. In a list context, it gives the list of elements. But in a scalar context, it returns the number of elements in the array:

```
@people = qw( fred barney betty );
@sorted = sort @people; # list context: barney, betty, fred
$number = 5 + @people;   # scalar context: 5 + 3 gives 8
```

---

[*] If you aren't a native speaker of English, this analogy may not be obvious to you. But context sensitivity happens in every spoken language, so you may be able to think of an example in your own language.

[†] Or maybe they were asking what the word "red" means, if they were speaking rather than writing a book. It's ambiguous either way. As Douglas Hofstadter said, no language can express every thought unambiguously, especially this one.

[‡] Unless, of course, Perl is expecting something else entirely. There are other contexts that aren't covered here. In fact, nobody knows how many contexts Perl uses; the biggest brains in all of Perl haven't agreed on an answer to that yet.

[§] This is no different than what you're used to in human languages. If I make a grammatical mistake, you notice it right away, because you expect certain words in places certain. Eventually, you'll read Perl this way, too, but at first you have to think about it.

[**] The list may be just one element long, of course. It could also be empty, or it could have any number of elements.

[††] Well, the true name of the array `@people` is just `people`. The @-sign is just a qualifier.

Even ordinary assignment (to a scalar or a list) causes different contexts:

```
@list = @people; # a list of three people
$n = @people;    # the number 3
```

But please don't jump to the conclusion that scalar context always gives the number of elements that would have been returned in list context. Most list-producing expressions* return something *much* more interesting than that.

Using List-Producing Expressions in Scalar Context

There are many expressions that would typically be used to produce a list. If you use one in a scalar context, what do you get? See what the author of that operation says about it. Usually, that person is Larry, and usually the documentation gives the whole story. In fact, a big part of learning Perl is actually learning how Larry thinks.† Therefore, once you can think like Larry does, you know what Perl should do. But while you're learning, you'll probably need to look into the documentation.

Some expressions don't have a scalar-context value at all. For example, what should **sort** return in a scalar context? You wouldn't need to sort a list to count its elements, so until someone implements something else, **sort** in a scalar context always returns **undef**.

Another example is **reverse**. In a list context, it gives a reversed list. In a scalar context, it returns a reversed string (or reversing the result of concatenating all the strings of a list, if given one):

```
@backwards = reverse qw/ yabba dabba doo /;
   # gives doo, dabba, yabba
$backwards = reverse qw/ yabba dabba doo /;
   # gives oodabbadabbay
```

At first, it's not always obvious whether an expression is being used in a scalar or a list context. But, trust us, it *will* get to be second nature for you eventually.

Here are some common contexts to start you off:

```
$fred = something;          # scalar context
@pebbles = something;       # list context
($wilma, $betty) = something; # list context
($dino) = something;        # still list context!
```

---

* But with regard to the point of this section, there's no difference between a "list-producing" expression and a "scalar-producing" one; any expression can produce a list or a scalar, depending upon context. So when we say "list-producing expressions," we mean expressions that are typically used in a list context and that therefore might surprise you when they're used unexpectedly in a scalar context (like reverse or @fred).

† This is only fair, since while writing Perl he tried to think like you do to predict what you would want!

Don't be fooled by the one-element list; that last one is a list context, not a scalar one. If you're assigning to a list (no matter the number of elements), it's a list context. If you're assigning to an array, it's a list context.

Here are some other expressions we've seen, and the contexts they provide. First, some that provide scalar context to *something*:

```
$fred = something;
$fred[3] = something;
123 + something
something + 654
if (something) { ... }
while (something) { ... }
$fred[something] = something;
```

And here are some that provide a list context:

```
@fred = something;
($fred, $barney) = something;
($fred) = something;
push @fred, something;
foreach $fred (something) { ... }
sort something
reverse something
print something
```

Using Scalar-Producing Expressions in List Context

Going this direction is straightforward: if an expression doesn't normally have a list value, the scalar value is automatically promoted to make a one-element list:

```
@fred = 6 * 7; # gets the one-element list (42)
@barney = "hello" . ' ' . "world";
```

Well, there's one possible catch:

```
@wilma = undef; # OOPS! Gets the one-element list (undef)
   # which is not the same as this:
@betty = ();    # A correct way to empty an array
```

Since **undef** is a scalar value, assigning **undef** to an array doesn't clear the array. The better way to do that is to assign an empty list.[*]

Forcing Scalar Context

On occasion, you may need to force scalar context where Perl is expecting a list. In that case, you can use the fake function **scalar**. It's not a true function, because it just tells Perl to provide a scalar context:

---

[*] Well, in most real-world algorithms, if the variable is declared in the proper scope, it will never need to be explicitly emptied. So this type of assignment is rare in well-written Perl programs. We'll learn about scoping in the next chapter.

```
@rocks = qw( talc quartz jade obsidian );
print "How many rocks do you have?\n";
print "I have ", @rocks, " rocks!\n";        # WRONG, prints names of rocks
print "I have ", scalar @rocks, " rocks!\n"; # Correct, gives a number
```

Oddly enough, there's no corresponding function to force list context. It turns out never to be needed. Trust us on this, too.

<STDIN> in List Context

One previously seen operator that returns a different value in an array context is the line-input operator, <STDIN>. As described earlier, <STDIN> returns the next line of input in a scalar context. Now, in list context, this operator returns *all* of the remaining lines up to the end of file. Each line is returned as a separate element of the list. For example:

```
@lines = <STDIN>; # read standard input in list context
```

When the input is coming from a file, this will read the rest of the file. But how can there be an end-of-file when the input comes from the keyboard? On Unix and similar systems, including Linux and Mac OS X, you'll normally type a Control-D* to indicate to the system that there's no more input; the special character itself is never seen by Perl,† even though it may be echoed to the screen. On DOS/Windows systems, use Ctrl-Z instead.‡ You'll need to check the documentation for your system or ask your local expert, if it's different from these.

If the person running the program types three lines, then presses the proper keys needed to indicate end-of-file, the array ends up with three elements. Each element will be a string that ends in a newline, corresponding to the three newline-terminated lines entered.

Wouldn't it be nice if, having read those lines, you could chomp the newlines all at once? It turns out that if you give chomp a list of lines, it will remove the newlines from each item in the list. For example:

```
@lines = <STDIN>; # Read all the lines
chomp(@lines);    # discard all the newline characters
```

But the more common way to write that is with code similar to what we used earlier:

```
chomp(@lines = <STDIN>); # Read the lines, not the newlines
```

---

* This is merely the default; it can be changed by the stty command. But it's pretty dependable—we've never seen a Unix system where a different character was used to mean end-of-file from the keyboard.

† It's the OS that "sees" the control key and reports "end of file" to the application.

‡ There's a bug affecting some ports of Perl for DOS/Windows where the first line of output to the terminal following the use of Control-Z is obscured. On these systems, you can work around this problem by simply printing a blank line ("\n") after reading the input.

Although you're welcome to write your code either way in the privacy of your own cubicle, most Perl programmers will expect the second, more compact, notation.

It may be obvious to you (but it's not obvious to everyone) that once these lines of input have been read, they can't be re-read.* Once you've reached end-of-file, there's no more input out there to read.

And what happens if the input is coming from a 400MB log file? The line input operator reads all of the lines, gobbling up lots of memory.† Perl tries not to limit you in what you can do, but the other users of your system (not to mention your system administrator) are likely to object. If the input data is large, you should generally find a way to deal with it without reading it all into memory at once.

Exercises

See Appendix A for answers to the following exercises:

1. [6] Write a program that reads a list of strings on separate lines until end-of-input and prints out the list in reverse order. If the input comes from the keyboard, you'll probably need to signal the end of the input by pressing Control-D on Unix, or Control-Z on Windows.

2. [12] Write a program that reads a list of numbers (on separate lines) until end-of-input and then prints for each number the corresponding person's name from the list shown below. (Hardcode this list of names into your program. That is, it should appear in your program's source code.) For example, if the input numbers were 1, 2, 4, and 2, the output names would be fred, betty, dino, and betty.

   ```
   fred betty barney dino wilma pebbles bamm-bamm
   ```

3. [8] Write a program that reads a list of strings (on separate lines) until end-of-input. Then it should print the strings in ASCIIbetical order. That is, if you enter the strings fred, barney, wilma, betty, the output should show barney betty fred wilma. Are all of the strings on one line in the output, or on separate lines? Could you make the output appear in either style?

---

* Well, yes, if the input is from a source upon which you can **seek**, then you'll be able to go back and read again. But that's not what we're talking about here.

† Typically, that's much more memory than the size of the file, too. That is, a 400MB file will typically take up at least a full gigabyte of memory when read into an array. This is because Perl will generally waste memory to save time. This is a good tradeoff; if you're short of memory, you can buy more; if you're short on time, you're hosed.

4

Subroutines

System and User Functions

We've already seen and used some of the builtin system functions, such as `chomp`, `reverse`, `print`, and so on. But, as other languages do, Perl has the ability to make *subroutines*, which are user-defined functions.* These let us recycle one chunk of code many times in one program.†

The name of a subroutine is another Perl identifier (letters, digits, and underscores, but can't start with a digit) with a sometimes-optional ampersand (&) in front. There's a rule about when you can omit the ampersand and when you cannot; we'll see that rule by the end of the chapter. For now, we'll just use it every time that it's not forbidden, which is always a safe rule. And we'll tell you every place where it's forbidden, of course.

That subroutine name comes from a separate namespace, so Perl won't be confused if you have a subroutine called `&fred` and a scalar called `$fred` in the same program—although there's no reason to do that under normal circumstances.

---

* In Perl, we don't generally make the distinction that Pascal programmers are used to, between *functions*, which return a value, and *procedures*, which don't. But a *subroutine* is always user-defined, while a *function* may or may not be. That is, the word *function* may be used as a synonym for *subroutine*, or it may mean one of Perl's builtin functions. That's why this chapter is titled *Subroutines*, because it's about the ones you can define, not the builtins. Mostly.

† The code examples used in this book are recycled from at least 40% post-consumer programming, and are at least 75% recyclable into your programs when properly decomposed.

Defining a Subroutine

To define your own subroutine, use the keyword `sub`, the name of the subroutine (without the ampersand), then the indented* block of code (in curly braces) which makes up the *body* of the subroutine, something like this:

```
sub marine {
    $n += 1;   # Global variable $n
    print "Hello, sailor number $n!\n";
}
```

Subroutine definitions can be anywhere in your program text, but programmers who come from a background of languages like C or Pascal like to put them at the start of the file. Others may prefer to put them at the end of the file, so that the main part of the program appears at the beginning. It's up to you. In any case, you don't normally need any kind of forward declaration.†

Subroutine definitions are global; without some powerful trickiness, there are no private subroutines.‡ If you have two subroutine definitions with the same name, the later one overwrites the earlier one.§ That's generally considered bad form, or the sign of a confused maintenance programmer.

As you may have noticed in the previous example, you may use any global variables within the subroutine body. In fact, all of the variables we've seen so far are globals; that is, they are accessible from every part of your program. This horrifies linguistic purists, but the Perl development team formed an angry mob with torches and ran them out of town years ago. We'll see how to make private variables in the section "Private Variables in Subroutines" later in this chapter.

Invoking a Subroutine

Invoke a subroutine from within any expression by using the subroutine name (with the ampersand):**

```
&marine;   # says Hello, sailor number 1!
&marine;   # says Hello, sailor number 2!
```

---

* Okay, purists, we admit it: the curly braces are part of the block, properly speaking. And Perl doesn't require the indentation of the block—but your maintenance programmer will. So please be stylish.

† Unless your subroutine is being particularly tricky and declares a "prototype," which dictates how a compiler will parse and interpret its invocation arguments. This is rare—see the *perlsub* manpage for more information.

‡ If you wish to be powerfully tricky, read the Perl documentation about coderefs stored in private (lexical) variables.

§ A warnable offense, however.

**And frequently a pair of parentheses, even if empty. As written, the subroutine inherits the caller's @_ value, which we'll be discussing shortly. So don't stop reading here, or you'll be writing code with unintended effects!

```
&marine;   # says Hello, sailor number 3!
&marine;   # says Hello, sailor number 4!
```

Sometimes, we refer to the invocation as *calling* the subroutine.

Return Values

The subroutine is always invoked as part of an expression, even if the result of the expression isn't being used. When we invoked &marine earlier, we were calculating the value of the expression containing the invocation, but then throwing away the result.

Many times, we'll call a subroutine and actually do something with the result. This means that we'll be paying attention to the *return value* of the subroutine. All Perl subroutines have a return value—there's no distinction between those that return values and those that don't. Not all Perl subroutines have a *useful* return value, however.

Since all Perl subroutines can be called in a way that needs a return value, it'd be a bit wasteful to have to declare special syntax to "return" a particular value for the majority of the cases. So Larry made it simple. Every subroutine is chugging along, calculating values as part of its series of actions. Whatever calculation is *last* performed in a subroutine is *automatically* also the return value.

For example, let's define this subroutine:

```
sub sum_of_fred_and_barney {
  print "Hey, you called the sum_of_fred_and_barney subroutine!\n";
  $fred + $barney;  # That's the return value
}
```

The last expression evaluated in the body of this subroutine is the sum of $fred and $barney, so the sum of $fred and $barney will be the return value. Here's that in action:

```
$fred = 3;
$barney = 4;
$c = &sum_of_fred_and_barney; # $c gets 7
print "\$c is $c.\n";
$d = 3 * &sum_of_fred_and_barney; # $d gets 21
print "\$d is $d.\n";
```

That code will produce this output:

```
Hey, you called the sum_of_fred_and_barney subroutine!
$c is 7.
Hey, you called the sum_of_fred_and_barney subroutine!
$d is 21.
```

That **print** statement is just a debugging aid, so that we can see that we called
the subroutine. You'd take it out when the program is finished. But suppose you
added another line to the end of the code, like this:

```
sub sum_of_fred_and_barney {
    print "Hey, you called the sum_of_fred_and_barney subroutine!\n";
    $fred + $barney;  # That's not really the return value!
    print "Hey, I'm returning a value now!\n"; # Oops!
}
```

In this example, the last expression evaluated is not the addition; it's the **print**
statement. Its return value will normally be 1, meaning "printing was successful,"*
but that's not the return value we actually wanted. So be careful when adding
additional code to a subroutine to ensure that the last expression *evaluated* will be
the desired return value.

So, what happened to the sum of $fred and $barney in that subroutine? We
didn't put it anywhere, so Perl discarded it. If you had requested warnings, Perl
(noticing that there's nothing useful about adding two variables and discarding the
result) would likely warn you about something like "a useless use of addition in a
void context." The term *void context* is just a fancy of saying that the answer isn't
being stored in a variable or used by another function.

"The last expression evaluated" really means the last expression *evaluated*, rather
than the last line of text. For example, this subroutine returns the larger value of
$fred or $barney:

```
sub larger_of_fred_or_barney {
    if ($fred > $barney) {
        $fred;
    } else {
        $barney;
    }
}
```

The last expression evaluated is the single $fred or $barney, which becomes the
return value. We won't know whether the return value will be $fred or $barney
until we see what those variables hold at runtime.

A subroutine can also return a list of values when evaluated in a list context.† Suppose you wanted to get a range of numbers (as from the range operator, ..),

---

* The return value of **print** is true for a successful operation and false for a failure. We'll see how to
determine the kind of failure later in Chapter 11, *Filehandles and File Tests.*

† You can detect whether a subroutine is being evaluated in a scalar or list context using the **wantarray**
function, which lets you easily write subroutines with specific list or scalar context values.

except that you want to be able to count down as well as up. The range operator only counts upwards, but that's easily fixed:

```
sub list_from_fred_to_barney {
  if ($fred < $barney) {
    # Count upwards from $fred to $barney
    $fred..$barney;
  } else {
    # Count downwards from $fred to $barney
    reverse $barney..$fred;
  }
}
$fred = 11;
$barney = 6;
@c = &list_from_fred_to_barney; # @c gets (11, 10, 9, 8, 7, 6)
```

In this case, the range operator gives us the list from 6 to 11, then `reverse` reverses the list, so that it goes from `$fred` (11) to `$barney` (6), just as we wanted.

These are all rather trivial examples. It gets better when we can pass values that are different for each invocation into a subroutine instead of relying on global variables. In fact, that's coming right up.

Arguments

That subroutine called `larger_of_fred_or_barney` would be much more useful if it didn't force us to use the global variables `$fred` and `$barney`. That's because, if we wanted to get the larger value from `$wilma` and `$betty`, we currently have to copy those into `$fred` and `$barney` before we can use `larger_of_fred_or_barney`. And if we had something useful in those variables, we'd have to first copy those to other variables, say `$save_fred` and `$save_barney`. And then, when we're done with the subroutine, we'd have to copy those back to `$fred` and `$barney` again.

Luckily, Perl has subroutine arguments. To pass an argument list to the subroutine, simply place the list expression, in parentheses, after the subroutine invocation, like this:

```
$n = &max(10, 15);  # This sub call has two parameters
```

That list is *passed* to the subroutine; that is, it's made available for the subroutine to use however it needs to. Of course, this list has to be stored into a variable, so the parameter list (another name for the argument list) is automatically assigned to a special array variable named `@_` for the duration of the subroutine. The subroutine can access this variable to determine both the number of arguments and the value of those arguments.

So, that means that the first subroutine parameter is stored in $_[0], the second one is stored in $_[1], and so on. But—and here's an important note—these variables have nothing whatsoever to do with the $_ variable, any more than $dino[3] (an element of the @dino array) has to do with $dino (a completely distinct scalar variable). It's just that the parameter list must be stored into some array variable for the subroutine to use it, and Perl uses the array @_ for this purpose.

Now, you *could* write the subroutine &max to look a little like the subroutine &larger_of_fred_or_barney, but instead of using $a you *could* use the first subroutine parameter ($_[0]), and instead of using $b, you *could* use the second subroutine parameter ($_[1]). And so you *could* end up with code something like this:

```
sub max {
  # Compare this to &larger_of_fred_or_barney
  if ($_[0] > $_[1]) {
    $_[0];
  } else {
    $_[1];
  }
}
```

Well, as we said, you *could* do that. But it's pretty ugly with all of those subscripts, and hard to read, write, check, and debug, too. We'll see a better way in a moment.

There's another problem with this subroutine. The name &max is nice and short, but it doesn't remind us that this subroutine works properly only if called with exactly two parameters:

```
$n = &max(10, 15, 27);  # Oops!
```

Excess parameters are ignored—since the subroutine never looks at $_[2], Perl doesn't care whether there's something in there or not. And insufficient parameters are also ignored—you simply get **undef** if you look beyond the end of the @_ array, as with any other array. We'll see how to make a better &max, which works with any number of parameters, later in this chapter.

The @_ variable is local to the subroutine;[*] if there's a global value in @_, it is saved away before the subroutine is invoked and restored to its previous value upon return from the subroutine.[†] This also means that a subroutine can pass

---

[*] Unless there's an ampersand in front of the name for the invocation, and no parentheses (or arguments) afterward, in which case the @_ array is inherited from the caller's context. That's generally a bad idea, but is occasionally useful.

[†] You might recognize that this is the same mechanism as used with the control variable of the foreach loop, as seen in the previous chapter. In either case, the variable's value is saved and automatically restored by Perl. We'll see this again with the **local** operator later in this chapter.

arguments to another subroutine without fear of losing its own @_ variable—the nested subroutine invocation gets its own @_ in the same way. Even if the subroutine calls itself recursively, each invocation gets a new @_, so @_ is always the parameter list for the current subroutine invocation.

Private Variables in Subroutines

But if Perl can give us a new @_ for every invocation, can't it give us variables for our own use as well? Of course it can.

By default, all variables in Perl are global variables; that is, they are accessable from every part of the program. But you can create private variables called *lexical variables* at any time with the my operator:

```
sub max {
  my($a, $b);      # new, private variables for this block
  ($a, $b) = @_;   # give names to the parameters
  if ($a > $b) { $a } else { $b }
}
```

These variables are private (or *scoped*) to the enclosing block; any other $a or $b is totally unaffected by these two. And that goes the other way, too—no other code can access or modify these private variables, by accident or design.* So, we could drop this subroutine into any Perl program in the world and know that we wouldn't mess up that program's $a and $b (if any).†

It's also worth pointing out that, inside the if's blocks, there's no semicolon needed after the return value expression. Although Perl allows for the last semicolon in a block to be omitted, in practice that's omitted only when the code is so simple that the block is written in a single line, like the previous ones.

The subroutine in the previous example could be made even simpler. Did you notice that the list ($a, $b) was written twice? That my operator can also be applied to a list of variables enclosed in parentheses, so it's more customary to combine those first two statements in the subroutine:

```
my($a, $b) = @_;  # Name the subroutine parameters
```

That one statement creates the private variables and sets their values, so the first parameter now has the easier-to-use name $a and the second has $b. Nearly every subroutine will start with a line much like that one, naming its parameters. When you see that line, you'll know that the subroutine expects two scalar parameters, which we'll call $a and $b inside the subroutine.

---

* Advanced programmers will realize that a lexical variable may be accessible by reference from outside its scope, but never by name.

† Of course, if that program already had a subroutine called &max, we'd mess *that* up.

The local Operator

You might consider this next section a giant footnote, but then we couldn't have footnotes on footnotes, so we decided to put it up in the main text. Skip over this text on first reading, and pop right on down to "Variable Length Parameter Lists" below. You won't need any of it to do the exercises or write Perl code for a long time. But someone invariably asks us in class something like "What is that `local` thing I see in some programs?" so we're including what we normally say as an aside in class for your enjoyment and edification.

Occasionally, mostly in older code or older Perl books, you'll see the `local` operator used instead of `my`. It often looks much the same as `my`:

```
sub max {
  local($a, $b) = @_;  # looks a lot like my
  if ($a > $b) { $a } else { $b }
}
```

But `local` is misnamed, or at least *misleadingly* named. Our friend Chip Salzenberg says that if he ever gets a chance to go back in a time machine to 1986 and give Larry one piece of advice, he'd tell Larry to call `local` by the name "save" instead.* That's because `local` actually will save the given global variable's value away, so it will later automatically be restored to the global variable. (That's right: these so-called "`local`" variables are actually globals!) This save-and-restore mechanism is the same one we've already seen twice now, in the control variable of a `foreach` loop, and in the `@_` array of subroutine parameters.

What `local` actually does, then, is to save away a copy of the variable's value in a secret place (called the stack). That value can't be accessed, modified, or deleted† while it is saved. Then `local` sets the variable to an empty value (`undef` for scalars, or empty list for arrays), or to whatever value is being assigned. When Perl returns from the subroutine,‡ the variable is automatically restored to its original value. In effect, the variable was borrowed for a time and given back (hopefully) before anyone noticed that it was borrowed.

The Difference Between local and my

But what if the subroutine called another subroutine, one that *did* notice that the variable was being borrowed by `local`? For example:

---

* We would tell Larry to buy stock in Yahoo!, but Chip is more idealistic than we are.

† Or damaged, defiled, read, checked, touched, seen, changed, or printed, for that matter. There's no way from within Perl to get at the saved value.

‡ Or when it finishes execution of the smallest enclosing block or file, to be more precise.

```
$office = "global";   # Global $office
&say();                                 # says "global", accessing $office directly

&fred();                                # says "fred", dynamic scope,
    # because fred's local $office hides the global

&barney();                              # says "global", lexical scope;
    # barney's $office is visible only in that block

sub say { print "$office\n"; }          # print the currently visible $office
sub fred { local($office) = "fred"; &say(); }
sub barney { my($office) = "barney"; &say(); }
```

First, we call the subroutine &say, which tells us which $office it sees—the global $office. That's normal.

But then we call Fred's subroutine. Fred has made his own local $office, so he has actually changed the behavior of the &say subroutine; now it tells us what's in Fred's $office. We can't tell whether that's what Fred wanted to do or not without understanding the meaning of his code. But it's a little odd.

Barney, however, is a little smarter, as well as being shorter, so he uses the shorter (and smarter) operator, my. Barney's variable $office is private, and Barney's private $office can't be accessed from outside his subroutine, so the &say subroutine is back to normal; it can see only the global $office. Barney didn't change the way &say works, which is more like what most programmers would want and expect.

Now, if you're confused about these two operators at this point, that's to be expected. But any time that you see local, think "save," and that may help. In any new code, just use my, since my variables (lexical variables) are faster than globals—remember, so-called local variables are really globals—and they'll work more like the traditional variables in other modern programming languages. But when you're maintaining someone else's old code, you can't necessarily change every local to my without checking upon whether the programmer was using that save-and-restore functionality.

Variable-length Parameter Lists

In real-world Perl code, subroutines are often given parameter lists of arbitrary length. That's because of Perl's "no unnecessary limits" philosophy that we've already seen. Of course, this is unlike many traditional programming languages, which require every subroutine to be strictly typed; that is, to permit only a certain, predefined number of parameters of predefined types. It's nice that Perl is so flexible, but (as we saw with the &max routine earlier) that may cause problems when a subroutine is called with a different number of arguments than the author expected.

Of course, the subroutine can easily check that it has the right number of arguments by examining the @_ array. For example, we could have written &max to check its argument list like this:[*]

```
sub max {
  if (@_ != 2) {
    print "WARNING! &max should get exactly two arguments!\n";
  }
  # continue as before...
  .
  .
  .
}
```

That if-test uses the "name" of the array in a scalar context to find out the number of array elements, as we saw in Chapter 3.

But in real-world Perl programming, this sort of check is hardly ever used; it's better to make the subroutine adapt to the parameters.

A Better &max Routine

So let's rewrite &max to allow for any number of arguments:

```
$maximum = &max(3, 5, 10, 4, 6);

sub max {
  my($max_so_far) = shift @_;   # the first one is the largest yet seen
  foreach (@_) {                # look at the remaining arguments
    if ($_ > $max_so_far) {     # could this one be bigger yet?
      $max_so_far = $_;
    }
  }
  $max_so_far;
}
```

This code uses what has often been called the "high-water mark" algorithm: after a flood, when the waters have surged and receded for the last time, the high-water mark shows where the highest water was seen. In this routine, $max_so_far keeps track of our high-water mark, the largest number yet seen.

The first line sets $max_so_far to 3 (the first parameter in the example code) by shifting that parameter from the parameter array, @_. So @_ now holds (5, 10, 4, 6), since the 3 has been shifted off. And the largest number yet seen is the *only* one yet seen: 3, the first parameter.

---

[*] As soon as you learn about warn (in Chapter 11), you'll see that you can use it to turn improper usage like this into a proper warning. Or perhaps you'll decide that this case is severe enough to warrant using die, described in the same chapter.

Now, the `foreach` loop will step through the remaining values in the parameter list, from `@_`. The control variable of the loop is, by default, `$_`. (But, remember, there's no automatic connection between `@_` and `$_`; it's just a coincidence that they have such similar names.) The first time through the loop, `$_` is 5. The `if` test sees that it is larger than `$max_so_far`, so `$max_so_far` is set to 5—the new high-water mark.

The next time through the loop, `$_` is 10. That's a new record high, so it's stored in `$max_so_far` as well.

The next time, `$_` is 4. The `if` test fails, since that's no larger than `$max_so_far`, which is 10, so the body of the `if` is skipped.

The next time, `$_` is 6, and the body of the `if` is skipped again. And that was the last time through the loop, so the loop is done.

Now, `$max_so_far` becomes the return value. It's the largest number we've seen, and we've seen them all, so it must be the largest from the list: 10.

Empty Parameter Lists

That improved `&max` algorithm works fine now, even if there are more than two parameters. But what happens if there are none?

At first, it may seem too esoteric to worry about. After all, why would someone call `&max` without giving it any parameters? But maybe someone wrote a line like this one:

```
$maximum = &max(@numbers);
```

And the array `@numbers` might sometimes be an empty list; perhaps it was read in from a file that turned out to be empty, for example. So what does `&max` do in that case?

The first line of the subroutine sets `$max_so_far` by using `shift` on `@_`, the (now empty) parameter array. That's harmless; the array is left empty, and `shift` returns `undef` to `$max_so_far`.

Now the `foreach` loop wants to iterate over `@_`, but since that's empty, the loop body is executed zero times.

So in short order, Perl returns the value of `$max_so_far`—`undef`—as the return value of the subroutine. In some sense, that's the right answer, because there is no largest value in an empty list.

Of course, whoever is calling this subroutine should be aware that the return value may be `undef`—or they could simply ensure that the parameter list is never empty.

Notes on Lexical (my) Variables

Those lexical variables can actually be used in any block, not merely in a subroutine's block. For example, they can be used in the block of an `if`, `while`, or `foreach`:

```
foreach (1..10) {
  my($square) = $_ * $_;  # private variable in this loop
  print "$_ squared is $square.\n";
}
```

The variable `$square` is private to the enclosing block; in this case, that's the block of the `foreach` loop. If there's no block, the variable is private to the entire source file. For now, your programs aren't going to use more than one source file, so this isn't an issue. But the important concept is that the *scope* of a lexical variable's name is limited to the smallest enclosing block or file. The *only* code that can say `$square` and mean that variable is the code inside that textual scope. This is a big win for maintainability—if the wrong value is found in `$square`, the culprit will be found within a limited amount of source code. As experienced programmers have learned (often the hard way), limiting the scope of a variable to a page of code, or even to a few lines of code, really speeds along the development and testing cycle.

Note also that the `my` operator doesn't change the context of an assignment:

```
my($num) = @_;  # list context, same as ($num) = @_;
my $num  = @_;  # scalar context, same as $num = @_;
```

In the first one, `$num` gets the first parameter, as a list-context assignment; in the second, it gets the number of parameters, in a scalar context. Either line of code could be what the programmer wanted; we can't tell from that one line alone, and so Perl can't warn you if you use the wrong one. (Of course, you wouldn't have *both* of those lines in the same subroutine, since you can't have two lexical variables with the same name declared in the same scope; this is just an example.) So, when reading code like this, you can always tell the context of the assignment by seeing what the context would be without the word `my`.

Of course, you can use `my` to create new, private arrays as well:[*]

```
my @phone_number;
```

Any new variable will start out empty—`undef` for scalars, or the empty list for arrays.

---

[*] Or hashes, which we'll see in the next chapter.

The use strict Pragma

Perl tends to be a pretty permissive language. But maybe you want Perl to impose a little discipline; that can be arranged with the **use strict** pragma.

A *pragma* is a hint to a compiler, telling it something about the code. In this case, the **use strict** pragma tells Perl's internal compiler that it should enforce some good programming rules for the rest of this block or source file.

Why would this be important? Well, imagine that you're composing your program, and you type a line like this one:

```
$bamm_bamm = 3;  # Perl creates that variable automatically
```

Now, you keep typing for a while. After that line has scrolled off the top of the screen, you type this line to increment the variable:

```
$bammbamm += 1;  # Oops!
```

Since Perl sees a new variable name (the underscore *is* significant in a variable name), it creates a new variable and increments that one. If you're lucky and smart, you've turned on warnings, and Perl can tell you that you used one or both of those global variable names only once in your program. But if you're merely smart, you used each name more than once, and Perl won't be able to warn you.

To tell Perl that you're ready to be more restrictive, put the **use strict** pragma at the top of your program (or in any block or file where you want to enforce these rules):

```
use strict;  # Enforce some good programming rules
```

Now, among other restrictions,* Perl will insist that you declare every new variable with **my**:†

```
my $bamm_bamm = 3;  # New lexical variable
```

Now if you try to spell it the other way, Perl can complain that you haven't declared any variable called **$bammbamm**, so your mistake is automatically caught at compile time.

```
$bammbamm += 1;  # No such variable: Compile time error
```

---

* To learn about the other restrictions, see the documentation for strict. The documentation for any pragma is filed under that pragma's name, so the command *perldoc strict* (or your system's native documentation method) should find it for you. In brief, the other restrictions require that strings be quoted in most cases, and that references be true (hard) references. Neither of these restrictions should affect beginners in Perl.

† There are some other ways to declare variables, too.

Of course, this applies only to new variables; Perl's builtin variables, such as $_ and @_ never need to be declared.*

If you add **use strict** to an already-written program, you'll generally get a flood of warning messages, so it's better to use it from the start, when it's needed.

Most people recommend that programs that are longer than a screenful of text generally need **use strict**. And we agree.

From here on, most (but not all) of our examples will be written as if **use strict** is in effect, even where we don't show it. That is, we'll generally declare variables with **my** where it's appropriate. But, even though we don't always do so here, we encourage you to include **use strict** in your programs as often as possible.

The return Operator

The **return** operator immediately returns a value from a subroutine:

```
my @names = qw/ fred barney betty dino wilma pebbles bamm-bamm /;
my $result = &which_element_is("dino", @names);

sub which_element_is {
  my($what, @list) = @_;
  foreach (0..$#list) {  # indices of @list's elements
    if ($what eq $list[$_]) {
      return $_;            # return early once found
    }
  }
  -1;                       # element not found (return is optional here)
}
```

This subroutine is being used to find the index of "dino" in the array @names. First, the **my** declaration names the parameters: there's $what, which is what we're searching for, and @list, a list of values to search within. That's a copy of the array @names, in this case. The foreach loop steps through the indices of @list (the first index is 0, and the last one is $#list, as we saw in Chapter 3).

Each time through the **foreach** loop, we check to see whether the string in $what is equal† to the element from @list at the current index. If it's equal, we return that index at once. This is the most common use of the keyword **return** in Perl—to return a value immediately, without executing the rest of the subroutine.

---

* And, at least in some circumstances, $a and $b won't need to be declared, because they're used internally by **sort**. So if you're testing this feature, use other variable names than those two. The fact that **use strict** doesn't forbid these two is one of the most frequently reported non-bugs in Perl.

† You noticed that we used the string equality test, eq, instead of the numeric equality test, ==, didn't you?

But what if we never found that element? In that case, the author of this subroutine has chosen to return −1 as a "value not found" code. It would be more Perlish, perhaps, to return `undef` in that case, but this programmer used −1. Saying `return` −1 on that last line would be correct, but the word `return` isn't really needed.

Some programmers like to use `return` every time there's a return value, as a means of documenting that it is a return value. For example, you might use `return` when the return value is not the last line of the subroutine, such as in the subroutine `&list_from_fred_to_barney`, earlier in this chapter. It's not really needed, but it doesn't hurt anything. However, many Perl programmers believe it's just an extra seven characters of typing. So you'll need to be able to read code written by both kinds of programmers.

If `return` is used with no expression, that will return an empty value—`undef` in a scalar context, or an empty list in a list context. `return` ( ) does the same, in case you want to be explicit.

Omitting the Ampersand

As promised, now we'll tell you the rule for when a subroutine call can omit the ampersand. If the compiler sees the subroutine definition before invocation, or if Perl can tell from the syntax that it's a subroutine call, the subroutine can be called without an ampersand, just like a builtin function. (But there's a catch hidden in that rule, as we'll see in a moment.)

This means that if Perl can see that it's a subroutine call without the ampersand, from the syntax alone, that's generally fine. That is, if you've got the parameter list in parentheses, it's got to be a function[*] call:

```
my @cards = shuffle(@deck_of_cards);   # No & necessary on &shuffle
```

Or if Perl's internal compiler has already seen the subroutine definition, that's generally okay, too; in that case, you can even omit the parentheses around the argument list:

```
sub division {
  $_[0] / $_[1];                       # Divide first param by second
}

my $quotient = division 355, 113;  # Uses &division
```

This works because of the rule that parentheses may always be omitted, except when doing so would change the meaning of the code.

---

[*] In this case, the function is the subroutine `&shuffle`. But it may be a built-in function, as we'll see in a moment.

But don't put that subroutine declaration *after* the invocation, or the compiler won't know what the attempted invocation of `division` is all about. The compiler has to see the definition before the invocation in order to use the subroutine call as if it were a builtin.

That's not the catch, though. The catch is this: if the subroutine has the same name as a Perl builtin, you *must* use the ampersand to call it. With an ampersand, you're sure to call the subroutine; without it, you can get the subroutine *only* if there's no builtin with the same name:

```
sub chomp {
  print "Munch, munch!";
}

&chomp;  # That ampersand is not optional!
```

Without the ampersand, we'd be calling the builtin `chomp`, even though we've defined the subroutine `&chomp`. So, the real rule to use is this one: until you know the names of all of Perl's builtin functions, *always* use the ampersand on function calls. That means that you will use it for your first hundred programs or so. But when you see someone else has omitted the ampersand in their own code, it's not necessarily a mistake; perhaps they simply know that Perl has no builtin with that name.*

When programmers plan to call their subroutines as if they were calling Perl's builtins, often when writing *modules*, they often use *prototypes* to tell Perl about the parameters to expect. Making modules is an advanced topic, though; when you're ready for that, see Perl's documentation (in particular, the *perlmod* and *perlsub* documents) for more information about subroutine prototypes and making modules.

Exercises

See Appendix A for answers to the following exercises:

1. [12] Write a subroutine, called `&total`, which returns the total of a list of numbers. Hint: the subroutine should not perform any I/O; it should simply process its parameters and return a value to its caller. Try it out in this sample program, which merely exercises the subroutine to see that it works. The first group of numbers should add up to 25.

---

* Then again, maybe it *is* a mistake; you can search the `perlfunc` and `perlop` manpages for that name, though, to see whether it's the same as a builtin. And Perl will usually be able to warn you about this, when you have warnings turned on.

```
my @fred = qw{ 1 3 5 7 9 };
my $fred_total = &total(@fred);
print "The total of \@fred is $fred_total.\n";
print "Enter some numbers on separate lines: ";
my $user_total = &total(<STDIN>);
print "The total of those numbers is $user_total.\n";
```

2. [5] Using the subroutine from the previous problem, make a program to calculate the sum of the numbers from 1 to 1000.

5

Hashes

In this chapter, we will see one of Perl's features that makes Perl one of the world's truly great programming languages—*hashes*.* Although hashes are a powerful and useful feature, you may have used other powerful languages for years without ever hearing of hashes. But you'll use hashes in nearly every Perl program you'll write from now on; they're that important.

What Is a Hash?

A hash is a data structure, not unlike an array in that it can hold any number of values and retrieve them at will. But instead of indexing the values by *number*, as we did with arrays, we'll look up the values by *name*. That is, the *indices* (here, we'll call them *keys*) aren't numbers, but instead they are arbitrary unique strings (see Figure 5-1).

The keys are *strings*, first of all, so instead of getting element number 3 from an array, we'll be accessing the hash element named wilma.

These keys are arbitrary strings—you can use any string expression for a hash key. And they are unique strings—just as there's only one array element numbered 3, there's only one hash element named wilma.

Another way to think of a hash is that it's like a barrel of data, where each piece of data has a tag attached. You can reach into the barrel and pull out any tag and see what piece of data is attached. But there's no "first" item in the barrel; it's just a jumble. In an array, we'd start with element 0, then element 1, then element 2,

---

* In the olden days, we called these "associative arrays." But the Perl community decided in about 1995 this was too many letters to type and too many syllables to say, so we changed the name to "hashes."

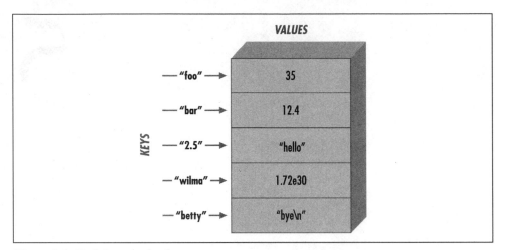

Figure 5-1. Hash keys and values

and so on. But in a hash, there's no fixed order, no first element. It's just a collection of key-value pairs.

The keys and values are both arbitrary scalars, but the keys are always converted to strings. So, if you used the numeric expression 50/20 as the key,* it would be turned into the three-character string "2.5", which is one of the keys shown in the diagram above.

As usual, Perl's no-unnecessary-limits philosophy applies: a hash may be of any size, from an empty hash with zero key-value pairs, up to whatever fills up your memory.

Some implementations of hashes (such as in the original *awk* language, from where Larry borrowed the idea) slow down as the hashes get larger and larger. This is not the case in Perl—it has a good, efficient, scalable algorithm.† So, if a hash has only three key-value pairs, it's very quick to "reach into the barrel" and pull out any one of those. If the hash has three *million* key-value pairs, it should be just about as quick to pull out any one of those. A big hash is nothing to fear.

It's worth mentioning again that the keys are always unique, although the values may be duplicated. The values of a hash may be all numbers, all strings, undef values, or a mixture.‡ But the keys are all arbitrary, unique strings.

---

* That's a numeric expression, not the five-character string "50/20". If we used that five-character string as a hash key, it would stay the same five-character string, of course.

† Technically, Perl rebuilds the hash table as needed for larger hashes. In fact, the term "hashes" comes from the fact that a hash table is used for implementing them.

‡ Or, in fact, any scalar values, including other scalar types than the ones we'll see in this book.

Why Use a Hash?

When you first hear about hashes, especially if you've lived a long and productive life as a programmer using other languages that don't have hashes, you may wonder why anyone would want one of these strange beasts. Well, the general idea is that you'll have one set of data "related to" another set of data. For example, here are some hashes you might find in typical applications of Perl:

Given name, family name

The given name (first name) is the key, and the family name is the value. This requires unique given names, of course; if there were two people named randal, this wouldn't work. With this hash, you can look up anyone's given name, and find the corresponding family name. If you use the key tom, you get the value phoenix.

Host name, IP address

You may know that each computer on the Internet has both a host name (like *www.stonehenge.com*) and an IP address number (like 123.45.67.89). That's because machines like working with the numbers, but we humans have an easier time remembering the names. The host names are unique strings, so they can be used to make this hash. With this hash, you could look up a host name and find the corresponding IP address number.

IP address, host name

Or you could go in the opposite direction. We generally think of the IP address as a number, but it can also be a unique string, so it's suitable for use as a hash key. In this hash, we can look up the IP address number to determine the corresponding host name. Note that this is *not* the same hash as the previous example: hashes are a one-way street, running from key to value; there's no way to look up a value in a hash and find the corresponding key! So these two are a *pair* of hashes, one for storing IP addresses, one for host names. It's easy enough to create one of these given the other, though, as we'll see below.

Word, count of number of times that word appears[*]

The idea here is that you want to know how often each word appears in a given document. Perhaps you're building an index to a number of documents, so that when a user searches for fred, you'll know that a certain document mentions fred five times, another mentions fred seven times, and yet another doesn't mention fred at all—so you'll know which documents the user is likely to want. As the index-making program reads through a given document, each time it sees a mention of fred, it adds one to the value filed

---

[*] This is a very common use of a hash. It's so common, in fact, that it just might turn up in the exercises at the end of the chapter!

under the key of **fred**. That is, if we had seen **fred** twice already in this document, the value would be 2, but now we'll increment it to 3. If we had never seen **fred** before, we'd change the value from **undef** (the implicit, default value) to 1.

Username, number of disk blocks they are using [wasting]

System administrators like this one: the usernames on a given system are all unique strings, so they can be used as keys in a hash to look up information about that user.

Driver's license number, name

There may be many, many people named John Smith, but we hope that each one has a different driver's license number. That number makes for a unique key, and the person's name is the value.

So, yet another way to think of a hash is as a *very* simple database, in which just one piece of data may be filed under each key. In fact, if your task description includes phrases like "finding duplicates," "unique," "cross-reference," or "lookup table," it's likely that a hash will be useful in the implementation.

Hash Element Access

To access an element of a hash, use syntax that looks like this:

```
$hash{$some_key}
```

This is similar to what we used for array access, but here we use curly braces instead of square brackets around the subscript (key).* And that key expression is now a string, rather than a number:

```
$family_name{"fred"} = "flintstone";
$family_name{"barney"} = "rubble";
```

Figure 5-2 shows how the resulting hash keys are assigned.

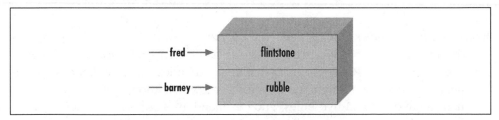

Figure 5-2. Assigned hash keys

---

* Here's a peek into the mind of Larry Wall: Larry says that we use curly braces instead of square brackets because we're doing something fancier than ordinary array access, so we should use fancier punctuation.

This lets us use code like this:

```
foreach $person (qw< barney fred >) {
  print "I've heard of $person $family_name{$person}.\n";
}
```

The name of the hash is like any other Perl identifier (letters, digits, and under-scores, but can't start with a digit). And it's from a separate namespace; that is, there's no connection between the hash element `$family_name{"fred"}` and a subroutine `&family_name`, for example. Of course, there's no reason to confuse everyone by giving everything the same name. But Perl won't mind if you also have a scalar called `$family_name` and array elements like `$family_name[5]`. We humans will have to do as Perl does; that is, we'll have to look to see what punctuation appears before and after the identifier to see what it means. When there is a dollar sign in front of the name and curly braces afterwards, it's a hash element that's being accessed.

When choosing the name of a hash, it's often nice to think of the word "of" between the name of the hash and the key. As in, "the `family_name` of `fred` is `flintstone`". So the hash is named `family_name`. Then it becomes clear what the relationship is between the keys and their values.

Of course, the hash key may be any expression, not just the literal strings and simple scalar variables that we're showing here:

```
$foo = "bar";
print $family_name{ $foo . "ney" };  # prints "rubble"
```

When you store something into an existing hash element, that overwrites the pre-vious value:

```
$family_name{"fred"} = "astaire";  # gives new value to existing element
$bedrock = $family_name{"fred"};   # gets "astaire"; old value is lost
```

That's analogous to what happens with arrays and scalars; if you store something new into `$pebbles[17]` or `$dino`, the old value is replaced. If you store some-thing new into `$family_name{"fred"}`, the old value is replaced as well.

Hash elements will spring into existence by assignment:

```
$family_name{"wilma"} = "flintstone";               # adds a new key (and value)
$family_name{"betty"} .= $family_name{"barney"};   # creates the element if needed
```

That's also just like what happens with arrays and scalars; if you didn't have `$pebbles[17]` or `$dino` before, you will have it after you assign to it. If you didn't have `$family_name{"betty"}` before, you do now.

And accessing outside the hash gives **undef**:

```
$granite = $family_name{"larry"};  # No larry here: undef
```

Once again, this is just like what happens with arrays and scalars; if there's nothing yet stored in `$pebbles[17]` or `$dino`, accessing them will yield `undef`. If there's nothing yet stored in `$family_name{"larry"}`, accessing it will yield `undef`.

The Hash as a Whole

To refer to the entire hash, use the percent sign ("`%`") as a prefix. So, the hash we've been using for the last few pages is actually called `%family_name`.

For convenience, a hash may be converted into a list, and back again. Assigning to a hash (in this case, the one from Figure 5-1) is a list-context assignment, where the list is made of key-value pairs:[*]

```
%some_hash = ("foo", 35, "bar", 12.4, 2.5, "hello",
      "wilma", 1.72e30, "betty", "bye\n");
```

The value of the hash (in a list context) is a simple list of key-value pairs:

```
@any_array = %some_hash;
```

We call this *unwinding* the hash; turning it back into a list of key-value pairs. Of course, the pairs won't necessarily be in the same order as the original list:

```
print "@any_array\n";
  # might give something like this:
  #  betty bye (and a newline) wilma 1.72e+30 foo 35 2.5 hello bar 12.4
```

The order is jumbled because Perl keeps the key-value pairs in an order that's convenient for Perl, so that it can look up any item quickly. So you'd normally use a hash either when you don't care what order the items are in, or when you have an easy way to put them into the order you want.

Of course, even though the order of the key-value pairs is jumbled, each key "sticks" with its corresponding value in the resulting list. So, even though we don't know where the key `foo` will appear in the list, we know that its value, `35`, will be right after it.

Hash Assignment

It's rare to do so, but a hash may be copied using the obvious syntax:

```
%new_hash = %old_hash;
```

This is actually more work for Perl than meets the eye. Unlike what happens in languages like Pascal or C, where such an operation would be a simple matter of

---

[*] Although any list expression may be used, it must have an even number of elements, because the hash is made of key-value *pairs*. An odd element will likely do something unreliable, although it's a warnable offense.

copying a block of memory, Perl's data structures are more complex. So, that line of code tells Perl to unwind the %old_hash into a list of key-value pairs, then assign those to %new_hash, building it up one key-value pair at a time.

It's more common to transform the hash in some way, though. For example, we could make an inverse hash:

```
%inverse_hash = reverse %any_hash;
```

This takes %any_hash and unwinds it into a list of key-value pairs, making a list like (*key, value, key, value, key, value, ...*). Then **reverse** turns that list end-for-end, making a list like (*value, key, value, key, value, key, ...*). Now the keys are where the values used to be, and the values are where the keys used to be. When that's stored into %inverse_hash, we'll be able to look up a string that was a value in %any_hash—it's now a key of %inverse_hash. And the value we'll find is one that was one of the keys from %any_hash. So, we have a way to look up a "value" (now a key), and find a "key" (now a value).

Of course, you might guess (or determine from scientific principles, if you're clever) that this will work properly only if the values in the original hash were unique—otherwise we'd have duplicate keys in the new hash, and keys are always unique. Here's the rule that Perl uses: the last one in wins. That is, the later items in the list overwrite any earlier ones. Of course, we don't know what order the key-value pairs will have in this list, so there's no telling which ones would win. You'd use this technique only if you know there are no duplicates among the original values.* But that's the case for the IP address and host name examples given earlier:

```
%ip_address = reverse %host_name;
```

Now we can look up a host name or IP address with equal ease, to find the corresponding IP address or host name.

The Big Arrow

When assigning a list to a hash, sometimes it's not obvious which elements are keys and which are values. For example, in this assignment (which we saw earlier), we humans have to count through the list, saying, "key, value, key, value...", in order to determine whether 2.5 is a key or a value:

```
%some_hash = ("foo", 35, "bar", 12.4, 2.5, "hello",
        "wilma", 1.72e30, "betty", "bye\n");
```

---

* Or if you don't care that there are duplicates. For example, we could invert the %family_name hash (in which the keys are people's given names and values are their family names) to make it easy to determine whether there is or is not anyone with a given family name in the group. Thus, in the inverted hash, if there's no key of slate, we'd know that there's no one with that name in the original hash.

Wouldn't it be nice if Perl gave us a way to pair up keys and values in that kind of a list, so that it would be easy to see which ones were which? Larry thought so, too, which is why he invented the big arrow, (=>).* To Perl, it's just a different way to "spell" a comma. That is, in the Perl grammar, any time that you need a comma (,), you can use the big arrow instead; it's all the same to Perl.† So here's another way to set up the hash of last names:

```
my %last_name = (  # a hash may be a lexical variable
  "fred" => "flintstone",
  "dino" => undef,
  "barney" => "rubble",
  "betty" => "rubble",
);
```

Here, it's easy (or perhaps at least easier) to see whose name pairs with which value, even if we end up putting many pairs on one line. And notice that there's an extra comma at the end of the list. As we saw earlier, this is harmless, but convenient; if we need to add additional people to this hash, we'll simply make sure that each line has a key-value pair and a trailing comma. Perl will see that there is a comma between each item and the next, and one extra (harmless) comma at the end of the list.

Hash Functions

Naturally, there are some useful functions that can work on an entire hash at once.

The keys and values Functions

The keys function yields a list of all the current keys in a hash, while the values function gives the corresponding values. If there are no elements to the hash, then either function returns an empty list:

```
my %hash = ("a" => 1, "b" => 2, "c" => 3);
my @k = keys %hash;
my @v = values %hash;
```

So, @k will contain "a", "b", and "c", and @v will contain 1, 2, and 3—in *some* order. Remember, Perl doesn't maintain the order of elements in a hash. But, whatever order the keys are in, the values will be in the corresponding order: If "b" is last in the keys, 2 will be last in the values; if "c" is the first key, 3 will be

---

* Yes, there's also a *little* arrow, (->). It's used with references, which are an advanced topic; see the *perlreftut* and *perlref* manpage when you're ready for that.

† Well, there's one technical difference: any bareword (a sequence of nothing but letters, digits, and underscores not starting with a digit) to the left of the big arrow is implicitly quoted. So you can leave off the quote marks on a bareword to the left of the big arrow. You may also omit the quote marks if there's nothing but a bareword as a key inside the curly braces of a hash.

the first value. That's true as long as you don't modify the hash between the request for the keys and the one for the values. If you add elements to the hash, Perl reserves the right to rearrange it as needed, to keep the access quick.[*]

In a scalar context, these functions give the number of elements (key-value pairs) in the hash. They do this quite efficiently, without having to visit each element of the hash:

```
my $count = keys %hash;  # gets 3, meaning three key-value pairs
```

Once in a long while, you'll see that someone has used a hash as a Boolean (true/false) expression, something like this:

```
if (%hash) {
   print "That was a true value!\n";
}
```

That will be true if (and only if) the hash has at least one key-value pair.[†] So, it's just saying, "if the hash is not empty...". But this is a pretty rare construct, as such things go.

The each Function

If you wish to iterate over (that is, examine every element of) an entire hash, one of the usual ways is to use the **each** function, which returns a key-value pair as a two-element list.[‡] On each evaluation of this function for the same array, the next successive key-value pair is returned, until all the elements have been accessed. When there are no more pairs, **each** returns an empty list.

In practice, the only way to use **each** is in a **while** loop, something like this:

```
while ( ($key, $value) = each %hash ) {
   print "$key => $value\n";
}
```

There's a lot going on here. First, each %hash returns a key-value pair from the hash, as a two-element list; let's say that the key is "c" and the value is 3, so the list is ("c", 3). That list is assigned to the list ($key, $value), so $key becomes "c", and $value becomes 3.

---

[*] Of course, if you started adding elements to the hash between **keys** and **values**, your list of values (or keys, whichever you did second) would have additional items, which would be tough to match up with the first list. So no normal programmer would do that.

[†] The actual result is an internal debugging string useful to the people who maintain Perl. It looks something like "4/16", but the value is guaranteed to be true when the hash is non-empty, and false when it's empty, so the rest of us can still use it for that.

[‡] The other usual way to iterate over an entire hash is to use **foreach** on a list of keys from the hash; we'll see that by the end of this section.

But that list assignment is happening in the conditional expression of the `while` loop, which is a scalar context. (Specifically, it's a Boolean context, looking for a true/false value; and a Boolean context is a particular kind of scalar context.) The value of a list assignment in a scalar context is the number of elements in the source list—2, in this case. Since 2 is a true value, we enter the body of the loop and print the message `c => 3`.

The next time through the loop, `each %hash` gives a new key-value pair; let's say it's (`"a", 1`) this time. (It knows to return a different pair than previously because it keeps track of where it is; in technical jargon, there's an iterator stored in with each hash.*) Those two items are stored into (`$key, $value`). Since the number of elements in the source list was again 2, a true value, the `while` condition is true, and the loop body runs again, telling us `a => 1`.

We go one more time through the loop, and by now we know what to expect, so it's no surprise to see `b => 2` appear in the output.

But we knew it couldn't go on forever. Now, when Perl evaluates `each %hash`, there are no more key-value pairs available. So, `each` has to return an empty list.† The empty list is assigned to (`$key, $value`), so `$key` gets `undef`, and `$value` also gets `undef`.

But that hardly matters, because the whole thing is being evaluated in the conditional expression of the `while` loop. The value of a list assignment in a scalar context is the number of elements in the source list—in this case, that's 0. Since 0 is a false value, the `while` loop is done, and execution continues with the rest of the program.

Of course, `each` returns the key-value pairs in a jumbled order. (It's the same order as `keys` and `values` would give, incidentally; the "natural" order of the hash.) If you need to go through the hash in order, simply sort the keys, perhaps something like this:

```
foreach $key (sort keys %hash) {
  $value = $hash{$key};
  print "$key => $value\n";
  # Or, we could have avoided the extra $value variable:
  #  print "$key => $hash{$key}\n";
}
```

We'll see more about sorting hashes in Chapter 15.

---

* Since each hash has its own private iterator, loops using `each` may be nested, as long as they are iterating over *different* hashes. And, as long as we're already in a footnote, we may as well tell you: it's unlikely you'll ever need to do so, but you may reset the iterator of a hash by using the `keys` or `values` function on the hash. The iterator is also automatically reset if a new list is stored into the entire hash, or if `each` has iterated through all of the items to the "end" of the hash. On the other hand, adding new key-value pairs to the hash while iterating over it is generally a bad idea, since that won't necessarily reset the iterator. That's likely to confuse you, your maintenance programmer, and `each` as well.

† It's being used in list context, so it can't return `undef` to signal failure; that would be the one-element list (`undef`) instead of the empty (zero-element) list (`)`.

Typical Use of a Hash

At this point, you may find it helpful to see a more concrete example.

The Bedrock library uses a Perl program in which a hash keeps track of how many books each person has checked out, among other information:

```
$books{"fred"} = 3;
$books{"wilma"} = 1;
```

It's easy to see whether an element of the hash is true or false, do this:

```
if ($books{$someone}) {
  print "$someone has at least one book checked out.\n";
}
```

But there are some elements of the hash that aren't true:

```
$books{"barney"} = 0;       # no books currently checked out
$books{"pebbles"} = undef;  # no books EVER checked out - a new library card
```

Since Pebbles has never checked out any books, her entry has the value of **undef**, rather than 0.

There's a key in the hash for everyone who has a library card. For each key (that is, for each library patron), there's a value that is either a number of books checked out, or **undef** if that person's library card has never been used.

The exists Function

To see whether a key exists in the hash, (that is, whether someone has a library card or not), use the **exists** function, which returns a true value if the given key exists in the hash, whether the corresponding value is true or not:

```
if (exists $books{"dino"}) {
  print "Hey, there's a library card for dino!\n";
}
```

That is to say, **exists $books{"dino"}** will return a true value if (and only if) **dino** is found in the list of keys from **keys %books**.

The delete Function

The **delete** function removes the given key (and its corresponding value) from the hash. (If there's no such key, its work is done; there's no warning or error in that case.)

```
my $person = "betty";
delete $books{$person};  # Revoke the library card for $person
```

Note that this is *not* the same as storing `undef` into that hash element—in fact, it's precisely the opposite! Checking `exists($books{"betty"})` will give opposite results in these two cases; after a `delete`, the key *can't* exist in the hash, but after storing `undef`, the key *must* exist.

Hash Element Interpolation

You can interpolate a single hash element into a double-quoted string just as you'd expect:

```
foreach $person (sort keys %books) {          # for each library patron,in order
  if ($books{$person}) {
    print "$person has $books{$person} items\n";# fred has 3 items
  }
}
```

But there's no support for entire hash interpolation; `"%books"` is just the six char-arcters of (literally) `%books`.* So we've seen all of the magical characters that need backslashing in double quotes: `$` and `@`, because they introduce a variable to be interpolated; `"`, since that's the quoting character that would otherwise end the double-quoted string; and `\`, the backslash itself. Any other characters in a double-quoted string are non-magical and should simply stand for themselves.†

Exercises

See Appendix A for answers to the following exercises:

1. [7] Write a program that will ask the user for a given name and report the corresponding family name. Use the names of people you know, or (if you spend so much time on the computer that you don't know any actual people) use the following table:

Input	Output
fred	flintstone
barney	rubble
wilma	flintstone

---

* Well, it couldn't really be anything else; if we tried to print out the entire hash, as a series of key-value pairs, that would be nearly useless. And, as we'll see in Chapter 6, *I/O Basics*, the percent sign is frequently used in `printf` format strings; giving it another meaning here would be terribly inconvenient.

† But do beware of the apostrophe (`'`), left square bracket (`[`), left curly brace (`{`), the small arrow (`->`), or double-colon (`::`) following a variable name in a double-quoted string, as they could perhaps mean something you didn't intend.

2. [15] Write a program that reads a series of words (with one word per line*) until end-of-input, then prints a summary of how many times each word was seen. (Hint: remember that when an undefined value is used as if it were a number, Perl automatically converts it to 0. It may help to look back at the earlier exercise that kept a running total.) So, if the input words were fred, barney, fred, dino, wilma, fred (all on separate lines), the output should tell us that fred was seen 3 times. For extra credit, sort the summary words in ASCII order in the output.

---

* It has to be one word per line, because we still haven't shown you how to extract individual words from a line of input.

6

I/O Basics

We've already seen how to do some input/output (I/O), in order to make some of the earlier exercises possible. But now we'll learn a little more about those operations. As the title of this chapter implies, there will be more about Perl's I/O operations in Chapter 11.

Input from Standard Input

Reading from the standard input stream is easy.* We've been doing it already with the `<STDIN>` operator.† Evaluating this operator in a scalar context gives you the next line of input:

```
$line = <STDIN>;              # read the next line
chomp($line);                 # and chomp it

chomp($line = <STDIN>);       # same thing, more idiomatically
```

Since the line-input operator will return **undef** when you reach end-of-file, this is handy for dropping out of loops:

```
while (defined($line = <STDIN>)) {
  print "I saw $line";
{
```

There's a lot going on in that first line: we're reading the input into a variable, checking that it's defined, and if it is (meaning that we haven't reached the end of

---

* If you're already familiar with the workings of standard input, output, and error streams, you're ahead of the game. If not, we'll get you caught up when we get to Chapter 14. For now, just think of "standard input" as being "the keyboard," and "standard output" as being "the display screen."

† What we're calling the line-input operator here, `<STDIN>`, is actually a line-input operator (represented by the angle brackets) around a *filehandle*. We'll learn about filehandles in Chapter 11.

the input) we're running the body of the `while` loop. So, inside the body of the loop, we'll see each line, one after another, in `$line.`* This is something you'll want to do fairly often, so naturally Perl has a shortcut for it. The shortcut looks like this:

```
while (<STDIN>) {
    print "I saw $_";
}
```

Now, to make this shortcut, Larry chose some useless syntax. That is, this is *literally* saying, "Read a line of input, and see if it's true. (Normally it is.) And if it is true, enter the `while` loop, but *throw away that line of input!*" Larry knew that it was a useless thing to do; nobody should ever need to do that in a real Perl program. So, Larry took this useless syntax and made it useful.

What this is *actually* saying is that Perl should do the same thing as we saw in our earlier loop: it tells Perl to read the input into a variable, and (as long as the result was defined, so we haven't reached end-of file) then enter the `while` loop. However, instead of storing the input into `$line`, Perl will use its favorite default variable, `$_`, just as if you had written this:

```
while (defined($_ = <STDIN>)) {
    print "I saw $_";
}
```

Now, before we go any further, we must be very clear about something: this shortcut works *only* if you write it just as we did. If you put a line-input operator anywhere else (in particular, as a statement all on its own) it won't read a line into `$_` by default. It works *only* if there's nothing but the line-input operator in the conditional of a `while` loop.† If you put anything else into the conditional expression, this shortcut won't apply.

There's no connection between the line-input operator (`<STDIN>`) and Perl's favorite default variable (`$_`). In this case, though, it just happens that the input is being stored in that variable.

On the other hand, evaluating the line-input operator in a list context gives you all of the (remaining) lines of input as a list—each element of the list is one line:

```
foreach (<STDIN>) {
    print "I saw $_";
}
```

Once again, there's no connection between the line-input operator and Perl's favorite default variable. In this case, though, the default control variable for

---

* You probably noticed that we never chomped that input. In this kind of a loop, you can't really put chomp into the conditional expression, so it's often the first item in the loop body, when it's needed. We'll see examples of that in the next section.

† Well, okay, the conditional of a `for` loop is just a `while` conditional in disguise, so it works there, too.

foreach is $_. So in this loop, we'll see each line of input in $_, one after the other.

That may sound familiar, and for good reason: That's the same behavior as the while loop would do. Isn't it?

The difference is under the hood. In the while loop, Perl reads a line of input, puts it into a variable, and runs the body of the loop. Then, it goes back to find another line of input. But in the foreach loop, the line-input operator is being used in a list context (since foreach needs a list to iterate through). So it has to read all of the input before the loop can start running. That difference will become apparent when the input is coming from your 400MB web server log file! It's generally best to use code like the while loop's shortcut, which will process input a line at a time, whenever possible.

Input from the Diamond Operator

Another way to read input is with the diamond* operator: <>. This is useful for making programs that work like standard Unix† utilities, with respect to the invocation arguments (which we'll see in a moment). If you want to make a Perl program that can be used like the utilities *cat, sed, awk, sort, grep, lpr*, and many others, the diamond operator will be your friend. If you want to make anything else, the diamond operator probably won't help.

The *invocation arguments* to a program are normally a number of "words" on the command line after the name of the program.‡ In this case, they give the names of a number of files to be processed in sequence:

```
$ ./my_program fred barney betty
```

That command means to run the command *my_program* (which will be found in the current directory), and that it should process file *fred*, followed by file *barney*, followed by file *betty*.

If you give no invocation arguments, the program should process the standard input stream. Or, as a special case, if you give just a hyphen as one of the argu-

---

* The diamond operator was named by Larry's daughter, Heidi, when Randal went over to Larry's house one day to show off the new training materials he'd been writing, and complained that there was no spoken name for "that thing". Larry didn't have a name for it, either. Heidi (eight years old at the time) quickly chimed in, "That's a diamond, Daddy." So the name stuck. Thanks, Heidi!

† But not just on Unix systems. Many other systems have adopted this way of using invocation arguments.

‡ Whenever a program is started, it has a list of zero or more invocation arguments, supplied by whatever program is starting it. Often this is the shell, which makes up the list depending upon what you type on the command line. But we'll see in a later chapter that you can invoke a program with pretty much any strings as the invocation arguments. Because they often come from the shell's command line, they are sometimes called "command-line arguments" as well.

ments, that means standard input as well.* So, if the invocation arguments had been `fred - betty`, that would have meant that the program should process file *fred*, followed by the standard input stream, followed by file *betty*.

The benefit of making your programs work like this is that you may choose where the program gets its input at run time; for example, you won't have to rewrite the program to use it in a pipeline (which we'll discuss more later). Larry put this feature into Perl because he wanted to make it easy for you to write your own programs that work like standard Unix utilities—even on non-Unix machines. Actually, he did it so he could make his *own* programs work like standard Unix utilities; since some vendors' utilities don't work just like others', Larry could make his own utilities, deploy them on a number of machines, and know that they'd all have the same behavior. Of course, this meant porting Perl to every machine he could find.

The diamond operator is actually a special kind of line-input operator. But instead of getting the input from the keyboard, it comes from the user's choice of input:†

```
while (defined($line = <>)) {
  chomp($line);
  print "It was $line that I saw!\n";
}
```

So, if we run this program with the invocation arguments **fred**, **barney**, and **betty**, it will say something like: "It was [a line from file *fred*] that I saw!", "It was [another line from file *fred*] that I saw!", on and on until it reaches the end of file **fred**. Then, it will automatically go on to file **barney**, printing out one line after another, and then on to file **betty**. Note that there's no break when we go from one file to another; when you use the diamond, it's as if the input files have been merged into one big file.‡ The diamond will return **undef** (and we'll drop out of the **while** loop) only at the end of all of the input.

In fact, since this is just a special kind of line-input operator, we may use the same shortcut we saw earlier, to read the input into $_ by default:

```
while (<>) {
  chomp;
  print "It was $_ that I saw!\n";
}
```

---

* Here's a possibly unfamilar Unix fact: most of those standard utilities, like *cat* and *sed* use this same convention, where a hyphen stands for the standard input stream.

† Which may or may not include getting input from the keyboard.

‡ If it matters to you, or even if it doesn't, the current file's name is kept in Perl's special variable $ARGV. This name may be "-" instead of a real filename if the input is coming from the standard input stream, though.

This works like the loop above, but with less typing. And you may have noticed that we're using the default for chomp; without an argument, chomp will work on $_. Every little bit of saved typing helps!

Since the diamond operator is generally being used to process all of the input, it's typically a mistake to use it in more than one place in your program. If you find yourself putting two diamonds into the same program, especially using the second diamond inside the while loop that is reading from the first one, it's almost certainly not going to do what you would like.* In our experience, when beginners put a second diamond into a program, they meant to use $_ instead. Remember, the diamond operator *reads* the input, but the input itself is (generally, by default) found in $_.

If the diamond operator can't open one of the files and read from it, it'll print an allegedly helpful diagnostic message, such as:

```
can't open wimla: No such file or directory
```

The diamond operator will then go on to the next file automatically, much like what you'd expect from *cat* or another standard utility.

The Invocation Arguments

Technically, the diamond operator isn't looking literally at the invocation arguments—it works from the @ARGV array. This array is a special array that is preset by the Perl interpreter to be a list of the invocation arguments. In other words, this is just like any other array, (except for its funny, all-caps name), but when your program starts, @ARGV is already stuffed full of the list of invocation arguments.†

You can use @ARGV just like any other array; you could shift items off of it, perhaps, or use foreach to iterate over it. You could even check to see if any arguments start with a hyphen, so that you could process them as invocation options (like Perl does with its own -w option).‡

---

* If you re-initialize @ARGV before using the second diamond, then you're on solid ground. We'll see @ARGV in the next section.

† C programmers may be wondering about argc (there isn't one in Perl), and what happened to the program's own name (that's found in Perl's special variable $0, not @ARGV). Also, depending upon how you've invoked your program, there may be a little more happening than we say here. See the *perlrun* manpage for the full details.

‡ If you need more than just one or two such options, you should almost certainly use a module to process them in a standard way. See the documentation for the Getopt::Long and Getopt::Std modules, which are part of the standard distribution.

This is how the diamond operator knows what filenames it should use: it looks in @ARGV. If it finds an empty list, it uses the standard input stream; otherwise it uses the list of files that it finds. This means that after your program starts and before you start using the diamond, you've got a chance to tinker with @ARGV. For example, here we can process three specific files, regardless of what the user chose on the command line:

```
@ARGV = qw# larry moe curly #;  # force these three files to be read
while (<>) {
  chomp;
  print "It was $_ that I saw in some stooge-like file!\n";
}
```

In Chapter 11, we'll see how to open and close specific filenames at specific times. But this technique will suffice for the next few chapters.

Output to Standard Output

The `print` operator takes a list of values and sends each item (as a string, of course) to standard output in turn, one after another. It doesn't add any extra characters before, after, or in between the items;* if you want spaces between items and a newline at the end, you have to say so:

```
$name = "Larry Wall";
print "Hello there, $name, did you know that 3+4 is ", 3+4, "?\n";
```

Of course, that means that there's a difference between printing an array and interpolating an array:

```
print @array;     # print a list of items
print "@array";   # print a string (containing an interpolated array)
```

That first `print` statement will print a list of items, one after another, with no spaces in between. The second one will print exactly one item, which is the string you get by interpolating @array into the empty string—that is, it prints the contents of @array, separated by spaces.† So, if @array holds qw/ fred barney betty /,‡ the first one prints fredbarneybetty, while the second prints fred barney betty separated by spaces.

But before you decide to always use the second form, imagine that @array is a list of unchomped lines of input. That is, imagine that each of its strings has a

---

* Well, it doesn't add anything extra *by default*, but this default (like so many others in Perl) may be changed. Changing these defaults will likely confuse your maintenance programmer, though, so avoid doing so except in small, quick-and-dirty programs, or (rarely) in a small section of a normal program. See the *perlvar* manpage to learn about changing the defaults.

† Yes, the spaces are another default; see the *perlvar* manpage again.

‡ You know that we mean a three-element list here, right? This is just Perl notation.

trailing newline character. Now, the first `print` statement prints `fred`, `barney`, and `betty` on three separate lines. But the second one prints this:

```
fred
 barney
 betty
```

Do you see where the spaces come from? Perl is interpolating an array, so it puts spaces between the elements. So, we get the first element of the array (`fred` and a newline character), then a space, then the next element of the array (`barney` and a newline character), then a space, then the last element of the array (`betty` and a newline character). The result is that the lines seem to have become indented, except for the first one. Every week or two, a message appears on the newsgroup *comp.lang.perl.misc* with a subject line something like:

> Perl indents everything after the first line

Without even reading the message, we can immediately see that the program used double quotes around an array containing unchomped strings. "Did you perhaps put an array of unchomped strings inside double quotes?" we ask, and the answer is always yes.

Generally, if your strings contain newlines, you simply want to print them, after all:

```
print @array;
```

But if they don't contain newlines, you'll generally want to add one at the end:

```
print "@array\n";
```

So, if you're using the quote marks, you'll be (generally) adding the `\n` at the end of the string anyway; this should help you to remember which is which.

It's normal for your program's output to be *buffered*. That is, instead of sending out every little bit of output at once, it'll be saved until there's enough to bother with. That's because if (for example) the output were going to be saved on disk, it would be (relatively) slow and inefficient to spin the disk every time that one or two characters need to be added to the file. Generally, then, the output will go into a buffer that is *flushed* (that is, actually written to disk, or wherever) only when the buffer gets full, or when the output is otherwise finished (such as at the end of runtime). Usually, that's what you want.

But if you (or a program) may be waiting impatiently for the output, you may wish to take that performance hit and flush the output buffer each time you `print`. See the Perl manpages for more information on controlling buffering in that case.

Since **print** is looking for a list of strings to print, its arguments are evaluated in list context. Since the diamond operator (as a special kind of line-input operator) will return a list of lines in a list context, these can work well together:

```
print <>;          # source code for 'cat'

print sort <>;  # source code for 'sort'
```

Well, to be fair, the standard Unix commands *cat* and *sort* do have some additional functionality that these replacements lack. But you can't beat them for the price! You can now re-implement all of your standard Unix utilities in Perl, and painlessly port them to any machine that has Perl, whether that machine is running Unix or not. And you can be sure that the programs on every different type of machine will nevertheless have the same behavior.*

What might not be obvious is that **print** has optional parentheses, which can sometimes cause confusion. Remember the rule that parentheses in Perl may always be omitted, except when doing so would change the meaning of a statement. So, here are two ways to print the same thing:

```
print("Hello, world!\n");
print "Hello, world!\n";
```

So far, so good. But another rule in Perl is that if the invocation of **print** *looks* like a function call, then it *is* a function call. It's a simple rule, but what does it mean for something to look like a function call?

In a function call, there's a function name immediately† followed by parentheses around the function's arguments, like this:

```
print (2+3);
```

That looks like a function call, so it is a function call. It prints 5, but then it returns a value like any other function. The return value of **print** is a true or false value, indicating the success of the print. It nearly always succeeds, unless you get some I/O error, so the $result in the following statement will normally be 1:

```
$result = print("hello world!\n");
```

But what if you used the result in some other way? Let's suppose you decide to multiply the return value times four:

---

* In fact, there was even an endeavor started, called the PPT (Perl Power Tools) project, whose goal is to implement all of the classic Unix utilities in Perl. They actually completed nearly all the utilities (and most of the games!), but got bogged down when they got to reimplementing the shell. The PPT project has been helpful because it has made these standard utilities available on many non-Unix machines.

† We say "immediately" here because Perl won't permit a newline character between the function name and the opening parenthesis in this kind of function call. If there is a newline there, Perl sees your code as making a list operator, rather than a function call. This is the kind of piddling technical detail that we mention only for completeness. If you're terminally curious, see the full story in the manpages.

```
print (2+3)*4;  # Oops!
```

When Perl sees this line of code, it prints 5, just as you asked. Then it takes the return value from **print**, which is 1, and multiplies that times 4. It then throws away the product, wondering why you didn't tell it to do something else with it. And at this point, someone looking over your shoulder says, "Hey, Perl can't do math! That should have printed 20, rather than 5!"

This is the problem with allowing the parentheses to be optional; sometimes we humans forget where the parentheses really belong. When there are no parentheses, **print** is a list operator, printing all of the items in the following list; that's generally what you'd expect. But when the first thing after **print** is a left parenthesis, **print** is a function call, and it will print only what's found inside the parentheses. Since that line had parentheses, it's the same to Perl as if you'd said this:

```
( print(2+3) ) * 4;  # Oops!
```

Fortunately, Perl itself can almost always help you with this, if you ask for warnings—so use **-w**, at least during program development and debugging.

Actually, this rule—"If it looks like a function call, it is a function call"—applies to all list functions* in Perl, not just to **print**. It's just that you're most likely to notice it with **print**. If **print** (or another function name) is followed by an open parenthesis, make sure that the corresponding close parenthesis comes after *all* of the arguments to that function.

Formatted Output with printf

You may wish to have a little more control with your output than **print** provides. In fact, you may be accustomed to the formatted output of C's **printf** function. Fear not—Perl provides a comparable operation with the same name.

The **printf** operator takes a format string followed by a list of things to print. The format† string is a fill-in-the-blanks template showing the desired form of the output:

```
printf "Hello, %s; your password expires in %d days!\n",
    $user, $days_to_die;
```

The format string holds a number of so-called *conversions*; each conversion begins with a percent sign (%) and ends with a letter. (As we'll see in a moment, there

---

* Functions that take zero or one arguments don't suffer from this problem.

† Here, we're using "format" in the generic sense. Perl has a report-generating feature called "formats" that we won't even be mentioning (except in this footnote) until Appendix B, and then only to say that we really aren't going to talk about them. So, you're on your own there. Just wanted to keep you from getting lost.

may be significant extra characters between these two symbols.) There should be the same number of items in the following list as there are conversions; if these don't match up, it won't work correctly. In the example above, there are two items and two conversions, so the output might look something like this:

```
Hello, merlyn; your password expires in 3 days!
```

There are many possible `printf` conversions, so we'll take time here to describe just the most common ones. Of course, the full details are available in the `perlfunc` manpage.

To print a number in what's generally a good way, use `%g`,[*] which automatically chooses floating-point, integer, or even exponential notation as needed:

```
printf "%g %g %g\n", 5/2, 51/17, 51 ** 17;  # 2.5 3 1.0683e+29
```

The `%d` format means a decimal[†] integer, truncated as needed:

```
printf "in %d days!\n", 17.85;  # in 17 days!
```

Note that this is truncated, not rounded; we'll see how to round off a number in a moment.

In Perl, `printf` is most often used for columnar data, since most formats accept a field width. If the data won't fit, the field will generally be expanded as needed:

```
printf "%6d\n", 42;  # output like ⌣⌣⌣⌣42 (the ⌣ symbol stands for a space)
printf "%2d\n", 2e3 + 1.95;  # 2001
```

The `%s` conversion means a string, so it effectively interpolates the given value as a string, but with a given field width:

```
printf "%10s\n", "wilma";  # looks like ⌣⌣⌣⌣⌣wilma
```

A negative field width is left-justified (in any of these conversions):

```
printf "%-15s\n", "flintstone";  # looks like flintstone⌣⌣⌣⌣⌣
```

The `%f` conversion (floating-point) rounds off its output as needed, and even lets you request a certain number of digits after the decimal point:

```
printf "%12f\n", 6 * 7 + 2/3;    # looks like ⌣⌣⌣42.666667
printf "%12.3f\n", 6 * 7 + 2/3;  # looks like ⌣⌣⌣⌣⌣⌣42.667
printf "%12.0f\n", 6 * 7 + 2/3;  # looks like ⌣⌣⌣⌣⌣⌣⌣⌣⌣⌣43
```

---

[*] "General" numeric conversion. Or maybe a "Good conversion for this number" or "Guess what I want the output to look like."

[†] There's also `%x` for hexadecimal and `%o` for octal, if you need those. But we really say "decimal" here as a memory aid: `%d` for Decimal integer.

To print a real percent sign, use `%%`, which is special in that it uses no element from the list:*

```
printf "Monthly interest rate: %.2f%%\n",
    5.25/12;  # the value looks like "0.44%"
```

Arrays and printf

Generally, you won't use an array as an argument to `printf`. That's because an array may hold any number of items, and a given format string will work with only a certain fixed number of items: if there are three conversions in the format, there must be exactly three items.

But there's no reason you can't whip up a format string on the fly, since it may be any expression. This can be tricky to get right, though, so it may be handy (especially when debugging) to store the format into a variable:

```
my @items = qw( wilma dino pebbles );
my $format = "The items are:\n" . ("%10s\n" x @items);
## print "the format is <<$format>>\n"; # for debugging
printf $format, @items;
```

This uses the **x** operator (which we learned about in Chapter 2, *Scalar Data*) to replicate the given string a number of times given by `@items` (which is being used in a scalar context). In this case, that's **3**, since there are three items, so the resulting format string is the same as if we had written it as `"The items are:\`
`n%10s\n%10s\n%10s\n."` And the output prints each item on its own line, right-justified in a ten-character column, under a heading line. Pretty cool, huh? But not cool enough, because you can even combine these:

```
printf "The items are:\n".("%10s\n" x @items), @items;
```

Note that here we have `@items` being used once in a scalar context, to get its length, and once in a list context, to get its contents. Context is important.

---

* Maybe you thought you could simply put a backslash in front of the percent sign. Nice try, but no. The reason that won't work is that the format is an *expression*, and the expression `"\%"` means the one-character string `'%'`. Even if we got a backslash into the format string, `printf` wouldn't know what to do with it. Besides, C programmers are used to `printf` working like this.

Exercises

See Appendix A for answers to the following exercises:

1. [7] Write a program that acts like *cat*, but reverses the order of the output lines. (Some systems have a utility like this named *tac*.) If you run yours as `./tac fred barney betty`, the output should be all of file *betty* from last line to first, then *barney* and then *fred*, also from last line to first. (Be sure to use the `./` in your program's invocation if you call it *tac*, so that you don't get the system's utility instead!)

2. [8] Write a program that asks the user to enter a list of strings on separate lines, printing each string in a right-justified 20-character column. To be certain that the output is in the proper columns, print a "ruler line" of digits as well. (This is simply a debugging aid.) Make sure that you're not using a 19-character column by mistake! For example, entering `hello`, `good-bye` should give output something like this:

```
1234567890123456789012345678901234567890123456789012345678901234567890
               hello
            good-bye
```

3. [8] Modify the previous program to let the user choose the column width, so that entering 30, `hello`, `good-bye` (on separate lines) would put the strings at the 30th column. (Hint: see the section "Interpolation of Scalar Variables into Strings" in Chapter 2 about controlling variable interpolation.) For extra credit, make the ruler line longer when the selected width is larger.

7

Concepts of Regular Expressions

Perl has many features that set it apart from other languages. Of all those features, one of the most important is its strong support for regular expressions. These allow fast, flexible, and reliable string handling.

But that power comes at a price. Regular expressions are actually tiny programs in their own special language, built inside Perl. (Yes, you're about to learn *another* programming language!* Fortunately it's a simple one.) So for the next two chapters, we'll be learning that language; then we'll take what we've learned back to the world of Perl in Chapter 9.

Regular expressions aren't merely part of Perl; they're also found in *sed* and *awk*, *procmail*, *grep*, most programmers' text editors like *vi* and *emacs*, and even in more esoteric places. If you've seen some of these already, you're ahead of the game. Keep watching, and you'll see many more tools that use or support regular expressions, such as search engines on the Web (often written in Perl), email clients, and others.

What Are Regular Expressions?

A *regular expression*, often called a *pattern* in Perl, is a template that either matches or doesn't match a given string.† That is, there are an infinite number of possible text strings; a given pattern divides that infinite set into two groups: the ones that match, and the ones that don't. There's never any kinda-sorta-almost-up-

---

* Some might argue that regular expressions are not a *complete* programming language. We won't argue.

† Purists would ask for a more rigorous definition. But then again, purists say that Perl's patterns aren't really regular expressions. If you're serious about regular expressions, we highly recommend the book *Mastering Regular Expressions* by Jeffrey Friedl (O'Reilly & Associates, Inc.).

to-here wishy-washy matching: either it matches or it doesn't. A pattern may match just one possible string, or just two or three, or a dozen, or a hundred, or an infinite number. Or it may match all strings *except* for one, or except for some, or except for an infinite number.*

We already referred to regular expressions as being little programs in their own simple programming language. It's a simple language because the programs have just one task: to look at a string and say "it matches" or "it doesn't match".† That's all they do.

One of the places you're likely to have seen regular expressions is in the Unix *grep* command, which prints out text lines matching a given pattern. For example, if you wanted to see which lines in a given file mention `flint` and, somewhere later on the same line, `stone`, you might do something like this, with the Unix *grep* command:

```
$ grep 'flint.*stone' some_file
a piece of flint, a stone which may be used to start a fire by striking
found obsidian, flint, granite, and small stones of basaltic rock, which
a flintlock rifle in poor condition. The sandstone mantle held several
```

Now, if you've used regular expressions somewhere else, that's good, because you have a head start on these three chapters. But Perl's regular expressions have somewhat different syntax than most other implementations; in fact, everybody's regular expressions are a little different. So, if you needed to use a backslash to do something in another implementation, maybe you'll need to leave it off in Perl, or maybe vice versa.

Don't confuse regular expressions with shell filename-matching patterns, called *globs*. A typical glob is what you use when you type `*.pm` to the Unix shell to match all filenames that end in `.pm`. Globs use a lot of the same characters that we use in regular expressions, but those characters are used in totally different ways.‡ We'll visit globs later, in Chapter 12, *Directory Operations*, but for now try to put them totally out of your mind.

---

* And as we'll see, you could have a pattern that always matches or that never does. In rare cases, even these may be useful. Generally, though, they're mistakes.

† The programs also pass back some information that Perl can use later. One such piece of information is the "regular expressions memories" that we'll learn about a little later.

‡ Globs are also (alas) sometimes called patterns. What's worse, though, is that some bad Unix books for beginners (and possibly *written* by beginners) have taken to calling globs "regular expressions", which they certainly are not. This confuses many folks at the start of their work with Unix.

Using Simple Patterns

To compare a pattern (regular expression) to the contents of $_, simply put the pattern between a pair of forward slashes (/), like we do here:

```
$_ = "yabba dabba doo";
if (/abba/) {
  print "It matched!\n";
}
```

The expression /abba/ looks for that four-letter string in $_; if it finds it, it returns a true value. In this case, it's found more than once, but that doesn't make any difference. If it's found at all, it's a match; if it's not in there at all, it fails.

Because the pattern match is generally being used to return a true or false value, it is almost always found in the conditional expression of if or while.

All of the usual backslash escapes that you can put into double-quoted strings are available in patterns, so you could use the pattern /coke\tsprite/ to match the eleven characters of coke, a tab, and sprite.

About Metacharacters

Of course, if patterns matched only simple literal strings, they wouldn't be very useful. That's why there are a number of special characters, called *metacharacters*, that have special meanings in regular expressions.

For example, the dot (.) is a wildcard character—it matches any single character except a newline (which is represented by "\n"). So, the pattern /bet.y/ would match betty. Or it would match betsy, or bet=y, or bet.y, or any other string that has bet, followed by any one character (except a newline), followed by y. It wouldn't match bety or betsey, though, since those don't have exactly one character between the t and the y. The dot always matches exactly one character.

So, if you wanted to match a period in the string, you *could* use the dot. But that would match any possible character (except a newline), which might be more than you wanted. If you wanted the dot to match *just* a period, you can simply backslash it. In fact, that rule goes for all of Perl's regular expression metacharacters: a backslash in front of any metacharacter makes it nonspecial. So, the pattern /3\.14159/ doesn't have a wildcard character.

So the backslash is our second metacharacter. If you mean a real backslash, just use a pair of them—a rule that applies just as well everywhere else in Perl.

Simple Quantifiers

It often happens that you'll need to repeat something in a pattern. The star (*) means to match the preceding item zero or more times. So, /fred\t*barney/ matches any number of tab characters between fred and barney. That is, it matches "fred\tbarney" with one tab, or "fred\t\tbarney" with two tabs, or "fred\t\t\tbarney" with three tabs, or even "fredbarney" with nothing in between at all. That's because the star means "zero or more"—so you could even have hundreds of tab characters in between, but nothing other than tabs. You may find it helpful to think of star as saying, "that previous thing, any number of *times*, even zero times."

What if you wanted to allow something besides tab characters? The dot matches any character*, so .* will match any character, any number of times. That means that the pattern /fred.*barney/ matches "any old junk" between fred and barney. Any line that mentions fred and (somewhere later) barney will match that pattern. We often call .* the "any old junk" pattern, because it can match any old junk in your strings.

The star is formally called a *quantifier*, meaning that it specifies a quantity of the preceding item. But it's not the only quantifier; the plus ("+") is another. The plus means to match the preceding item *one* or more times: /fred +barney/ matches if fred and barney are separated by spaces and only spaces. (The space is not a metacharacter.) This won't match fredbarney, since the plus means that there must be one or more spaces between the two names, so at least one space is required. It may be helpful to think of the plus as saying, "that last thing, *plus* any number more of the same thing."

There's a third quantifier like the star and plus, but more limited. It's the question mark ("?"), which means that the preceding item is optional. That is, the preceding item may occur once or not at all. Like the other two quantifiers, the question mark means that the preceding item appears a certain number of times. It's just that in this case the item may match one time (if it's there) or zero times (if it's not). There aren't any other possibilities. So, /bamm-?bamm/ matches either spelling: bamm-bamm or bammbamm. This is easy to remember, since it's saying "that last thing, maybe? Or maybe not?"

All three of these quantifiers must follow something, since they tell how many times the *previous* item may repeat.

---

* Except newline. But we're going to stop reminding you of that so often, because you know it by now. Most of the time it doesn't matter, anyway, because your strings will most-often not have newlines. But don't forget this detail, because someday a newline will sneak into your string and you'll need to remember that the dot doesn't match newline.

Grouping in Patterns

As in mathematics, parentheses ("()") may be used for grouping. So, parentheses are also metacharacters. As an example, the pattern /fred+/ matches strings like freddddddddd, but strings like that don't show up often in real life. But the pattern /(fred)+/ matches strings like fredfredfred, which is more likely to be what you wanted. And what about the pattern /(fred)*/? That matches strings like hello, world.*

Alternatives

The vertical bar (|), often pronounced "or" in this usage, means that either the left side may match, or the right side. That is, if the part of the pattern on the left of the bar fails, the part on the right gets a chance to match. So, /fred|barney|betty/ will match any string that mentions fred, or barney, or betty.

Now we can make patterns like /fred(|\t)+barney/, which matches if fred and barney are separated by spaces, tabs, or a mixture of the two. The plus means to repeat one or more times; each time it repeats, the (|\t) has the chance to match either a space or a tab.† There must be at least one character between the two names.

If you wanted the characters between fred and barney to all be the same, you could rewrite that pattern as /fred(+|\t+)barney/. In this case, the separators must be all spaces, or all tabs.

The pattern /fred (and|or) barney/ matches any string containing either of the two possible strings: fred and barney, or fred or barney.‡ We could match the same two strings with the pattern /fred and barney|fred or barney/, but that would be too much typing. It would probably also be less efficient, depending upon what optimizations are built into the regular expression engine.

A Pattern Test Program

When in the course of Perl events it becomes necessary for a programmer to write a regular expression, it may be difficult to tell just what the pattern will do. It's normal to find that a pattern matches more than you expected, or less. Or it may match earlier in the string than you expected, or later, or not at all.

---

* The star means to match *zero* or more repetitions of fred. When you're willing to settle for zero, it's hard to be disappointed! That pattern will match any string, even the empty string.

† This particular match would normally be done more efficiently with a character class, as we'll see in the next chapter.

‡ Note that the words and and or are *not* operators in regular expressions! They are shown here in a fixed-width typeface because they're part of the strings.

This program is useful to test out a pattern on some strings and see just what it matches, and where:

```
#!/usr/bin/perl
while (<>) {                          # take one input line at a time
  chomp;
  if (/YOUR_PATTERN_GOES_HERE/) {
    print "Matched: |$`<$&>$'|\n";   # Mystery code! See the text.
  } else {
    print "No match.\n";
  }
}
```

This pattern test program is written for programmers to use, not endusers; you can tell because it doesn't have any prompts or usage information. It will take any number of input lines and check each one against the pattern that you'll put in place of the string saying YOUR_PATTERN_GOES_HERE. For each line that matches, the line with "mystery code" will be run. We'll learn about what that line is really doing in Chapter 9. But what you'll see is this: if the pattern is /match/ and the input is beforematchafter, the output will say "|before<match>after|", using angle brackets to show you just what part of the string was matched by your pattern. Try it and see! If you pattern matches something you didn't expect, you'll be able to see that right away.

Exercises

See Appendix A for answers to the following exercises:

Remember, it's normal to be surprised by some of the things that regular expressions do; that's one reason that the exercises in this chapter are even more important than the others. Expect the unexpected.

Several of these exercises ask you to use the test program from this chapter. You *could* manually type up this program, taking great care to get all of the odd punctuation marks correct.* But you'll probably find it faster and easier to simply download the program and some other goodies from the O'Reilly website, as we mentioned in the Preface. You'll find this program under the name *pattern_test*.†

1. [6] Use the test program to make and test a pattern that matches any string containing fred. Does it match if your string is Fred, frederick, or Alfred?

---

* If you *do* type it up on your own, remember that the backtick character (`) is not the same as the apostrophe ('). On most full-sized computer keyboards these days (in the U.S., at least), the backtick is found on a key immediately to the left of the 1 key. Try out the program with the pattern /match/and the string beforematchafter, as the text describes, and see that it works correctly before you do the exercises.

† Don't be surprised if the program you download is a little fancier than what we have in the book. The commented-out extra features you see will come in handy in later exercises.

2. [6] Use the test program to make and test a pattern that matches any string containing at least one **a** followed by any number of **b**'s. Remember that "any number" might be zero. Does it match if your string is **barney**, **fred**, **abba**, or **dinosaur**?

3. [5] Use the test program to make and test a pattern that matches any string containing any number of backslashes followed by any number of asterisks. Does it match if your string is **, **fred**, **barney** ***, or ***wilma**\? (Note the typography; those are four separate test strings.)

4. [6] Write a new program (*not* the test program) that prints out any input line that mentions **wilma**. (Any other lines should simply be skipped.) For extra credit, allow it to match **Wilma** with a capital **W** as well.

5. [8] Extra credit exercise: write a program that prints out any input line that mentions *both* **wilma** and **fred**.

8

More About Regular Expressions

In the previous chapter, we saw the beginnings of what regular expressions can do. Here we'll see some of their other common features.

Character Classes

A *character class*, a list of possible characters inside square brackets ([ ]), matches any single character from within the class. It matches just one single character, but that one character may be any of the ones listed.

For example, the character class [abcwxyz] may match any one of those seven characters. For convenience, you may specify a range of characters with a hyphen (-), so that class may also be written as [a-cw-z]. That didn't save much typing, but it's more usual to make a character class like [a-zA-Z], to match any one letter out of that set of 52.* You may use the same character shortcuts as in any double-quotish string to define a character, so the class [\000-\177] matches any seven-bit ASCII character.†

Of course, a character class will be just part of a full pattern; it will never stand on its own in Perl. For example, you might see code that says something like this:

```
$_ = "The HAL-9000 requires authorization to continue.";
if (/HAL-[0-9]+/) {
  print "The string mentions some model of HAL computer.\n";
}
```

---

* Notice that those 52 don't include letters like Å and É and Î and Ø and Ü. But when Unicode processing is available, that particular character range is noticed and enhanced to automatically do the right thing.

† At least, if you use ASCII and not EBCDIC.

Sometimes, it's easier to specify the characters left out, rather than the ones within the character class. A caret ("^") at the start of the character class negates it. That is, [^def] will match any single character *except* one of those three. And [^n\-z] matches any character except for n, hyphen, or z. (Note that the hyphen is backslashed, because it's special inside a character class. But the first hyphen in /HAL-[0-9]+/ doesn't need a backslash, because hyphens aren't special *outside* a character class.)

Character Class Shortcuts

Some character classes appear so frequently that they have shortcuts. For example, the character class for any digit, [0-9], may be abbreviated as \d. Thus, the pattern from the example about HAL could be written /HAL-\d+/ instead.

The shortcut \w is a so-called "word" character: [A-Za-z0-9_]. If your "words" are made up of ordinary letters, digits, and underscores, you'll be happy with this. Most of the rest of us have words made up of ordinary letters, hyphens, and apostrophes,* and we'd like to change this. As of this writing, the Perl developers are working on it, but it's not available yet.† So use this one only when you want ordinary letters, digits, and underscores.

Of course, \w doesn't match a "word"; it merely matches a single "word" character. To match an entire word, though, the plus modifier is handy. A pattern like /fred \w+ barney/ will match fred and a space, then a "word", then a space and barney. That is, it'll match if there's one word‡ between fred and barney, set off by single spaces.

As you may have noticed in that previous example, it might be handy to be able to match spaces more flexibly. The \s shortcut is good for whitespace; it's the same as [\f\t\n\r]. That is, it's the same as a class containing the five whitespace characters form-feed, tab, newline, carriage return, and the space character itself. These are the characters that merely move the printing position around; they don't use any ink. Still, like the other shortcuts we've just seen, \s matches just a single character from the class, so it's usual to use either \s* for any amount of whitespace (including none at all), or \s+ for one or more

---

* At least, in usual English we do. In other languages, you may have different components of words. And when looking at ASCII-encoded English text, we have the problem that the single quote and the apostrophe are the same character, so it's not possible in isolation to tell whether cats' is a word with an apostrophe or a word at the end of a quotation. This is probably one reason that computers haven't been able to take over the world yet.

† Except to a limited (but nevertheless useful) extent in connection with locales; see the *perllocale* manpage.

‡ We're going to stop saying "word" in quotes so much; you know by now that these letter-digit-underscore words are the ones we mean.

whitespace characters. (In fact, it's rare to see \s without one of those quantifiers.) Since all of those whitespace characters look about the same to us humans, we can treat them all in the same way with this shortcut.

Negating the Shortcuts

Sometimes you may want the opposite of one of these three shortcuts. That is, you may want [^\d], [^\w], or [^\s], meaning a nondigit character, a nonword character, or a nonwhitespace character. That's easy enough to accomplish by using their uppercase counterparts: \D, \W, or \S. These match any character that their counterpart would *not* match.

Any of these shortcuts will work either in place of a character class (standing on their own in a pattern), or inside the square brackets of a larger character class. That means that you could now use /[\dA-Fa-f]+/ to match hexadecimal (base 16) numbers, which use letters ABCDEF (or the same letters in lowercase) as additional digits.

Another compound character class is [\d\D], which means any digit, or any non-digit. That is to say, any character at all! This is a common way to match any character, even a newline. (As opposed to ., which matches any character *except* a newline.) And then there's the totally useless [^\d\D], which matches anything that's not either a digit or a non-digit. Right—nothing!

General Quantifiers

A *quantifier* in a pattern means to repeat the preceding item a certain number of times. We've already seen three quantifiers: *, +, and ?. But if none of those three suits your needs, just use a comma-separated pair of numbers inside curly braces ({}) to specify exactly how few and how many repetitions are allowed.

So the pattern /a{5,15}/ will match from five to fifteen repetitions of the letter a. If the a appears three times, that's too few, so it won't match. If it appears five times, it's a match. If it appears ten times, that's still a match. If it appears twenty times, just the first fifteen will match, since that's the upper limit.

If you omit the second number (but include the comma), there's no upper limit to the number of times the item will match. So, /(fred){3,}/ will match if there are three or more instances of fred in a row (with no extra characters, like spaces, allowed between each fred and the next). There's no upper limit, so that would match eighty-eight instances of fred, if you had a string with that many.

If you omit the comma as well as the upper bound, the number given is an exact count: /\w{8}/ will match exactly eight word characters (occuring as part of a larger string, perhaps).

In fact, the three quantifier characters that we saw earlier are just common short-cuts. The star is the same as the quantifier {0,}, meaning zero or more. The plus is the same as {1,}, meaning one or more. And the question mark could be written as {0,1}. In practice, it's unusual to need any curly-brace quantifiers, since the three shortcut characters are nearly always the only ones needed.

Anchors

By default, if a pattern doesn't match at the start of the string, it can "float" on down the string, trying to match somewhere else. But there are a number of anchors that may be used to hold the pattern at a particular point in a string.

The caret* anchor (^) marks the beginning of the string, while the dollar sign ($) marks the end.† So the pattern /^fred/ will match **fred** only at the start of the string; it wouldn't match **manfred mann**. And /rock$/ will match **rock** only at the end of the string; it wouldn't match **knute rockne**.

Sometimes, you'll want to use both of these anchors, to ensure that the pattern matches an entire string. A common example is /^\s*$/, which matches a blank line. But this "blank" line may include some whitespace characters, like tabs and spaces, which are invisible to you and me. Any line that matches that pattern looks just like any other one on paper, so this pattern treats all blank lines as equivalent. Without the anchors, it would match nonblank lines as well.

Word Anchors

Anchors aren't just at the ends of the string. The word-boundary anchor, \b, matches at either end of a word.‡ So we can use /\bfred\b/ to match the word **fred** but not **frederick** or **alfred** or **manfred mann**. This is similar to the feature often called something like "match whole words only" in a word processor's search command.

Alas, these aren't words as you and I are likely to think of them; they're those \w-type words made up of ordinary letters, digits, and underscores. The \b anchor matches at the start or end of a group of \w characters.

---

* Yes, you've seen that caret is already used in another way in patterns. As the first character of a character class, it negates the class. But *outside* of a character class, it's a metacharacter in a different way, being the start-of-string anchor. There are only so many characters, so we have to use some of them twice.

† Actually, it matches either the end of the string, or at a newline at the end of the string. That's so that you can match the end of the string whether it has a trailing newline or not. Most folks don't worry about this distinction much, but once in a long while it's important to remember that /^fred$/will match either "fred" or "fred\n" with equal ease.

‡ Some regular expression implementations have one anchor for start-of-word and another for end-of-word, but Perl uses \b for both.

In Figure 8-1, there's a grey underline under each "word," and the arrows show the corresponding places where \b could match. There are always an even number of word boundaries in a given string, since there's an end-of-word for every start-of-word.

The "words" are sequences of letters, digits, and underscores; that is, a word in this sense is what's matched by /\w+/. There are five words in that sentence: That, s, a, word, and boundary.* Notice that the quote marks around word don't change the word boundaries; these words are made of \w characters.

Each arrow points to the beginning or the end of one of the grey underlines, since the word boundary anchor \b matches only at the beginning or the end of a group of word characters.

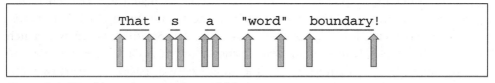

Figure 8-1. Word-boundary matches with \b

The word-boundary anchor is useful to ensure that we don't accidentally find cat in delicatessen, dog in boondoggle, or fish in selfishness. Sometimes you'll want just one word-boundary anchor, as when using /\bhunt/ to match words like hunt or hunting or hunter, but not shunt, or when using /stone\b/ to match words like sandstone or flintstone but not capstones.

The nonword-boundary anchor is \B; it matches at any point where \b would not match. So the pattern /\bsearch\B/ will match searches, searching, and searched, but not search or researching.

Memory Parentheses

You remember that parentheses ("( )") may be used for grouping together parts of a pattern. They also have a second function: they tell the regular expression engine to remember what was in the substring matched by the pattern in the parentheses. That is to say, it doesn't remember what was in the pattern itself; it remembers what was in the corresponding part of the string. Whenever you use parentheses for grouping, they automatically work as memory parentheses as well.

---

* You can see why we wish that we could change the definition of "word"; That's should be one word, not two words with an apostrophe in-between. And even in text that may be mostly ordinary English, it's normal to find a soupçon of other characters spicing things up.

So, if you use `/./`, you'll match any single character (except newline); if you use `/(.)/`, you'll still match any single character, but now it will be kept in a regular expression memory. For each pair of parentheses in the pattern, you'll have one regular expression memory.

Backreferences

A *backreference* refers back to a memory that was saved earlier in the current pattern's processing. Backreferences are made with a backslash, which is easy to remember. For example, `\1` contains the first regular expression memory (that is, the part of the string matched by the first pair of parentheses).

Backreferences are used to go back and match the exact same* string that was matched earlier in the pattern. So, `/(.)\1/` means to match any one character, remember it as memory one, then match memory one again. In other words, match any character, followed by the *same* character. So, this pattern will match strings with doubled-letters, as in **bamm-bamm** and **betty**. Of course, the dot will match characters other than letters, so if a string has two spaces in a row, two tabs in a row, or two asterisks in a row, it will match.

That's not the same as the pattern `/../`, which will match any character followed by any character—those two could be the same, or they could be different. `/(.)\1/` means to match any character followed by the *same* character.

A typical usage of these memories might be if you have some HTML-like† text to process. For example, maybe you want to match a tag like these two, which may use either single quotes or double quotes:

```
<image source='fred.png'>
<image source="fred's-birthday.png">
```

The tag may have either single quotes or double quotes, since the quoted data may include the other kind of mark (as with the apostrophe in the second example tag). So the pattern might look like this: `/<image source=(['"]).*\1>/`. That says that the opening quote mark may be of either type, but there must be a matching mark at the end of the quote.‡

---

* Well, if the pattern is case-insensitive, as we'll learn in the next chapter, the capitalization doesn't have to match. Other than that, though, the string must be the same.

† These examples are intentionally *not* HTML, because there are too many tricky things that crop up in real HTML, or any similar markup language like XML or SGML. If you need to work with HTML, don't use simple patterns like these. Get a robust module from CPAN, so that you can start with code that's already written and debugged. If you don't, we promise that you'll be sorry. Don't say we didn't warn you.

‡ If you realize that there may be problems with using this pattern on a markup language like HTML, that's okay. There are lots of problems with that! This is just an example to illustrate a use of a backreference. You shouldn't use simple patterns to parse anything as complex as HTML anyway.

If you have more sets of parentheses, you can have more backreferences. As you might guess, \17 is the contents of the seventeenth regular expression memory, if you have at least that many sets of parentheses.[*]

In numbering backreferences, you can just count the left (opening) parentheses. The pattern `/((fred|wilma) (flintstone)) \1/` says to match strings like `fred flintstone fred flintstone`, since the first opening parenthesis and its corresponding closing parenthesis hold a pattern that matches `fred flintstone`.[†]

If we wrote `/((fred|wilma) (flintstone)) \2/` instead, we would match strings like `fred flintstone fred`; memory two is the choice of `fred` or `wilma`. (Notice that it wouldn't match `fred flintsone wilma`, since the backreference can match only the same name that was matched earlier: either `fred` or `wilma`. But it could match `wilma flintstone wilma`, since that one uses the same name.) And the pattern `/((fred|wilma) (flintstone)) \3/` would match strings like `fred flintstone flintstone`. It's uncommon to have a literal string like `flintstone` in memory parentheses, though; we did that one just to have a third example.

Memory Variables

When we get to the next chapter and back into the world of Perl, we'll see that the contents of these regular expression memories are available to us in special variables like `$1` after the pattern match is done. We mention this here just so you'll know that the memories aren't merely used for backreferences; if you see what seem to be unnecessary parentheses in a pattern, they may actually be setting up those memories.

Precedence

With all of these metacharacters in regular expressions, you may feel that you can't keep track of the players without a scorecard. That's the precedence chart, which shows us which parts of the pattern "stick together" the most tightly. Unlike the precedence chart for operators, the regular expression precedence chart is simple, with only four levels. As a bonus, this section will review all of the metacharacters that Perl uses in patterns.

---

[*] If you don't have that many sets of parentheses before that point in the pattern, backreferences \10 and beyond will be treated as octal character escapes. To keep an octal character escape like \12 from accidentally meaning a backreference, just use a leading zero: \012 is always a character, never a backreference.

[†] This pattern would also match `wilma flintstone wilma flintstone`.

1. At the top of the precedence chart are the parentheses, ("()"), used for grouping and memory. Anything in parentheses will "stick together" more tightly than anything else.

2. The second level is the quantifiers. These are the repeat operators—star (*), plus (+), and question mark (?)—as well as the quantifiers made with curly braces, like {5,15}, {3,}, and {5}. These always stick to the item they're following.

3. The third level of the precedence chart holds anchors and sequence. The anchors are the caret (^) start-of-string anchor, the dollar-sign ($) end-of-string anchor, the \b word-boundary anchor, and the \B nonword-boundary anchor. Sequence (putting one item after another) is actually an operator, even though it doesn't use a metacharacter. That means that letters in a word will stick together just as tightly as the anchors stick to the letters.

4. The lowest level of precedence is the vertical bar (|) of alternation. Since this is at the bottom of the chart, it effectively cuts the pattern into pieces. It's at the bottom of the chart because we want the letters in the words in /fred|barney/ to stick together more tightly than the alternation. If alternation were higher priority than sequence, that pattern would mean to match fre, followed by a choice of d or b, followed by arney. So, alternation is at the bottom of the chart, and the letters within the names stick together.

Besides the precedence chart, there are the so-called *atoms* that make up the most basic pieces of the pattern. These are the individual characters, character classes, and backreferences.

Examples of Precedence

When you need to decipher a complex regular expression, you'll need to do as Perl does, and use the precedence chart to see what's really going on.

For example, /^fred|barney$/ is probably not what the programmer intended. That's because the vertical bar of alternation is very low precedence; it cuts the pattern in two. That pattern matches either fred at the beginning of the string or barney at the end. It's much more likely that the programmer wanted /^(fred|barney)$/, which will match if the whole line has nothing but fred, or nothing but barney.[*]

And what will /(wilma|pebbles?)/ match? The question mark applies to the previous character,[†] so that will match either wilma or pebbles or pebble, perhaps as part of a larger string (since there are no anchors).

---

[*] And, perhaps, a newline at the end of the string, as we mentioned earlier in connection with the $ anchor.

[†] Because a quantifier sticks to the letter s more tightly than the s sticks to the other letters in pebbles.

The pattern /^(\w+)\s+(\w+)$/ matches lines that have a "word," some required whitespace, and another "word," with nothing else before or after. That might be used to match lines like `fred flintstone`, for example. The parentheses around the words aren't needed for grouping, so they may be intended to save those substrings into the regular expression memories, which we'll see more about in the next chapter.

When you're trying to understand a complex pattern, it may be helpful to add parentheses to clarify the precedence. That's okay, but remember that grouping parentheses are also automatically memory parentheses; you may need to change the numbering of other memories when you add the parentheses.[*]

And There's More

Although we've covered all of the regular expression features that most people are likely to need for everyday programming, there are more features being added all the time. Check the *perlre*, *perlrequick*, and *perlretut* manpages for the latest news about what patterns in Perl can do.[†]

Exercises

See Appendix A for answers to the following exercises. These exercises are among the most challenging in the entire book. But don't get too discouraged! The following chapters will actually be easier, partly because you'll have the power of regular expressions to help you.

1. [4] Using the test program from the previous chapter, make a pattern that matches only lines containing either the word `fred` or `wilma`, followed by some whitespace, and then the word `flintstone`. So it should match the string `I am fred   flintstone` (with one or more spaces or tabs between the names).

2. [10] Here, we give you the answer; you decide what problem it's trying to solve. What do these real-world patterns match? What might they be used for?

   ```
   /"([^"]*)"/
   /^0?[0-3]?[0-7]{1,2}$/
   /^\b[\w.]{1,12}\b$/
   ```

   Try each of them in the test program. It may help to find some strings that match (and that fail to match) each one.

---

[*] But look in the *perlre* manpage for information about nonmemory parentheses, which are used for grouping without memory.

[†] And check out `YAPE::Regexp::Explain` in CPAN as a regular-expression-to-English translator.

3. [8] Make a pattern that will match a string containing nothing but a scalar variable's name (not its value!), like $fred, $barney, or $_ (but you shouldn't match special variables like $0). That is, if the line of input has the six characters $wilma, the pattern should match. If the input says wilma, it should not match.

4. [12] Make a pattern that matches any line of input that has the same word repeated two or more times in a row. Words in this problem can be considered to be sequences of letters a to z or A to Z, digits, and underscores. Whitespace between words may differ. For example, the classic observation-test string Paris in the the spring should match, since it has a doubled word. Also, I thought that that was the problem should match, even though that may be a correct use of a doubled word. Does your pattern match all *three* words in I thought that that that was the problem (with extra spaces between only some of the words)? Does it match This is a test? How about This shouldn't match, according to the theory of regular expressions?

9

Using Regular Expressions

Now that we've seen what goes inside a regular expression, let's take what we've learned back into Perl.

Matches with m//

We've been writing patterns in pairs of forward slashes, like /fred/. But this is actually a shortcut for the m// (pattern match) operator. As we saw with the qw// operator, you may choose any pair of delimiters to quote the contents. So, we could write that same expression as m(fred), m<fred>, m{fred}, or m[fred] using those paired delimiters, or as m,fred,, m!fred!, m^fred^, or many other ways using nonpaired delimiters.[*]

The shortcut is that if you choose the forward slash as the delimiter, you may omit the initial m. Since Perl folks love to avoid typing extra characters, you'll see most pattern matches written using slashes, as in /fred/.

Of course, you should wisely choose a delimiter that doesn't appear in your pattern.[†] If you wanted to make a pattern to match the beginning of an ordinary web URL, you might start to write /^http:\/\// to match the initial "http://". But

---

[*] Nonpaired delimiters are the ones that don't have a different "left" and "right" variety; the same punctuation mark is used for both ends.

[†] If you're using paired delimiters, you shouldn't generally have to worry about using the delimiter inside the pattern, since that delimiter will generally be paired inside your pattern. That is, m(fred(.*)barney) and m{\w{2,}} and m[wilma[\n \t]+betty] are all fine, even though the pattern contains the quoting character, since each "left" has a corresponding "right". But the angle brackets ("<" and ">") aren't regular expression metacharacters, so they may not be paired; if the pattern were m{(\d+)\s*>=?\s*(\d+)}, quoting it with angle brackets would mean having to backslash the greater-than sign so that it wouldn't prematurely end the pattern.

that's easier to read, write, maintain, and debug if you use a better choice of delimiter: m%^http://%.*

It's common to use curly braces as the delimiter. If you use a programmers' text editor, it probably has the ability to jump from an opening curly brace to the corresponding closing one, which can be handy in maintaining code.

Option Modifiers

There are several option modifier letters, sometimes called *flags*, which may be appended as a group right after the ending delimiter of a regular expression to change its behavior from the default.

Case-insensitive Matching with /i

To make a case-insensitive pattern match, so that you can match FRED as easily as fred or Fred, use the /i modifier:

```
print "Would you like to play a game? ";
chomp($_ = <STDIN>);
if (/\byes\b/i) {  # case-insensitive match
  print "In that case, I recommend that you go bowling.\n";
}
```

Matching Any Character with /s

Do you ever feel frustrated that the dot (.) won't match newline? If you might have newlines in your strings, and you want the dot to be able to match them, the /s modifier will do the job. It changes every dot† in the pattern to act like the character class [\d\D] does, which is to match any character, even if it is a newline. Of course, you have to have a string with newlines for this to make a difference:

```
$_ = "I saw Barney\ndown at the bowling alley\nwith Fred\nlast night.\n";
if (/\bBarney\b.*\bFred\b/s) {
  print "That string mentions Fred after Barney!\n";
}
```

Without the /s modifier, that match would fail, since the two names aren't on the same line.

---

* Remember, the forward slash is not a metacharacter, so it doesn't need to be backslashed when it's not the delimiter.

† If you wish to change just some of them, and not all, you'll probably want to replace just those few with [\d\D].

Combining Option Modifiers

If you have more than one option modifier to use on the same pattern, they may be used one after the other; their order isn't significant:

```
if (/\bbarney\b.*\bfred\b/si) {  # both /s and /i
  print "That string mentions Fred after Barney!\n";
}
```

Other Options

There are many other option modifiers available. We'll cover those as we get to them, or you can read about them in the *perlop* manpage and in the descriptions of m// and the other regular expression operators that we'll see later in this chapter.

The Binding Operator, =~

Matching against $_ is merely the default; the *binding operator* (=~) tells Perl to match the pattern on the right against the string on the left, instead of matching against $_.* For example:

```
my $some_other = "I dream of betty rubble.";
if ($some_other =~ /\brub/) {
  print "Aye, there's the rub.\n";
}
```

The first time you see it, the binding operator looks like some kind of assignment operator. But it's no such thing! It is simply saying, "this pattern match which would attach to $_ by default—make it work with this string on the left instead." If there's no binding operator, the expression is using $_ by default.

In the (somewhat unusual) example below, $likes_perl is set to a Boolean value according to what the user typed at the prompt. This is a little on the quick-and-dirty side, because the line of input itself is discarded. This code reads the line of input, tests that string against the pattern, then discards the line of input.† It doesn't use or change $_ at all.

```
print "Do you like Perl? ";
my $likes_perl = (<STDIN> =~ /\byes\b/i);
...  # Time passes...
if ($likes_perl) {
  print "You said earlier that you like Perl, so...\n";
  ...
}
```

---

* The binding operator is also used with some other operations besides the pattern match, as we'll see later.

† Remember, the line of input is not automatically stored into $_ unless the line-input operator (<STDIN>) is all alone in the conditional expression of a while loop.

The parentheses around the pattern-test expression aren't required, so the following line does the same thing as the one above—it stores the result of the test (and not the line of input) into the variable:

```
my $likes_perl = <STDIN> =~ /\byes\b/i;
```

Interpolating into Patterns

The regular expression is double-quote interpolated, just as if it were a double-quoted string. This allows us to write a quick *grep*-like program like this:

```
#!/usr/bin/perl -w
my $what = "larry";

while (<>) {
  if (/^($what)/) {  # pattern is anchored at beginning of string
    print "We saw $what in beginning of $_";
  }
}
```

The pattern will be built up out of whatever's in $what when we run the pattern match. In this case, it's the same as if we had written /^(larry)/, looking for larry at the start of each line.

But we didn't have to get the value of $what from a literal string; we could have gotten it instead from the command-line arguments in @ARGV:

```
my $what = shift @ARGV;
```

Now, if the first command-line argument were fred|barney, the pattern becomes /^(fred|barney)/, looking for fred or barney at the start of each line.* The parentheses (which weren't really necessary when searching for larry) are important, now, because without them we'd be matching fred at the start or barney anywhere in the string.

With that line changed to get the pattern from @ARGV, this program resembles the Unix *grep* command. But we have to watch out for metacharacters in the string. If $what contains 'fred(barney', the pattern would look like /^(fred(barney)/, and you know that can't work right—it'll crash your program with an invalid regular expression error. With some advanced techniques,† you can trap this kind of error (or prevent the magic of the metacharacters in the first place) so that it won't crash your program. But for now, just know that if you give your users the power of regular expressions, they'll also need the responsibility to use them correctly.

---

* The astute reader will know that you can't generally type fred|barney as an argument at the command line because the vertical bar is a shell metacharacter. See the documentation to your shell to learn about how to quote command-line arguments.

† In this case, you would use an **eval** block to trap the error, or you would quote the interpolated text using **quotemeta** (or its \Q equivalent form) so that it's no longer treated as a regular expression.

The Match Variables

Do you remember the regular expression memories, which we used with backreferences in the previous chapter? Those memories are also available after the pattern match is done, after we return to Perl. They're strings, so they are kept in scalar variables with names like $1 and $2. There are as many of these variables as there are pairs of memory parentheses in the pattern. As you'd expect, $4 means the string matched by the fourth set of parentheses. This is the same string that \4 referred to inside the pattern match.

Why are there two different ways to refer to that same string? They're not really referring to the same string at the same time; $4 means the fourth memory of an *already completed* pattern match, while \4 is a backreference referring back to the fourth memory of the *currently matching* regular expression. Besides, backreferences work inside regular expressions only; once we're back in the world of Perl, we'll use $4.

These match variables are a big part of the power of regular expressions, because they let us pull out the parts of a string:

```
$_ = "Hello there, neighbor";
if (/\s(\w+),/) {                     # memorize the word between space and comma
  print "the word was $1\n";  # the word was there
}
```

Or you could use more than one memory at once:

```
$_ = "Hello there, neighbor";
if (/(\S+) (\S+), (\S+)/) {
  print "words were $1 $2 $3\n";
}
```

That tells us that the **words were Hello there neighbor**. Notice that there's no comma in the output (because the comma is outside of the memory parentheses). That leaves the comma out of memory two. Using this technique, we can choose exactly what we want in the memories, as well as what we want to leave out.

You could even have an empty match variable,[*] if that part of the pattern might be empty. That is, a match variable may contain the empty string:

```
my $dino = "I fear that I'll be extinct after 1000 years.";
if ($dino =~ /(\d*) years/) {
  print "That said '$1' years.\n";  # 1000
}
```

---

[*] As opposed to an undefined one. If you have three or fewer sets of parentheses in the pattern, $4 will be undef.

```
$dino = "I fear that I'll be extinct after a few million years.";
if ($dino =~ /(\d*) years/) {
  print "That said '$1' years.\n";  # empty string
}
```

The Persistence of Memory

These match variables generally stay around until the next *successful* pattern
match.* That is, an unsuccessful match leaves the previous memories intact, but a
successful one resets them all. But this correctly implies that you shouldn't use
these match variables unless the match succeeded; otherwise, you could be seeing
a memory from some previous pattern. The following (bad) example is supposed
to print a word matched from $_. But if the match fails, it's using whatever left-
over string happens to be found in $1:

```
$wilma =~ /(\w+)/;  # BAD! Untested match result
print "Wilma's word was $1... or was it?\n";
```

This is another reason that a pattern match is almost always found in the conditional expression of an `if` or `while`:

```
if ($wilma =~ /(\w+)/) {
  print "Wilma's word was $1.\n";
} else {
  print "Wilma doesn't have a word.\n";
}
```

Since these memories don't stay around forever, you shouldn't use a match variable like $1 more than a few lines after its pattern match. If your maintenance pro-
grammer adds a new regular expression between your regular expression and
your use of $1, you'll be getting the value of $1 for the second match, rather than
the first. For this reason, if you need a memory for more than a few lines, it's generally best to copy it into an ordinary variable. Doing this helps make the code
more readable at the same time:

```
if ($wilma =~ /(\w+)/) {
  my $wilma_word = $1;
  ...
}
```

Later, in Chapter 14, we'll see how to get the memory value *directly* into the variable at the same time as the pattern match happens, without having to use $1
explicitly.

---

* The actual scoping rule is much more complex (see the documentation if you need it), but as long as
  you don't expect the match variables to be untouched many lines after a pattern match, you shouldn't
  have problems.

The Automatic Match Variables

There are three more match variables that you get for free,* whether the pattern has memory parentheses or not. That's the good news; the bad news is that these variables have weird names.

Now, Larry probably would have been happy enough to call these by slightly-less-weird names, like perhaps $gazoo or $ozmodiar. But those are names that you just might want to use in your own code. To keep ordinary Perl programmers from having to memorize the names of *all* of Perl's special variables before choosing their first variable names in their first programs,† Larry has given strange names to many of Perl's builtin variables, names that "break the rules." In this case, the names are punctuation marks: $&, $`, and $'. They're strange, ugly, and weird, but those are their names.‡

The part of the string that actually matched the pattern is automatically stored in $&:

```
if ("Hello there, neighbor" =~ /\s(\w+),/) {
  print "That actually matched '$&'.\n";
}
```

That tells us that the part that matched was " **there,** " (with a space, a word, and a comma). Memory one, in $1, has just the five-letter word **there**, but $& has the entire matched section.

Whatever came before the matched section is in $`, and whatever was after it is in $'. Another way to say that is that $` holds whatever the regular expression engine had to skip over before it found the match, and $' has the remainder of the string that the pattern never got to. If you glue these three strings together in order, you'll always get back the original string:

```
if ("Hello there, neighbor" =~ /\s(\w+),/) {
  print "That was ($`)($&)($').\n";
}
```

The message shows the string as (Hello)(there,)(neighbor), showing the three automatic match variables in action. This may seem familiar, and for good reason: These automatic memory variables are what the pattern test program (from Chapter 7) was using in its line of "mystery" code, to show what part of the string was being matched by the pattern:

---

* Yeah, right. There's no such thing as a free match. These are "free" only in the sense that they don't require match parentheses. Don't worry; we'll mention their real cost a little later, though.

† You should still avoid a few classical variable names like $ARGV, but these few are all in all-caps. All of Perl's builtin variables are documented in the *perlvar* manpage.

‡ If you really can't stand these names, check out the English module, which attempts to give all of Perl's strangest variables nearly normal names. But the use of this module has never really caught on; instead, Perl programmers have grown to love the punctuation-mark variable names, strange as they are.

```
print "Matched: |$`<$&>$'|\n";   # The three automatic match variables
```

Any or all of these three automatic match variables may be empty, of course, just like the numbered match variables. And they have the same scope as the numbered match variables. Generally, that means that they'll stay around until the next successful pattern match.

Now, we said earlier that these three are "free." Well, freedom has its price. In this case, the price is that once you use any one of these automatic match variables anywhere in your entire program, other regular expressions will run a little more slowly. Now, this isn't a giant slowdown, but it's enough of a worry that many Perl programmers will simply never use these automatic match variables.* Instead, they'll use a workaround. For example, if the only one you need is $&, just put parentheses around the whole pattern and use $1 instead (you may need to renumber the pattern's memories, of course).

Match variables (both the automatic ones and the numbered ones) are most often used in substitutions, which are the topic of the next section.

Substitutions with s///

If you think of the m// pattern match as being like your word processor's "search" feature, the "search and replace" feature would have to be Perl's s/// substitution operator. This simply replaces whatever part of a variable† matches a pattern with a replacement string:

```
$_ = "He's out bowling with Barney tonight.";
s/Barney/Fred/;   # Replace Barney with Fred
print "$_\n";
```

If the match fails, nothing happens, and the variable is untouched:

```
# Continuing from above; $_ has "He's out bowling with Fred tonight."
s/Wilma/Betty/;   # Replace Wilma with Betty (fails)
```

Of course, both the pattern and the replacement string could be more complex. Here, the replacement string uses the first memory variable, which is set by the pattern match:

---

* Most of these folks haven't actually benchmarked their programs to see whether their workarounds actually save time, though; it's as though these variables were poisonous or something. But we can't blame them for not benchmarking—many programs that could benefit from these three variables take up only a few minutes of CPU time in a week, so benchmarking and optimizing would be a waste of time. But in that case, why fear a possible extra millisecond? By the way, the Perl developers are working on this problem, but there will probably be no solution before Perl 6.

† Unlike m//, which can match against any string expression, s/// is modifying data that must therefore be contained in what's known as an *lvalue*. This is nearly always a variable, although it could actually be anything that could be used on the left side of an assignment operator.

```
s/with (\w+)/against $1/;
print "$_\n";  # says "He's out bowling against Fred tonight."
```

Here are some other possible substitutions. (These are here only as samples; in the real world, it would not be typical to do so many unrelated substitutions in a row.)

```
$_ = "green scaly dinosaur";
s/(\w+) (\w+)/$2, $1/;    # Now it's "scaly, green dinosaur"
s/^/huge, /;             # Now it's "huge, scaly, green dinosaur"
s/,.*een//;              # Empty replacement: Now it's "huge dinosaur"
s/green/red/;            # Failed match: still "huge dinosaur"
s/\w+$/($`!)$&/;         # Now it's "huge (huge !)dinosaur"
s/\s+(!\W+)/$1 /;        # Now it's "huge (huge!) dinosaur"
s/huge/gigantic/;        # Now it's "gigantic (huge!) dinosaur"
```

There's a return value from **s///**; it's true if a substitution was successful; otherwise it's false:

```
$_ = "fred flintstone";
if (s/fred/wilma/) {
  print "Successfully replaced fred with wilma!\n";
}
```

Global Replacements with /g

As you may have noticed in a previous example, **s///** will make just one replacement, even if others are possible. Of course, that's just the default. The **/g** modifier tells **s///** to make all possible nonoverlapping* replacements:

```
$_ = "home, sweet home!";
s/home/cave/g;
print "$_\n";  # "cave, sweet cave!"
```

A fairly common use of a global replacement is to collapse whitespace; that is, to turn any arbitrary whitespace into a single space:

```
$_ = "Input data\t may have    extra whitespace.";
s/\s+/ /g;  # Now it says "Input data may have extra whitespace."
```

Once we show collapsing whitespace, everyone wants to know about stripping leading and trailing whitespace. That's easy enough, in two steps:†

```
s/^\s+//;  # Replace leading whitespace with nothing
s/\s+$//;  # Replace trailing whitespace with nothing
```

Different Delimiters

Just as we did with **m//** and **qw//**, we can change the delimiters for **s///**. But the substitution uses three delimiter characters, so things are a little different.

---

* It's nonoverlapping because each new match starts looking just beyond the latest replacement.

† It could be done in one step, but this way is better.

With ordinary (non-paired) characters, which don't have a left and right variety, just use three of them, as we did with the forward slash. Here, we've chosen the pound sign* aSs the delimiter:

```
s#^https://#http://#;
```

But if you use paired characters, which have a left and right variety, you have to use two pairs: one to hold the pattern and one to hold the replacement string. In this case, the delimiters don't have to be the same kind around the string as they are around the pattern. In fact, the delimiters of the string could even be non-paired. These are all the same:

```
s{fred}{barney};
s[fred](barney);
s<fred>#barney#;
```

Option Modifiers

In addition to the /g modifier,† substitutions may use the /i and /s modifiers that we saw in ordinary pattern matching. The order of modifiers isn't significant.

```
s#wilma#Wilma#gi;  # replace every WiLmA or WILMA with Wilma
s{__END__.*}{}s;   # chop off the end marker and all following lines
```

The Binding Operator

Just as we saw with m//, we can choose a different target for s/// by using the binding operator:

```
$file_name =~ s#^.*/##s;  # In $file_name, remove any Unix-style path
```

Case Shifting

It often happens in a substitution that you'll want to make sure that a replacement word is properly capitalized (or not, as the case may be). That's easy to accomplish with Perl, by using some backslash escapes. The \U escape forces what follows to all uppercase:

```
$_ = "I saw Barney with Fred.";
s/(fred|barney)/\U$1/gi;  # $_ is now "I saw BARNEY with FRED."
```

Similarly, the \L escape forces lowercase. Continuing from the previous code:

```
s/(fred|barney)/\L$1/gi;  # $_ is now "I saw barney with fred."
```

---

* With apologies to our British friends, to whom the pound sign is something else! Although the pound sign is generally the start of a comment in Perl, it won't start a comment when the parser knows to expect a delimiter—in this case, immediately after the s that starts the substitution.

† We speak of the modifiers with names like "/i" , even if the delimiter is something different than a slash.

By default, these affect the rest of the (replacement) string; or you can turn off case shifting with \E:

```
s/(\w+) with (\w+)/\U$2\E with $1/i;  # $_ is now "I saw FRED with barney."
```

When written in lowercase (\l and \u), they affect only the next character:

```
s/(fred|barney)/\u$1/ig;  # $_ is now "I saw FRED with Barney."
```

You can even stack them up. Using \u with \L means "all lower case, but capitalize the first letter":[*]

```
s/(fred|barney)/\u\L$1/ig;  # $_ is now "I saw Fred with Barney."
```

As it happens, although we're covering case shifting in relation to substitutions, it's available in any double-quotish string:

```
print "Hello, \L\u$name\E, would you like to play a game?\n";
```

The split Operator

Another operator that uses regular expressions is **split**, which breaks up a string according to a separator. This is useful for tab-separated data, or colon-separated, whitespace-separated, or *anything*-separated data, really.[†] So long as you can specify the separator with a regular expression (and generally, it's a simple regular expression), you can use **split**. It looks like this:

```
@fields = split /separator/, $string;
```

The **split** operator[‡] drags the pattern through a string and returns a list of fields (substrings) that were separated by the separators. Whenever the pattern matches, that's the end of one field and the start of the next. So, anything that matches the pattern will never show up in the returned fields. Here's a typical **split** pattern, splitting on colons:

```
@fields = split /:/, "abc:def:g:h";  # gives ("abc", "def", "g", "h")
```

You could even have an empty field, if there were two delimiters together:

```
@fields = split /:/, "abc:def::g:h"; # gives ("abc", "def", "", "g", "h")
```

---

[*] The \L and \u may appear together in either order. Larry realized that people would sometimes get those two backwards, so he made Perl figure out that you want just the first letter capitalized and the rest lowercase. Larry is a pretty nice guy.

[†] Except "comma-separated values," normally called CSV files. Those are a pain to do with **split**; you're better off getting the Text::CSV module from CPAN.

[‡] It's an operator, even though it acts a lot like a function, and everyone generally calls it a function. But the technical details of the difference are beyond the scope of this book.

Here's a rule that seems odd at first, but it rarely causes problems: Leading empty fields are always returned, but trailing empty fields are discarded:[*]

```
@fields = split /:/, ":::a:b:c:::";  # gives ("", "", "", "a", "b", "c")
```

It's also common to `split` on whitespace, using /\s+/ as the pattern. Under that pattern, all whitespace runs are equivalent to a single space:

```
my $some_input = "This  is a \t       test.\n";
my @args = split /\s+/, $some_input;  # ("This", "is", "a", "test.")
```

The default for `split` is to break up $_ on whitespace:

```
my @fields = split;  # like split /\s+/, $_;
```

This is almost the same as using /\s+/ as the pattern, except that a leading empty field is suppressed—so, if the line starts with whitespace, you won't see an empty field at the start of the list. (If you'd like to get the same behavior when splitting another string on whitespace, just use a single space in place of the pattern: `split ' ', $other_string`. Using a space instead of the pattern is a special kind of `split`.)

Generally, the patterns used for `split` are as simple as the ones you see here. But if the pattern becomes more complex, be sure to avoid using memory parentheses in the pattern; see the `perlfunc` manpage for more information.[†]

The join Function

The `join` function doesn't use patterns. So why is it in this chapter? It's here because, in a sense, `join` performs the opposite function of `split`: `split` breaks up a string into a number of pieces, and `join` glues together a bunch of pieces to make a single string. The `join` function looks like this:

```
my $result = join $glue, @pieces;
```

The first argument to `join` is the glue, which may be any string. The remaining arguments are a list of pieces. `join` puts the glue string between the pieces and returns the resulting string:

```
my $x = join ":", 4, 6, 8, 10, 12;  # $x is "4:6:8:10:12"
```

In that example, we had five items, so there are only four colons. That is, there are four pieces of glue. The glue shows up only between the pieces, never before or after them. So, there will be one fewer piece of glue than the number of items in the list.

---

[*] This is merely the default. It's this way for efficiency. If you worry about losing trailing empty fields, use −1 as a third argument to `split` and they'll be kept; see the *perlfunc* manpage.

[†] And you might want to check out the nonmemory grouping-only parenthesis notation as well, in the *perlre* manpage.

This means that there may be no glue at all, if the list doesn't have at least two elements:

```
my $y = join "foo", "bar";        # gives just "bar", since no fooglue is needed
my @empty;                        # empty array
my $empty = join "baz", @empty;   # no items, so it's an empty string
```

Using `$x` from above, we can break up a string and put it back together with a different delimiter:

```
my @values = split /:/, $x;   # @values is (4, 6, 8, 10, 12)
my $z = join "-", @values;    # $z is "4-6-8-10-12"
```

Although `split` and `join` work well together, don't forget that the first argument to `join` is always a string, not a pattern.

Exercises

See Appendix A for answers to the following exercises:

1. [7] Make a pattern that will match three consecutive copies of whatever is currently contained in `$what`. That is, if `$what` is `fred`, your pattern should match `fredfredfred`. If `$what` is `fred|barney`, your pattern should match `fredfredbarney` or `barneyfredfred` or `barneybarneybarney` or many other variations. (Hint: You should set `$what` at the top of the pattern test program with a statement like `my $what = 'fred|barney';`.)

2. [15] Write a program that looks through the `perlfunc.pod` file for lines that start with `=item` and some whitespace, followed by a Perl identifier name (made of letters, digits, and underscores, but never starting with a digit), like the lines below. (There may be more text on the line after the identifier name; just ignore it.) You can locate the `perlfunc.pod` file on your system with the command `perldoc -l perlfunc`, or ask your local expert. (Hint: You'll need the diamond operator to open this file. How will it get the filename?) Have the program print each identifier name as it finds it; there will be hundreds of them, and many will appear more than once in the file.

   As an example, the following lines of input resemble what you'll find in `perlfunc.pod`. For the first line, the program should print `wilma`. For the second, it should print `fred` (ignoring the word `flintstone`, since we're interested only in the identifier name):

   ```
   =item wilma
   =item fred flintstone
   ```

3. [10] Modify the previous program to list only the identifier names that appear more than twice on those `=item` lines, and tell how many times each one appeared. (That is, we want to know which identifier names appear on at least three separate `=item` lines in the file.) There should be a couple of dozen, depending upon your version of Perl.

10

More Control
Structures

In this chapter, we'll see some alternative ways to write Perl code. For the most part, these techniques don't make the language more powerful, but they make it easier or more convenient to get the job done. You don't have to use these techniques in your own code, but don't be tempted to skip this chapter—you're certain to see these control structures in other people's code, sooner or later (in fact, you're absolutely certain to see these things in use by the time you finish reading this book).

The unless Control Structure

In an `if` control structure, the block of code is executed only when the conditional expression is true. If you want a block of code to be executed only when the conditional is false, change `if` to **unless**:

```
unless ($fred =~ /^[A-Z_]\w*$/i) {
  print "The value of \$fred doesn't look like a Perl identifier name.\n";
}
```

Using **unless** says to run the block of code *unless* this condition is true. It's just like using an `if` test with the opposite condition. Another way to say it is that it's like having the **else** clause on its own. That is, whenever you see an **unless** that you don't understand, you can rewrite it (either in your head or in reality) to be an `if` test:

```
if ($fred =~ /^[A-Z_]\w*$/i) {
  # Do nothing
} else {
  print "The value of \$fred doesn't look like a Perl identifier name.\n";
}
```

It's no more or less efficient, and it should compile to the same internal byte codes. Or, another way to rewrite it would be to negate the conditional expression by using the negation operator (!):

```
if ( ! ($fred =~ /^[A-Z_]\w*$/i) ) {
  print "The value of \$fred doesn't look like a Perl identifier name.\n";
}
```

Generally, you should pick the way of writing code that makes the most sense to you, since that will probably make the most sense to your maintenance programmer. If it makes the most sense to write **if** with a negation, do that. More often, however, you'll probably find it natural to use **unless**.

The else Clause with unless

You could even have an **else** clause with an **unless**. While this syntax is supported, it's potentially confusing:

```
unless ($mon =~ /^(Feb)/) {
  print "This month has at least thirty days.\n";
} else {
  print "Do you see what's going on here?\n";
}
```

Some people may wish to use this, especially when the first clause is very short (perhaps only one line) and the second is several lines of code. But we'd make this one a negated **if**, or maybe simply swap the clauses to make a normal **if**:

```
if ($mon =~ /^(Feb)/) {
  print "Do you see what's going on here?\n";
} else {
  print "This month has at least thirty days.\n";
}
```

It's important to remember that you're always writing code for two readers: the computer that will run the code and the human being who has to keep the code working. If the human can't understand what you've written, pretty soon the computer won't be doing the right thing either.

The until Control Structure

Sometimes you'll want to reverse the condition of a **while** loop. To do that, just use **until**:

```
until ($j > $i) {
  $j *= 2;
}
```

This loop runs until the conditional expression returns true. But it's really just a **while** loop in disguise, except that this one repeats as long as the conditional is

false, rather than true. The conditional expression is evaluated before the first iteration, so this is still a zero-or-more-times loop, just like the `while` loop.*

As with `if` and `unless`, you could rewrite any `until` loop to become a `while`
loop by negating the condition. But generally, you'll find it simple and natural to
use `until` from time to time.

Expression Modifiers

In order to have a more compact notation, an expression may be followed by a
modifier that controls it. For example, the `if` modifier works in a way analogous
to an `if` block:

```
print "$n is a negative number.\n" if $n < 0;
```

That gives exactly the same result as if we had used this code, except that we
saved some typing by leaving out the parentheses and curly braces:†

```
if ($n < 0) {
  print "$n is a negative number.\n";
}
```

As we've said, Perl folks generally like to avoid typing. And the shorter form reads
like in English: print this message, if $n is less than zero.

Notice that the conditional expression is still evaluated first, even though it's
written at the end. This is backwards from the usual left-to-right ordering; in
understanding Perl code, we'll have to do as Perl's internal compiler does, and
read to the end of the statement before we can tell what it's really doing.

There are other modifiers as well:

```
&error("Invalid input") unless &valid($input);
$i *= 2 until $i > $j;
print " ", ($n += 2) while $n < 10;
&greet($_) foreach @person;
```

These all work just as (we hope) you would expect. That is, each one could be
rewritten in a similar way to rewriting the `if`-modifier example earlier. Here is one:

```
while ($n < 10) {
  print " ", ($n += 2);
}
```

---

* Pascal programmers, take note: in Pascal, the repeat-until always runs at least one iteration, but an
`until` loop in Perl may not run at all, if the conditional expression is true before the loop starts.

† We also left out the line breaks. But we should mention that the curly-brace form does create a new
scope. In the rare case that you need the full details, check the documentation.

The expression in parentheses inside the `print` argument list is noteworthy because it adds two to $n, storing the result back into $n. Then it returns that new value, which will be printed.

These shorter forms read almost like a natural language: call the `&greet` subroutine for each `@person` in the list. Double $i until it's larger than $j.[*]

One of the common uses of these modifiers is in a statement like this one:

```
print "fred is '$fred', barney is '$barney'\n"             if $I_am_curious;
```

By writing the code "in reverse" like this, you can put the important part of the statement at the beginning. The point of that statement is to monitor some variables; the point is not to check whether you're curious.[†] Some people prefer to write the whole statement on one line, perhaps with some tab characters before the `if`, to move it over toward the right margin, as we showed in the previous example, while others put the `if` modifier indented on a new line:

```
print "fred is '$fred', barney is '$barney'\n"
    if $I_am_curious;
```

Although you can rewrite any of these expressions with modifiers as a block (the "old-fashioned" way), the converse isn't necessarily true. Only a single expression is allowed on either side of the modifier. So you can't write something `if` something `while` something `until` something `unless` something `foreach` something, which would just be too confusing. And you can't put multiple statements on the left of the modifier. If you need more than just a simple expression on each side, just write the code the old-fashioned way, with the parentheses and curly braces.

As we mentioned in relation to the `if` modifier, the control expression (on the right) is always evaluated first, just as it would be in the old-fashioned form.

With the `foreach` modifier, there's no way to choose a different control variable—it's always $_. Usually, that's no problem, but if you want to use a different variable, you'll need to rewrite it as a traditional `foreach` loop.

The Naked Block Control Structure

The so-called "naked" block is one without a keyword or condition. That is, suppose you start with a `while` loop, which looks something like this:

```
while (condition) {
  body;
  body;
  body;
}
```

---

[*] Well, it helps *us* to think of them like that.

[†] Of course, we made up the name $I_am_curious; it's not a builtin Perl variable. Generally, folks who use this technique will either call their variable $TRACING, or will use a constant declared with the `constant` pragma.

Now, take away the **while** keyword and the conditional expression, and you'll have a naked block:

```
{
    body;
    body;
    body;
}
```

The naked block is like a **while** or **foreach** loop, except that it doesn't loop; it just executes the body of the loop once, and it's done. It's an un-loop!

We'll see in a while that there are other uses for the naked block, but one of its features is that it provides a scope for temporary lexical variables:

```
{
    print "Please enter a number: ";
    chomp(my $n = <STDIN>);
    my $root = sqrt $n;   # calculate the square root
    print "The square root of $n is $root.\n";
}
```

In this block, **$n** and **$root** are temporary variables scoped to the block. As a general guideline, all variables should be declared in the smallest scope available. If you need a variable for just a few lines of code, you can put those lines into a naked block and declare the variable inside that block. Of course, if we would need the value of either **$n** or **$root** later, we would need to declare them in a larger scope.

You may have noticed the **sqrt** function in that code and wondered about it—yes, it's a function we haven't shown before. Perl has many builtin functions that are beyond the scope of this book. When you're ready, check the *perlfunc* manpage to learn about more of them.

The elsif Clause

Every so often, you may need to check a number of conditional expressions, one after another, to see which one of them is true. This can be done with the **if** control structure's **elsif** clause, as in this example:*

```
if ( ! defined $dino) {
    print "The value is undef.\n";
} elsif ($dino =~ /^-?\d+\.?$/) {
    print "The value is an integer.\n";
} elsif ($dino =~ /^-?\d*\.\d+$/) {
```

---

* The reason that one of the messages in this example talks about a *simple* floating-point number is that the regular expression isn't complete (it leaves out numbers like "1.2e34"), but it's complete enough for this example.

```
    print "The value is a _simple_ floating-point number.\n";
  } elsif ($dino eq '') {
    print "The value is the empty string.\n";
  } else {
    print "The value is the string '$dino'.\n";
  }
```

Perl will test the conditional expressions one after another. When one succeeds, the corresponding block of code is executed, and then the whole control structure is done,* and execution goes on to the rest of the program. If none has succeeded, the `else` block at the end is executed. (Of course, the `else` clause is still optional, although in this case it's often a good idea to include it.)

There's no limit to the number of `elsif` clauses, but remember that Perl has to evaluate the first ninety-nine tests before it can get to the hundredth. If you'll have more than half a dozen `elsif`s, you should consider whether there's a more efficient way to write it. The Perl FAQ (see the **perlfaq** manpage) has a number of suggestions for emulating the "case" or "switch" statements of other languages.

You may have noticed by this point that the keyword is spelled `elsif`, with only one `e`. If you write it as "elseif", with a second `e`, Perl will tell you that it is not the correct spelling. Why not? Because Larry says so.†

Autoincrement and Autodecrement

You'll often want a scalar variable to count up or down by one. Since these are frequent constructs, there are shortcuts for them, like nearly everything else we do frequently.

The autoincrement operator ("++") adds one to a scalar variable, like the same operator in C and similar languages:

```
my $bedrock = 42;
$bedrock++;  # add one to $bedrock; it's now 43
```

Just like other ways of adding one to a variable, the scalar will be created if necessary:

```
my @people - qw{ fred barney fred wilma dino barney fred pebbles };
my %count;                  # new empty hash
$count{$_}++ foreach @people;  # creates new keys and values as needed
```

---

* There's no "fall-through" to the next block, as in the "switch" structure of languages like C.

† In fact, he resists any suggestion that it even be permitted as a valid alternative spelling. "If you want to spell it with a second `e`, it's simple. Step 1—Make up your own language. Step 2—Make it popular." When you make your own programming language, you can spell the keywords in any way you'd like. We hope that you will decide that yours shouldn't be the first to have an "elseunless".

The first time through that `foreach` loop, `$count{$_}` is incremented. That's `$count{"fred"}`, which thus goes from **undef** (since it didn't previously exist in the hash) up to 1. The next time through the loop, `$count{"barney"}` becomes 1; after that, `$count{"fred"}` becomes 2. Each time through the loop, one element in `%count` is incremented, and possibly created as well. After that loop is done, `$count{"fred"}` is 3. This provides a quick and easy way to see which items are in a list and how many times each one appears.

Similarly, the autodecrement operator ("`--`") subtracts one from a scalar variable:

```
$bedrock--;  # subtract one from $bedrock; it's 42 again
```

The Value of Autoincrement

You can fetch the value of a variable and change that value at the same time. Put the ++ operator in front of the variable name to increment the variable first and then fetch its value. This is a *preincrement*:

```
my $a = 5;
my $b = ++$a;  # increment $a to 6, and put that value into $b
```

Or put the `--` operator in front to decrement the variable first and then fetch its value. This is a *predecrement*:

```
my $c = --$a;  # decrement $a to 5, and put that value into $c
```

Here's the tricky part. Put the variable name first to fetch the value first, and then do the increment or decrement. This is called a *postincrement* or *postdecrement*:

```
my $d = $a++;  # $d gets the old value (5), then increment $a to 6
my $e = $a--;  # $e gets the old value (6), then decrement $a to 5
```

It's tricky because we're doing two things at once. We're fetching the value, and we're changing it in the same expression. If the operator is first, we increment (or decrement) first, then use the new value. If the variable is first, we return its (old) value first, then do the increment or decrement. Another way to say it is that these operators return a value, but they also have the side effect of modifying the variable's value.

If you write these in an expression of their own,[*] not using the value but only the side effect, there's no difference[†] whether you put the operator before or after the variable:

```
$bedrock++;  # adds one to $bedrock
++$bedrock;  # just the same; adds one to $bedrock
```

---

[*] That is, in a void context.

[†] Programmers who get inside the implementations of languages may expect that postincrement and postdecrement would be less efficient than their counterparts, but Perl's not like that. Perl automatically optimizes the post- forms when they're used in a void context.

A common use of these operators is in connection with a hash, to identify when an item has been seen before:

```
my @people = qw{ fred barney bamm-bamm wilma dino barney betty pebbles };
my %seen;

foreach (@people) {
  print "I've seen you somewhere before, $_!\n"
    if $seen{$_}++;
}
```

When **barney** shows up for the first time, the value of `$seen{$_}++` is false, since it's the value of `$seen{$_}`, which is `$seen{"barney"}`, which is **undef**. But that expression has the side effect of incrementing `$seen{"barney"}`. When **barney** shows up again, `$seen{"barney"}` is now a true value, so the message is printed.

The for Control Structure

Perl's **for** control structure is like the common **for** control structure you may have seen in other languages such as C. It looks like this:

```
for (initialization; test; increment) {
  body;
  body;
}
```

To Perl, though, this kind of loop is really a **while** loop in disguise, something like this:*

```
initialization;
while (test) {
  body;
  body;
  increment;
}
```

The most common use of the **for** loop, by far, is for making computed iterations:

```
for ($i = 1; $i <= 10; $i++) {  # count from 1 to 10
  print "I can count to $i!\n";
}
```

When you've seen these before, you'll know what the first line is saying even before you read the comment. Before the loop starts, the control variable, `$i`, is set to 1. Then, the loop is really a **while** loop in disguise, looping while `$i` is less than or equal to 10. Between each iteration and the next is the increment, which here is a literal increment, adding one to the control variable, which is `$i`.

---

* Actually, the increment happens in a **continue** block, which is beyond the scope of this book. See the *perlsyn* manpage for the truth.

So, the first time through this loop, $i is 1. Since that's less than or equal to 10, we see the message. Although the increment is written at the top of the loop, it logically happens at the bottom of the loop, after printing the message. So, $i becomes 2, which is less than or equal to 10, so we print the message again, and $i is incremented to 3, which is less than or equal to 10, and so on.

Eventually, we print the message that our program can count to 9. Then $i is incremented to 10, which is less than or *equal* to 10, so we run the loop one last time and print that our program can count to 10. Finally, $i is incremented for the last time, to 11, which is not less than or equal to 10. So control drops out of the loop, and we're on to the rest of the program.

All three parts are together at the top of the loop so that it's easy for an experienced programmer to read that first line and say, "Ah, it's a loop that counts $i from one to ten."

Note that after the loop is done, the control variable has a value "after" the loop. That is, in this case, the control variable has gone all the way to 11.*

This loop is a very versatile loop, since you can make it count in all sorts of ways. This loop counts from –150 to 1000 by threes:†

```
for ($i = -150; $i <= 1000; $i += 3) {
  print "$i\n";
}
```

In fact, you could make any of the three control parts (initialization, test, or increment) empty, if you wish, but you still need the two semicolons. In this (quite unusual) example, the test is a substitution, and the increment is empty:

```
for ($_ = "bedrock"; s/(.)//; ) {  # loops while the s/// is successful
  print "One character is: $1\n";
}
```

The test expression (in the implied **while** loop) is the substitution, which will return a true value if it succeeded. In this case, the first time through the loop, the substitution will remove the **b** from **bedrock**. Each iteration will remove another letter. When the string is empty, the substitution will fail, and the loop is done.

If the test expression (the one between the two semicolons) is empty, it's automatically true, making an infinite loop. But don't make an infinite loop like this until you see how to break out of such a loop, which we'll discuss later in this chapter:

```
for (;;) {
  print "It's an infinite loop!\n";
}
```

---

* Obligatory *This is Spinal Tap* outdated pop-culture reference.

† Of course, it never gets to 1000 exactly. The last iteration uses 999, since each value of $i is a multiple of three.

A more Perl-like way to write an intentional infinite loop, when you really want one,* is with `while`:

```
while (1) {
  print "It's another infinite loop!\n";
}
```

Although C programmers are familiar with the first way, even a beginning Perl programmer should recognize that 1 is always true, making an intentional infinite loop, so the second is generally a better way to write it. Perl is smart enough to recognize a constant expression like that and optimize it away, so there's no difference in efficiency.

The Secret Connection Between foreach and for

It turns out that, inside the Perl grammar, the keyword `foreach` is exactly equivalent to the keyword `for`. That is, any time Perl sees one of them, it's the same as if you had typed the other. Perl can tell which you meant by looking inside the parentheses. If you've got the two semicolons, it's a computed `for` loop (like we've just been talking about). If you don't have the semicolons, it's really a `foreach` loop:

```
for (1..10) {  # Really a foreach loop from 1 to 10
  print "I can count to $_!\n";
}
```

That's really a `foreach` loop, but it's written `for`. Except for that one example, all through this book, we'll spell out `foreach` wherever it appears. But in the real world, do you think that Perl folks will type those extra four letters?† Excepting only beginners' code, it's always written `for`, and you'll have to do as Perl does and look for the semicolons to tell which kind of loop it is.

In Perl, the true `foreach` loop is almost always a better choice. In the `foreach` loop (written `for`) in that previous example, it's easy to see at a glance that the loop will go from 1 to 10. But do you see what's wrong with this computed loop

---

* If you somehow made an infinite loop that's gotten away from you, see whether Control-C will halt it. It's possible that you'll get a lot of output even after typing Control-C, depending upon your system's I/O and other factors. Hey, we warned you.

† If you think that, you haven't been paying attention. Among programmers, especially Perl programmers, laziness is one of the classical virtues. If you don't believe us, ask someone at the next Perl Mongers' meeting.

that's trying to do the same thing? Don't peek at the answer in the footnote until you think you've found what's wrong:*

```
for ($i = 1; $i < 10; $i++) {  # Oops! Something is wrong here!
  print "I can count to $_!\n";
}
```

Loop Controls

As you've surely noticed by now, Perl is one of the so-called "structured" program-ming languages. In particular, there's just one entrance to any block of code, which is at the top of that block. But there are times when you may need more control or versatility than what we've shown so far. For example, you may need to make a loop like a while loop, but one that always runs at least once. Or maybe you need to occasionally exit a block of code early. Perl has three loop-control operators you can use in loop blocks to make the loop do all sorts of tricks.

The last Operator

The last operator immediately ends execution of the loop. (If you've used the "break" operator in C or a similar language, it's like that.) It's the "emergency exit" for loop blocks. When you hit last, the loop is done. For example:

```
# Print all input lines mentioning fred, until the __END__ marker
while (<STDIN>) {
  if (/__END__/) {
    # No more input on or after this marker line
    last;
  } elsif (/fred/) {
    print;
  }
}
## last comes here ##
```

Once an input line has the __END__ marker, that loop is done. Of course, that comment line at the end is merely a comment—it's not required in any way. We just threw that in to make it clearer what's happening.

---

* There are two and one-half bugs. First, the conditional uses a less-than sign, so the loop will run nine times, instead of ten. It's easy to get a so-called "fencepost" bug with this kind of loop, like what hap-pened when the rancher needed enough fenceposts to make a 30-meter-long fence with a post every three meters. (The answer is not ten fenceposts.) Second, the control variable is $i, but the loop body is using $_. And second and a half, it's a lot more work to read, write, maintain, and debug this type of loop, which is why we say that the true foreach is generally a better choice in Perl.

There are five kinds of loop blocks in Perl. These are the blocks of `for`, `foreach`, `while`, `until`, or the naked block.* The curly braces of an `if` block or subroutine† don't qualify. As you may have noticed in the example above, the `last` operator applied to the entire loop block.

The `last` operator will apply to the innermost currently running loop block. To jump out of outer blocks, stay tuned; that's coming up in a little bit.

The next Operator

Sometimes you're not ready for the loop to finish, but you're done with the current iteration. That's what the **next** operator is good for. It jumps to the *inside* of the bottom of the current loop block.‡ After **next**, control continues with the next iteration of the loop (much like the "continue" operator in C or a similar language):

```
# Analyze words in the input file or files
while (<>) {
  foreach (split) {  # break $_ into words, assign each to $_ in turn
    $total++;
    next if /\W/;    # strange words skip the remainder of the loop
    $valid++;
    $count{$_}++;    # count each separate word
    ## next comes here ##
  }
}

print "total things = $total, valid words = $valid\n";
foreach $word (sort keys %count) {
  print "$word was seen $count{$word} times.\n";
}
```

This one is a little more complex than most of our examples up to this point, so let's take it step by step. The **while** loop is reading lines of input from the diamond operator, one after another, into $_; we've seen that before. Each time through that loop, another line of input will be in $_.

---

* Yes, you can use `last` to jump out of a naked block. Be sure to check your local laws before doing so.

† It's probably not a good idea, but you could use these loop control operators from inside a subroutine to control a loop that is *outside* the subroutine. That is, if a subroutine is called in a loop block, and the subroutine executes `last` when there's no loop block running inside the subroutine, the flow of control will jump to just after the loop block *in the main code*. This ability to use loop control from within a subroutine may go away in a future version of Perl, and no one is likely to miss it.

‡ This is another of our many lies. In truth, `next` jumps to the start of the (usually omitted) `continue` block for the loop. See the *perlsyn* manpage for the full details.

Inside that loop, the `foreach` loop is iterating over the return value `split`. Do you remember the default for `split` with no arguments?* That splits `$_` on whitespace, in effect breaking `$_` into a list of words. Since the `foreach` loop doesn't mention some other control variable, the control variable will be `$_`. So, we'll see one word after another in `$_`.

But didn't we just say that `$_` holds one line of input after another? Well, in the outer loop, that's what it is. But inside the `foreach` loop, it holds one word after another. It's no problem for Perl to reuse `$_` for a new purpose; this happens all the time.

Now, inside the `foreach` loop, we're seeing one word at a time in `$_`. `$total` is incremented, so it must be the total number of words. But the next line (which is the point of this example) checks to see whether the word has any nonword characters—anything but letters, digits, and underscores. So, if the word is `Tom's`, or if it is `full-sized`, or if it has an adjoining comma, quote mark, or any other strange character, it will match that pattern and we'll skip the rest of the loop, going on to the next word.

But let's say that it's an ordinary word, like `fred`. In that case, we count `$valid` up by one, and also `$count{$_}`, keeping a count for each different word. So, when we finish the two loops, we've counted every word in every line of input from every file the user wanted us to use.

We're not going to explain the last few lines. By now, we hope you've got stuff like that down already.

Like `last`, `next` may be used in any of the five kinds of loop blocks: `for`, `foreach`, `while`, `until`, or the naked block. Also, if loop blocks are nested, `next` works with the innermost one. We'll see how to change that at the end of this section.

The redo Operator

The third member of the loop control triad is `redo`. It says to go back to the top of the current loop block, without testing any conditional expression or advancing to the next iteration. (If you've used C or a similar language, you've never seen this one before. Those languages don't have this kind of operator.) Here's an example:

```
# Typing test
my @words = qw{ fred barney pebbles dino wilma betty };
my $errors = 0;
```

---

* If you don't remember it, don't worry too much. Don't waste any brain cells remembering things that you can look up with *perldoc*.

```
foreach (@words) {
  ## redo comes here ##
  print "Type the word '$_': ";
  chomp(my $try = <STDIN>);
  if ($try ne $_) {
    print "Sorry - That's not right.\n\n";
    $errors++;
    redo;  # jump back up to the top of the loop
  }
}
print "You've completed the test, with $errors errors.\n";
```

Like the other two operators, **redo** will work with any of the five kinds of loop blocks, and it will work with the innermost loop block when they're nested.

The big difference between **next** and **redo** is that **next** will advance to the next iteration, but **redo** will redo the current iteration. Here's an example program that you can play with to get a feel for how these three operators work:[*]

```
foreach (1..10) {
  print "Iteration number $_.\n\n";
  print "Please choose: last, next, redo, or none of the above? ";
  chomp(my $choice = <STDIN>);
  print "\n";
  last if $choice =~ /last/i;
  next if $choice =~ /next/i;
  redo if $choice =~ /redo/i;
  print "That wasn't any of the choices... onward!\n\n";
}
print "That's all, folks!\n";
```

If you just press return without typing anything (try it two or three times), the loop counts along from one number to the next. If you choose **last** when you get to number four, the loop is done, and you won't go on to number five. If you choose **next** when you're on four, you're on to number five without printing the "onward" message. And if you choose **redo** when you're on four, you're back to doing number four all over again.

Labeled Blocks

When you need to work with a loop block that's not the innermost one, use a label. Labels in Perl are like other identifiers—made of letters, digits, and underscores, but they can't start with a digit—however, since they have no prefix character, labels could be confused with the names of builtin function names, or even with your own subroutines' names. So, it would be a poor choice to make a label

---

[*] If you've downloaded the example files from the O'Reilly website (as described in the Preface), you'll find this program called *lnr-example*.

called `print` or `if`. Because of that, Larry recommends that they be all upper-case. That not only ensures that the label won't conflict with another identifier but it also makes it easy to spot the label in the code. In any case, labels are rare, only showing up in a small percentage of Perl programs.

To label a loop block, just put the label and a colon in front of the loop. Then, inside the loop, you may use the label after `last`, `next`, or `redo` as needed:

```
LINE: while (<>) {
  foreach (split) {
    last LINE if /_ _END_ _/;  # bail out of the LINE loop
    ...;
  }
}
```

For readability, it's generally nice to put the label at the left margin, even if the current code is at a higher indentation. Notice that the label names the entire block; it's not marking a target point in the code.*

In that previous snippet of sample code, the special `__END__` token marks the end of all input. Once that token shows up, the program will ignore any remaining lines (even from other files).

It often makes sense to choose a noun as the name of the loop.† That is, the outer loop is processing a line at a time, so we called it `LINE`. If we had to name the inner loop, we would have called it `WORD`, since it processes a word at a time. That makes it convenient to say things like "(move on to the) `next WORD`" or "`redo` (the current) `LINE`".

Logical Operators

As you might expect, Perl has all of the necessary logical operators needed to work with Boolean (true/false) values. For example, it's often useful to combine logical tests by using the logical AND operator (`&&`) and the logical OR operator (`||`):

```
if ($dessert{'cake'} && $dessert{'ice cream'}) {
  # Both are true
  print "Hooray! Cake and ice cream!\n";
} elsif ($dessert{'cake'} || $dessert{'ice cream'}) {
  # At least one is true
  print "That's still good...\n";
} else {
  # Neither is true - do nothing (we're sad)
}
```

---

* This isn't goto, after all.

† That is, it makes more sense to do that than not to do that. Perl doesn't care if you call your loop labels things like XYZZY or PLUGH. However, unless you were friendly with the Colossal Cave in the 70's, you might not get the reference.

There may be a shortcut. If the left side of a logical AND operation is false, the whole thing is false, since logical AND needs both sides to be true in order to return true. In that case, there's no reason to check the right side, so it will not even be evaluated. Consider what happens in this example if `$hour` is 3:

```
if ( (9 <= $hour) && ($hour < 17) ) {
  print "Aren't you supposed to be at work...?\n";
}
```

Similarly, if the left side of a logical OR operation is *true*, the right side will not be evaluated. Consider what happens here if `$name` is `fred`:

```
if ( ($name eq 'fred') || ($name eq 'barney') ) {
  print "You're my kind of guy!\n";
}
```

Because of this behavior, these operators are called "short-circuit" logical operators. They take a short circuit to the result whenever they can. In fact, it's fairly common to rely upon this short-circuit behavior. Suppose you need to calculate an average:

```
if ( ($n != 0) && ($total/$n < 5) ) {
  print "The average is below five.\n";
}
```

In that example, the right side will be evaluated only if the left side is true, so we can't accidentally divide by zero and crash the program.

The Value of a Short-Circuit Operator

Unlike what happens in C (and similar languages), the value of a short-circuit logical operator is the last part evaluated, not just a Boolean value. This provides the same result, in that the last part evaluated is always true when the whole thing should be true, and it's always false when the whole thing should be false.

But it's a much more useful return value. Among other things, the logical OR operator is quite handy for selecting a default value:

```
my $last_name = $last_name{$someone} || '(No last name)';
```

If `$someone` is not listed in the hash, the left side will be `undef`, which is false. So, the logical OR will have to look to the right side for the value, making the right side the default.* We'll see other uses for this behavior later.

---

* But do note that in this idiom the default value won't merely replace `undef`; it would replace any false value equally well. That's fine for most names, but don't forget that zero and the empty string are useful values that are nevertheless false. This idiom should be used only when you're willing to replace *any* false value with the expression on the right.

The Ternary Operator, ?:

When Larry was deciding which operators to make available in Perl, he didn't want former C programmers to be left wishing for something that C had and Perl didn't, so he brought over all of C's operators to Perl.* That meant bringing over C's most confusing operator: the ternary ?: operator. While it may be confusing, it can also be quite useful.

The ternary operator is like an if-then-else test, all rolled into an expression. It is called a "ternary" operator because it takes three operands. It looks like this:

```
expression ? if_true_expr : if_false_expr
```

First, the expression is evaluated to see whether it's true or false. If it's true, the second expression is used; otherwise, the third expression is used. Every time, one of the two expressions on the right is evaluated, and one is ignored. That is, if the first expression is true, then the second expression is evaluated, and the third is ignored. If the first expression is false, then the second is ignored, and the third is evaluated as the value of the whole thing.

In this example, the result of the subroutine &is_weekend determines which string expression will be assigned to the variable:

```
my $location = &is_weekend($day) ? "home" : "work";
```

And here, we calculate and print out an average—or just a placeholder line of hyphens, if there's no average available:

```
my $average = $n ? ($total/$n) : "-----";
print "Average: $average\n";
```

You could always rewrite any use of the ?: operator as an if structure, often much less conveniently and less concisely:

```
my $average;
if ($n) {
  $average = $total / $n;
} else {
  $average = "-----";
}
print "Average: $average\n";
```

Here's a trick you might see, used to code up a nice multiway branch:

```
my $size =
  ($width < 10) ? "small"  :
  ($width < 20) ? "medium" :
  ($width < 50) ? "large"  :
                  "extra-large"; # default
```

---

* Well, to be sure, he did leave out the ones that have no use in Perl, such as the operator that turns a number into the memory address of a variable. And he added several operators (like the string concatenation operator), which make C folks jealous of Perl.

That is really just three nested ?: operators, and it works quite well, once you get the hang of it.

Of course, you're not obliged to use this operator. Beginners may wish to avoid it. But you'll see it in others' code, sooner or later, and we hope that one day you'll find a good reason to use it in your own programs.

Control Structures Using Partial-Evaluation Operators

These three operators that we've just seen—&&, ||, and ?:—all share a peculiar property: depending upon whether the value on the left side is true or false, they may or may not evaluate an expression. Sometimes the expression is evaluated, and sometimes it isn't. For that reason, these are sometimes called *partial-evaluation* operators, since they may not evaluate all of the expressions around them. And partial-evaluation operators are automatically control structures.*

It's not as if Larry felt a burning need to add more control structures to Perl. But once he had decided to put these partial-evaluation operators into Perl, they automatically became control structures as well. After all, anything that can activate and deactivate a chunk of code is a control structure.

Fortunately, you'll notice this only when the controlled expression has side effects, like altering a variable's value or causing some output. For example, suppose you ran across this line of code:

```
($a < $b) && ($a = $b);
```

Right away, you should notice that the result of the logical AND isn't being assigned anywhere.† Why not?

If $a is really less than $b, the left side is true, so the right side will be evaluated, thereby doing the assignment. But if $a is not less than $b, the left side will be false, and thus the right side would be skipped. So that line of code would do essentially the same thing as this one, which is easier to understand:

```
if ($a < $b) { $a = $b; }
```

Or maybe you'll be maintaining a program, and you'll see a line like this one:

```
($a > 10) || print "why is it not greater?\n";
```

---

* Some of you were wondering why these logical operators are being covered in this chapter, weren't you?

† But don't forget to consider that it might be a return value, as the last expression in a subroutine.

If $a is really greater than ten, the left side is true, and the logical OR is done. But if it's not, the left side is false, and this will go on to print the message. Once again, this could (and probably should) be written in the traditional way, probably with if or **unless**.

If you have a particularly twisted brain, you might even learn to read these lines as if they were written in English. For example: check that $a is less than $b, *and if it is*, then do the assignment. Check that $a is more than ten, *or if it's not*, then print the message.

It's generally former C programmers or old-time Perl programmers who most often use these ways of writing control structures. Why do they do it? Some have the mistaken idea that these are more efficient. Some think these tricks make their code cooler. Some are merely copying what they saw someone else do.

In the same way, the ternary operator may be used for control. In this case, we want to assign $c to the smaller of two variables:

```
($a < $b) ? ($a = $c) : ($b = $c);
```

If $a is smaller, it gets $c. Otherwise, $b does.

There is another way to write the logical AND and logical OR operators. You may wish to write them out as words: **and** and **or**.* These word-operators have the same behaviors as the ones written with punctuation, but the words are much lower on the precedence chart. Since the words don't "stick" so tightly to the nearby parts of the expression, they may need fewer parentheses:

```
$a < $b and $a = $b;   # but better written as the corresponding if
```

Then again, you may need *more* parentheses. Precedence is a bugaboo. Be sure to use parentheses to say what you mean, unless you're sure of the precedence. Nevertheless, since the word forms are very low precedence, you can generally understand that they cut the expression into big pieces, doing everything on the left first, and then (if needed) everything on the right.

Despite the fact that using logical operators as control structures can be confusing, sometimes they're the accepted way to write code. We'll see a common use of the **or** operator starting in the next chapter.

So, using these operators as control structures is part of idiomatic Perl—Perl as she is spoken. Used properly, they can make your code more powerful; otherwise they can make your code unmaintainable. Don't overuse them.†

---

* There are also the low-precedence not (like the logical-negation operator, "!") and the rare xor.

† Using these weird forms more than once per month counts as overuse.

Exercise

See Appendix A for an answer to the following exercise:

1. [25] Make a program that will repeatedly ask the user to guess a secret number from 1 to 100 until the user guesses the secret number. Your program should pick the number at random by using the magical formula `int(1 + rand 100)`.* When the user guesses wrong, the program should respond "Too high" or "Too low". If the user enters the word `quit` or `exit`, or if the user enters a blank line, the program should quit. Of course, if the user guesses correctly, the program should quit then as well!

---

* See what the *perlfunc* manpage says about `int` and `rand` if you're curious about these functions.

11

Filehandles and File Tests

What Is a Filehandle?

A filehandle is the name in a Perl program for an I/O connection between your Perl process and the outside world. That is, it's the name of a *connection*, not necessarily the name of a file.

Filehandles are named like other Perl identifiers (letters, digits, and underscores, but they can't start with a digit), but since they don't have any prefix character, they might be confused with present or future reserved words, as we saw with labels. Once again, as with labels, the recommendation from Larry is that you use all uppercase letters in the name of your filehandle—not only will it stand out better, but it will also guarantee that your program won't fail when a future (lowercase) reserved word is introduced.

But there are also six special filehandle names that Perl already uses for its own purposes: STDIN, STDOUT, STDERR, DATA, ARGV, and ARGVOUT.* Although you may choose any filehandle name you'd like, you shouldn't choose one of those six unless you intend to use that one's special properties.†

Maybe you recognized some of those names already. When your program starts, STDIN is the filehandle naming the connection between the Perl process and wherever the program should get its input, known as the *standard input stream*. This is generally the user's keyboard unless the user asked for something else to

---

* Some people hate typing in all-caps, even for a moment, and will try spelling these in lowercase, like stdin. Perl may even let you get away with that from time to time, but not always. The details of when these work and when they fail are beyond the scope of this book. But the important thing is that programs that rely upon this kindness will one day break, so it is best to avoid lowercase here.

† In some cases, you could (re-)use these names without a problem. But your maintenance programmer may think that you're using the name for its builtin features, and thus may be confused.

be the source of input, such as reading the input from a file or reading the output of another program through a pipe.[*]

There's also the *standard output stream*, which is STDOUT. By default, this one goes to the user's display screen, but the user may send the output to a file or to another program, as we'll see shortly. These standard streams come to us from the Unix "standard I/O" library, but they work in much the same way on most modern operating systems.[†] The general idea is that your program should blindly read from STDIN and blindly write to STDOUT, trusting in the user (or generally whichever program is starting your program) to have set those up. In that way, the user can type a command like this one at the shell prompt:

```
$ ./your_program <dino >wilma
```

That command tells the shell that the program's input should be read from the file *dino*, and the output should go to the file *wilma*. As long as the program blindly reads its input from STDIN, processes it (in whatever way we need), and blindly writes its output to STDOUT, this will work just fine.

And at no extra charge, the program will work in a *pipeline*. This is another concept from Unix, which lets us write command lines like this one:

```
$ cat fred barney | sort | ./your_program | grep something | lpr
```

Now, if you're not familiar with these Unix commands, that's okay. This line says that the *cat* command should print out all of the lines of file *fred* followed by all of the lines of file *barney*. Then that output should be the input of the *sort* command, which sorts those lines and passes them on to *your_program*. After it has done its processing, *your_program* will send the data on to *grep*, which discards certain lines in the data, sending the others on to the *lpr* command, which should print everything that it gets on a printer. Whew!

But pipelines like that are common in Unix and many other systems today because they let you put together a powerful, complex command out of simple, standard building blocks.

There's one more standard I/O stream. If (in the previous example) *your_program* had to emit any warnings or other diagnostic messages, those shouldn't go down the pipeline. The *grep* command is set to discard anything that it hasn't specifically been told to look for, and so it will most likely discard the warnings. Even if

---

[*] The defaults we speak of in this chapter for the three main I/O streams are what the Unix shells do by default. But it's not just shells that launch programs, of course. We'll see in Chapter 14 what happens when you launch another program from Perl.

[†] If you're not already familiar with how your non-Unix system provides standard input and output, see the *perlport* manpage and the documentation for that system's equivalent to the Unix shell (the program that runs programs based upon your keyboard input).

it did keep the warnings, we probably don't want those to be passed downstream to the other programs in the pipeline. So that's why there's also the *standard error stream*: STDERR. Even if the standard output is going to another program or file, the errors will go to wherever the user desires. By default, the errors will generally go to the user's display screen,* but the user may send the errors to a file with a shell command like this one:

```
$ netstat | ./your_program 2>/tmp/my_errors
```

Opening a Filehandle

So we see that Perl provides three filehandles—STDIN, STDOUT, and STDERR—which are automatically open to files or devices established by the program's parent process (probably the shell). When you need other filehandles, use the **open** operator to tell Perl to ask the operating system to open the connection between your program and the outside world. Here are some examples:

```
open CONFIG, "dino";
open CONFIG, "<dino";
open BEDROCK, ">fred";    Open and wipe out contents
open LOG, ">>logfile";    Open for appending
```

The first one opens a filehandle called CONFIG to a file called *dino*. That is, the (existing) file *dino* will be opened and whatever it holds will come into our program through the filehandle named CONFIG. This is similar to the way that data from a file could come in through STDIN if the command line had a shell redirection like <dino. In fact, the second example uses exactly that sequence. The second does the same as the first, but the less-than sign explicitly says "this filename is to be used for input," even though that's the default.†

Although you don't have to use the less-than sign to open a file for input, we include that because, as you can see in the third example, a greater-than sign means to create a new file for output. This opens the filehandle BEDROCK for output to the new file *fred*. Just as when the greater-then sign is used in shell

---

* Also, generally, errors aren't buffered. That means that if the standard error and standard output streams are both going to the same place (such as the monitor), the errors may appear earlier than the normal output. For example, if your program prints a line of ordinary text, then tries to divide by zero, the output may show the message about dividing by zero first, and the ordinary text second.

† This may be important for security reasons. As we'll see in a moment (and in further detail in Chapter 14), there are a number of magical characters that may be used in filenames. If $name holds a user-chosen filename, simply opening $name will allow any of these magical characters to come into play. This could be a convenience to the user, or it could be a security hole. But opening "<$name" is much safer, since it explicitly says to open the given name for input. Still, this doesn't prevent all possible mischief. For more information on different ways of opening files, especially when security may be a concern, see the *perlopentut* manpage.

redirection, we're sending the output to a *new* file called *fred*. If there's already a file of that name, we're asking to wipe it out and replace it with this new one.

The fourth example shows how two greater-than signs may be used (again, as the shell does) to open a file for appending. That is, if the file already exists, we will add new data at the end. If it doesn't exist, it will be created in much the same way as if we had used just one greater-than sign. This is handy for log files; your program could write a few lines to the end of a log file each time it's run. So that's why the fourth example names the filehandle **LOG** and the file *logfile*.

You can use any scalar expression in place of the filename specifier, although typically you'll want to be explicit about the direction specification:

```
my $selected_output = "my_output";
open LOG, "> $selected_output";
```

Note the space after the greater-than. Perl ignores this,* but it keeps unexpected things from happening if **$selected_output** were **">passwd"** for example (which would make an append instead of a write).

We'll see how to use these filehandles later in this chapter.

Closing a Filehandle

When you are finished with a filehandle, you may close it with the **close** operator like this:

```
close BEDROCK;
```

Closing a filehandle tells Perl to inform the operating system that we're all done with the given data stream, so any last output data should be written to disk in case someone is waiting for it.†

Perl will automatically close a filehandle if you reopen it (that is, if you reuse the filehandle name in a new **open**) or if you exit the program.‡ Because of this, many simple Perl programs don't bother with **close**. But it's there if you want to be

---

* Yes, this means that if your filename were to have leading whitespace, that would also be ignored by Perl. See *perlfunc* and *perlopentut* if you're worried about this.

† If you know much about I/O systems, you'll know there's more to the story. Generally, though, when a filehandle is closed, here's what happens. If there's input remaining in a file, it's ignored. If there's input remaining in a pipeline, the writing program may get a signal that the pipeline is closed. If there's output going to a file or pipeline, the buffer is flushed (that is, pending output is sent on its way). If the filehandle had a lock, the lock is released. See your system's I/O documentation for further details.

‡ Any exit from the program will close all filehandles, but if Perl itself breaks, pending output buffers won't get flushed. That is to say, if you accidentally crash your program by dividing by zero, for example, Perl itself is still running. Perl will ensure that data you've written actually gets output in that case. But if Perl itself can't run (because you ran out of memory or caught an unexpected signal), the last few pieces of output may not be written to disk. Usually, this isn't a big issue.

tidy, with one `close` for every `open`. In general, it's best to close each filehandle soon after you're done with it, though the end of the program often arrives soon enough.*

Bad Filehandles

Perl can't actually open a file all by itself. Like any other programming language, Perl can merely ask the operating system to let us open a file. Of course, the operating system may refuse, because of permission settings, an incorrect filename, or other reasons.

If you try to read from a bad filehandle (that is, a filehandle that isn't properly open), you'll see an immediate end-of-file. (With the I/O methods we'll see in this chapter, end-of-file will be indicated by `undef` in a scalar context or an empty list in a list context.) If you try to write to a bad filehandle, the data is silently discarded.

Fortunately, these dire consequences are easy to avoid. First of all, if we ask for warnings with **-w**, Perl will generally be able to tell us with a warning when it sees that we're using a bad filehandle. But even before that, **open** always tells us if it succeeded or failed, by returning true for success or false for failure. So you could write code like this:

```
my $success = open LOG, ">>logfile";  # capture the return value
unless ($success) {
  # The open failed
  ...
}
```

Well, you *could* do it like that, but there's another way that we'll see in the next section.

Fatal Errors with die

Let's step aside for a moment. We need some stuff that isn't directly related to (or limited to) filehandles, but is more about getting out of a program earlier than normal.

When a fatal error happens inside Perl (for example, if you divide by zero, use an invalid regular expression, or call a subroutine that hasn't been declared) your

---

* Closing a filehandle will flush any output buffers and release any locks on the file. Since someone else may be waiting for those things, a long-running program should generally close each filehandle as soon as possible. But many of our programs will take only one or two seconds to run to completion, so this may not matter. Closing a filehandle also releases possibly limited resources, so it's more than just being tidy.

program stops with an error message telling why.* But this functionality is available to us with the die function, so we can make our own fatal errors.

The die function prints out the message you give it (to the standard error stream, where such messages should go) and makes sure that your program exits with a nonzero exit status.

You may not have known it, but every program that runs on Unix (and many other modern operating systems) has an exit status, telling whether it was successful or not. Programs that run other programs (like the *make* utility program) look at that exit status to see that everything is running correctly. The exit status is just a single byte, so it can't say much; traditionally, it is zero for success and a nonzero value for failure. Perhaps one means a syntax error in the command arguments, while two means that something went wrong during processing and three means the configuration file couldn't be found; the details differ from one command to the next. But zero always means that everything worked. When the exit status shows failure, a program like *make* knows not to go on to the next step.

So we could rewrite the previous example, perhaps something like this:

```
unless (open LOG, ">>logfile") {
    die "Cannot create logfile: $!";
}
```

If the open fails, die will terminate the program and tell us that it cannot create the logfile. But what's that $! in the message? That's the human-readable complaint from the system. In general, when the system refuses to do something we've requested (like opening a file), it will give us a reason (perhaps "permission denied" or "file not found," in this case). This is the string that you may have obtained with perror in C or a similar language. This human-readable complaint message will be available in Perl's special variable $!.† It's a good idea to include $! in the message when it could help the user to figure out what he or she did wrong. But if you use die to indicate an error that is not the failure of a system request, don't include $!, since it will generally hold an unrelated message left over from something Perl did internally. It will hold a useful value only immediately after a *failed* system request. A successful request won't leave anything useful there.

---

* Well, it does this by default, but errors may be trapped with an eval block, as we'll see in Chapter 17, *Some Advanced Perl Techniques*.

† On some non-Unix operating systems, $! may say something like error number 7, leaving it up to the user to look that one up in the documentation. On Windows and VMS, the variable $^E may have additional diagnostic information.

There's one more thing that die will do for you: it will automatically append the Perl program name and line number[*] to the end of the message, so you can easily identify which die in your program is responsible for the untimely exit. The error message from the previous code might look like this, if $! contained the message **permission denied**:

```
Cannot create logfile: permission denied at your_program line 1234.
```

That's pretty helpful—in fact, we always seem to want more information in our error messages than we put in the first time around. If you don't want the line number and file revealed, make sure that the dying words have a newline on the end. That is, another way you could use die is in a line like this, with a trailing newline:

```
die "Not enough arguments\n" if @ARGV < 2;
```

If there aren't at least two command-line arguments, that program will say so and quit. It won't include the program name and line number, since the line number is of no use to the user; this is the user's error, after all. As a rule of thumb, put the newline on messages that indicate a usage error and leave it off when it the error might be something you want to track down during debugging.[†]

When opening a file fails, though, there's an easier and more common way instead of the **unless** block:

```
open LOG, ">>logfile"
  or die "Cannot create logfile: $!";
```

This uses the low-precedence short-circuit **or** operator that we saw in Chapter 10. If the **open** succeeds, it returns true, and the **or** is done. If the **open** fails, it returns false, and the short-circuit **or** goes on to the right side and dies with the message. You can read this as if it were English: "Open this file, or die!" It may not be the battle cry that will win a war, but it's a good way to write code.

You should always check the return value of **open**, since the rest of the program is relying upon its success. That's why we say that this is really the only way to write

---

[*] If the error happened while reading from a file, the error message will include the "chunk number" (usually the line number) from the file and the name of the filehandle as well, since those are often useful in tracking down a bug.

[†] The program's name is in Perl's special variable $0, so you may wish to include that in the string: "$0: Not enough arguments\n". This is useful if the program may be used in a pipeline or shell script, for example, where it's not obvious which command is complaining. $0 can be changed during the execution of the program, however. You might also want to look into the special __FILE__ and __LINE__ tokens (or the caller function) to get the information that is being left out by adding the newline, so you can print it in your own choice of format.

open—with or die after it.* Until you're ready to be extra tricky, you should simply think of this as the syntax for open. Typing or die and a message takes only a moment when you're writing the program, but it can save hours, or possibly days of debugging time when something goes wrong.

Warning Messages with warn

Just as die can indicate a fatal error that acts like one of Perl's builtin errors (like dividing by zero), you can use the warn function to cause a warning that acts like one of Perl's builtin warnings (like using an undef value as if it were defined, when warnings are enabled).

The warn function works just like die does, except for that last step—it doesn't actually quit the program. But it adds the program name and line number if needed, and it prints the message to standard error, just as die would.†

And having talked about death and dire warnings, we now return you to your regularly scheduled filehandle instructional material. Read on.

Using Filehandles

Once a filehandle is open for reading, you can read lines from it just like you can read from standard input with STDIN. So, for example, to read lines from the Unix password file:

```
open PASSWD, "/etc/passwd"
  or die "How did you get logged in? ($!)";

while (<PASSWD>) {
  chomp;
  if (/^root:/) {  # found root entry...
    ...;
  }
}
```

In this example, the die message uses parentheses around $!. Those are merely parentheses around the message in the output. (Sometimes a punctuation mark is just a punctuation mark.) As you can see, what we've been calling the "line-input operator" is really made of two components; the angle brackets (the *real* line-input

---

* Older code may use the higher-precedence || operator instead. The only difference is the precedence, but it's a big one! If the open is written without parentheses, the higher-precedence operator will bind to the filename argument, not to the return value—so the return value of open isn't being checked after all. If you use the ||, be sure to use the parentheses. Better yet, just use the low-precedence or as we've shown here whenever you're writing or die.

† Warnings can't be trapped with an eval block, like fatal errors can. But see the documentation for the _ _WARN_ _ pseudo-signal (in the *perlvar* manpage) if you need to trap a warning.

operator) are around an input filehandle. Each line of input is then tested to see if it begins with `root` followed by a colon, triggering unseen actions.

A filehandle open for writing or appending may be used with **print** or **printf**, appearing immediately after the keyword but before the list of arguments:

```
print LOG "Captain's log, stardate 3.14159\n";  # output goes to LOG
printf STDERR "%d percent complete.\n", $done/$total * 100;
```

Did you notice that there's no comma between the filehandle and the items to be printed?* This looks especially weird if you use parentheses. Either of these forms is correct:

```
printf (STDERR "%d percent complete.\n", $done/$total * 100);
printf STDERR ("%d percent complete.\n", $done/$total * 100);
```

Changing the Default Output Filehandle

By default, if you don't give a filehandle to **print** (or to **printf**, as everything we say here about one applies equally well to the other), the output will go to **STDOUT**. But that default may be changed with the **select** operator. Here we'll send some output lines to BEDROCK:

```
select BEDROCK;
print "I hope Mr. Slate doesn't find out about this.\n";
print "Wilma!\n";
```

Once you've selected a filehandle as the default for output, it will stay that way. But it's generally a bad idea to confuse the rest of the program, so you should generally set it back to **STDOUT** when you're done.†

Also by default, the output to each filehandle is buffered. Setting the special $| variable to 1 will set the currently selected filehandle (that is, the one selected at the time that the variable is modified) to always flush the buffer after each output operation. So if you wanted to be sure that the logfile gets its entries at once, in case you might be reading the log to monitor progress of your long-running program, you could use something like this:

```
select LOG;
$| = 1;  # don't keep LOG entries sitting in the buffer
```

---

* If you got straight A's in freshman English or Linguistics, when we say that this is called "indirect object syntax," you may say "Ah, of course! I see why there's no comma after the filehandle name—it's an indirect object!" We didn't get straight A's; we don't understand why there's no comma; we merely omit it because Larry told us that we should omit the comma.

† In the unlikely case that **STDOUT** might not be the selected filehandle, you could save and restore the filehandle, using the technique shown in the documentation for **select** in the *perlfunc* manpage. And as long as we're sending you to that manpage, we may as well tell you that there are actually *two* builtin functions in Perl named **select**, and both covered in the *perlfunc* manpage. The other **select** always has four arguments, so it's sometimes called "four-argument **select**".

```
select STDOUT;
# ... time passes, babies learn to walk, tectonic plates shift, and then...
print LOG "This gets written to the LOG at once!\n";
```

Reopening a Standard Filehandle

We mentioned earlier that if you were to reopen a filehandle (that is, if you were to open a filehandle FRED when you've already got an open filehandle named FRED, say), the old one would be closed for you automatically. And we said that you shouldn't reuse one of the six standard filehandle names unless you intended to get that one's special features. And we also said that the messages from **die** and **warn**, along with Perl's internally generated complaints, go automatically to STDERR. If you put those three pieces of information together, you now have an idea about how you could send error messages to a file, rather than to your program's standard error stream:*

```
# Send errors to my private error log
open STDERR, ">>/home/barney/.error_log"
    or die "Can't open error log for append: $!";
```

After reopening STDERR, any error messages from Perl will go into the new file. But what happens if the **or die** part is executed—where will *that* message go, if the new file couldn't be opened to accept the messages?

The answer is that if one of the three system filehandles—STDIN, STDOUT, or STDERR—fails to be reopened, Perl kindly restores the original one.† That is, Perl closes the original one (of those three) only when it sees that opening the new connection is successful. Thus, this technique could be used to redirect any (or all) of those three system filehandles from inside your program,‡ almost as if the program had been run with that I/O redirection from the shell in the first place.

File Tests

Now you know how to open a filehandle for output. Normally, that will create a new file, wiping out any existing file with the same name. Perhaps you want to check that there isn't a file by that name. Perhaps you need to know how old a

---

* Don't do this without a reason. It's nearly always better to let the user set up redirection when launching your program, rather than have redirection hardcoded. But this is handy in cases where your program is being run automatically by another program (say, by a web server or a scheduling utility like **cron** or **at**). Another reason might be that your program is going to start another process (probably with **system** or **exec**, which we'll see in Chapter 14), and you need that process to have different I/O connections.

† At least, this is true if you haven't changed Perl's special $^F variable, which tells Perl that only those three are special like this. But you'd never change that.

‡ But don't open STDIN for output or the others for input. Just thinking about that makes our heads hurt.

given file is. Or perhaps you want to go through a list of files to find which ones are larger than a certain number of bytes and not accessed for a certain amount of time. Perl has a complete set of tests you can use to find out information about files.

Let's try that first example, where we need to check that a given file doesn't exist, so that we don't accidentally overwrite a vital spreadsheet data file, or that important birthday calendar. For this, we need the −e file test, testing for existence:

```
die "Oops! A file called '$filename' already exists.\n"
  if -e $filename;
```

Notice that we don't include $! in this **die** message, since we're not reporting that the system refused a request in this case. Here's an example of checking whether a file is being kept up-to-date. Let's say that our program's configuration file should be updated every week or two. (Maybe it's checking for computer viruses, say.) If the file hasn't been modified in the past 28 days, then something is wrong:

```
warn "Config file is looking pretty old!\n"
  if -M CONFIG > 28;
```

The third example is more complex. Here, let's say that disk space is filling up and rather than buy more disks, we've decided to move any large, useless files to the backup tapes. So let's go through our list of files* to see which of them are larger than 100 K. But even if a file is large, we shouldn't move it to the backup tapes unless it hasn't been accessed in the last 90 days (so we know that it's not used too often):†

```
my @original_files = qw/ fred barney betty wilma pebbles dino bamm-bamm /;
my @big_old_files;  # The ones we want to put on backup tapes
foreach my $filename (@original_files) {
  push @big_old_files, $_
    if -s $filename > 100_000 and -A $filename > 90;
}
```

This is the first time that we've seen it, so maybe you noticed that the control variable of the foreach loop is a my variable. That declares it to have the scope of the loop itself, so this example should work under **use strict**. Without the my keyword, this would be using the global $filename.

The file tests all look like a hyphen and a letter, which is the name of the test, followed by either a filename or a filehandle to be tested. Many of them return a true/false value, but several give something more interesting. See Table 11-1 for the complete list, and then read the following discussion to learn more about the special cases.

---

* It's more likely that, instead of having the list of files in an array, as our example shows, you'll read it directly from the filesystem using a glob or directory handle, as shown in Chapter 12. Since we haven't seen that yet, we'll just start with the list and go from there.

† There's a way to make this example more efficient, as we'll see by the end of the chapter.

Table 11-1. File tests and their meanings

File test	Meaning
-r	File or directory is readable by this (effective) user or group
-w	File or directory is writable by this (effective) user or group
-x	File or directory is executable by this (effective) user or group
-o	File or directory is owned by this (effective) user
-R	File or directory is readable by this real user or group
-W	File or directory is writable by this real user or group
-X	File or directory is executable by this real user or group
-O	File or directory is owned by this real user
-e	File or directory name exists
-z	File exists and has zero size (always false for directories)
-s	File or directory exists and has nonzero size (the value is the size in bytes)
-f	Entry is a plain file
-d	Entry is a directory
-l	Entry is a symbolic link
-S	Entry is a socket
-p	Entry is a named pipe (a "fifo")
-b	Entry is a block-special file (like a mountable disk)
-c	Entry is a character-special file (like an I/O device)
-u	File or directory is setuid
-g	File or directory is setgid
-k	File or directory has the sticky bit set
-t	The filehandle is a TTY (as reported by the isatty() system function; filenames can't be tested by this test)
-T	File looks like a "text" file
-B	File looks like a "binary" file
-M	Modification age (measured in days)
-A	Access age (measured in days)
-C	Inode-modification age (measured in days)

The tests **-r**, **-w**, **-x**, and **-o** tell whether the given attribute is true for the effective user or group ID,* which essentially refers to the person who is "in charge of"

---

* The **-o** and **-O** tests relate only to the user ID and not to the group ID.

running the program.* These tests look at the "permission bits" on the file to see what is permitted. If your system uses Access Control Lists (ACLs), the tests will use those as well. These tests generally tell whether the system would *try* to permit something, but it doesn't mean that it really would be possible. For example, `-w` may be true for a file on a CD-ROM, even though you can't write to it, or `-x` may be true on an empty file, which can't truly be executed.

The `-s` test does return true if the file is nonempty, but it's a special kind of true. It's the length of the file, measured in bytes, which evaluates as true for a nonzero number.

On a Unix filesystem,† there are just seven types of items, represented by the seven file tests `-f`, `-d`, `-l`, `-S`, `-p`, `-b`, and `-c`. Any item should be one of those. But if you have a symbolic link pointing to a file, that will report true for both `-f` and `-l`. So if you want to know whether something is a symbolic link, you should generally test that first. (We'll learn more about symbolic links in Chapter 13.)

The age tests, `-M`, `-A`, and `-C` (yes, they're uppercase), return the number of days since the file was last modified, accessed, or had its inode changed.‡ (The inode contains all of the information about the file except for its contents—see the `stat` system call manpage or a good book on Unix internals for details.) This age value is a full floating-point number, so you might get a value of `2.00001` if a file were modified two days and one second ago. (These "days" aren't necessarily the same as a human would count; for example, if it's one thirty in the morning when you check a file modified at about an hour before midnight, the value of `-M` for this file would be around `0.1`, even though it was modified "yesterday.")

When checking the age of a file, you might even get a negative value like `-1.2`, which means that the file's last-access timestamp is set at about thirty hours in the future! The zero point on this timescale is the moment your program started running,§ so that value might mean that a long-running program was looking at a file that had just been accessed. Or a timestamp could be set (accidentally or intentionally) to a time in the future.

---

* Note for advanced students: the corresponding `-R`, `-W`, `-X`, and `-O` tests use the real user or group ID, which becomes important if your program may be running set-ID; in that case, it's generally the ID of the person who requested running it. See any good book about advanced Unix programming for a discussion of set-ID programs.

† This is the case on many non-Unix filesystems, but not all of the file tests are meaningful everywhere. For example, you aren't likely to have block special files on your non-Unix system.

‡ This information will be somewhat different on non-Unix systems, since not all keep track of the same times that Unix does. For example, on some systems, the ctime field (which the `-C` test looks at) is the file creation time (which Unix doesn't keep track of), rather than the inode change time; see the *perlport* manpage.

§ As recorded in the `$^T` variable, which you could update (with a statement like `$^T = time;`) if you needed to get the ages relative to a different starting time.

The tests $-T$ and $-B$ take a try at telling whether a file is text or binary. But people who know a lot about filesystems know that there's no bit (at least in Unix-like operating systems) to indicate that a file is a binary or text file—so how can Perl tell? The answer is that Perl cheats: it opens the file, looks at the first few thousand bytes, and makes an educated guess. If it sees a lot of null bytes, unusual control characters, and bytes with the high bit set, then that looks like a binary file. If there's not much weird stuff then it looks like text. As you might guess, it sometimes guesses wrong. If a text file has a lot of Swedish or French words (which may have characters represented with the high bit set, as some ISO-8859-something variant, or perhaps even a Unicode version), it may fool Perl into declaring it binary. So it's not perfect, but if you just need to separate your source code from compiled files, or HTML files from PNGs, these tests should do the trick.

You'd think that $-T$ and $-B$ would always disagree, since a text file isn't a binary and vice versa, but there are two special cases where they're in complete agreement. If the file doesn't exist, both are false, since it's neither a text file nor a binary. Alternatively, if the file is empty, it's an empty text file and an empty binary file at the same time, so they're both true.

The $-t$ file test returns true if the given filehandle is a TTY—in short, if it's able to be interactive because it's not a simple file or pipe. When $-t$ STDIN returns true, it generally means that you can interactively ask the user questions. If it's false, your program is probably getting input from a file or pipe, rather than a keyboard.

Don't worry if you don't know what some of the other file tests mean—if you've never heard of them, you won't be needing them. But if you're curious, get a good book about programming for Unix. (On non-Unix systems, these tests all try to give results analogous to what they do on Unix. Usually you'll be able to guess correctly what they'll do.)

If you omit the filename or filehandle parameter to a file test (that is, if you have just $-r$ or just $-s$, say), the default operand is the file named in $\$\_$.[*] So, to test a list of filenames to see which ones are readable, you simply type:

```
foreach (@lots_of_filenames) {
  print "$_ is readable\n" if -r;  # same as -r $_
}
```

But if you omit the parameter, be careful that whatever follows the file test doesn't look like it *could* be a parameter. For example, if you wanted to find out the size of a file in K rather than in bytes, you might be tempted to divide the result of $-s$ by 1000 (or 1024), like this:

---

[*] The $-t$ file test is an exception; since that test isn't useful with filenames (they're never TTYs). By default it tests STDIN.

```
# The filename is in $_
my $size_in_K = -s / 1000;   # Oops!
```

When the Perl parser sees the slash, it doesn't think about division; since it's looking for the optional operand for -s, it sees what looks like the start of a regular expression in forward slashes. One simple way to prevent this kind of confusion is to put parentheses around the file test:

```
my $size_in_k = (-s) / 1024;   # Uses $_ by default
```

Of course, it's always safe to explicitly give a file test a parameter.

The stat and lstat Functions

While these file tests are fine for testing various attributes regarding a particular file or filehandle, they don't tell the whole story. For example, there's no file test that returns the number of links to a file or the owner's user-ID (uid). To get at the remaining information about a file, merely call the **stat** function, which returns pretty much everything that the stat Unix system call returns (hopefully more than you want to know).*

The operand to **stat** is a filehandle, or an expression that evaluates to a filename. The return value is either the empty list, indicating that the **stat** failed (usually because the file doesn't exist), or a 13-element list of numbers, most easily described using the following list of scalar variables:

```
my($dev, $ino, $mode, $nlink, $uid, $gid, $rdev,
   $size, $atime, $mtime, $ctime, $blksize, $blocks)
     = stat($filename);
```

The names here refer to the parts of the stat structure, described in detail in the *stat(2)* manpage. You should probably look there for the detailed descriptions. But in short, here's a quick summary of the important ones:

$dev and $ino

The device number and inode number of the file. Together they make up a "license plate" for the file. Even if it has more than one name (hard link), the combination of device and inode numbers should always be unique.

---

* On a non-Unix system, both stat and lstat, as well as the file tests, should return "the closest thing available." For example, a system that doesn't have user IDs (that is, a system that has just one "user," in the Unix sense) might return zero for the user and group IDs, as if the one and only user is the system administrator. If stat or lstat fails, it will return an empty list. If the system call underlying a file test fails (or isn't available on the given system), that test will generally return undef. See the *perlport* manpage for the latest about what to expect on different systems.

$mode

The set of permission bits for the file, and some other bits. If you've ever used the Unix command *ls -l* to get a detailed (long) file listing, you'll see that each line of output starts with something like **-rwxr-xr-x**. The nine letters and hyphens of file permissions* correspond to the nine least-significant bits of $mode, which would in this case give the octal number 0755. The other bits, beyond the lowest nine, indicate other details about the file. So if you need to work with the mode, you'll generally want to use the bitwise operators covered later in this chapter.

$nlink

The number of (hard) links to the file or directory. This is the number of true names that the item has. This number is always 2 or more for directories and (usually) 1 for files. We'll see more about this when we talk about creating links to files in Chapter 13. In the listing from *ls -l*, this is the number just after the permission-bits string.

$uid and $gid

The numeric user-ID and group-ID showing the file's ownership.

$size

The size in bytes, as returned by the **-s** file test.

$atime, $mtime, and $ctime

The three timestamps, but here they're represented in the system's timestamp format: a 32-bit number telling how many seconds have passed since the *Epoch*, an arbitrary starting point for measuring system time. On Unix systems and some others, the Epoch is the beginning of 1970 at midnight Universal Time, but the Epoch is different on some machines. There's more information later in this chapter on turning that timestamp number into something useful.

Invoking **stat** on the name of a symbolic link returns information on what the symbolic link points at, not information about the symbolic link itself (unless the link just happens to be pointing at nothing currently accessible). If you need the (mostly useless) information about the symbolic link itself, use **lstat** rather than **stat** (which returns the same information in the same order). If the operand isn't a symbolic link, **lstat** returns the same things that **stat** would.

Like the file tests, the operand of **stat** or **lstat** defaults to $_, meaning that the underlying stat system call will be performed on the file named by the scalar variable $_.

---

* The first character in that string isn't a permission bit; it indicates the type of entry: a hyphen for an ordinary file, **d** for directory, or **l** for symbolic link, among others. The *ls* command determines this from the other bits past the least-significant nine.

The localtime Function

When you have a timestamp number (such as the ones from `stat`), it will typically look something like 1080630098. That's not very useful for most humans, unless you need to compare two timestamps by subtracting. You may need to convert it to something human-readable, such as a string like "`Tue Mar 30 07: 01:38 2004`". Perl can do that with the `localtime` function in a scalar context:

```
my $timestamp = 1080630098;
my $date = localtime $timestamp;
```

In a list context, `localtime` returns a list of numbers, several of which may not be quite what you'd expect:

```
my($sec, $min, $hour, $day, $mon, $year, $wday, $yday, $isdst)
  = localtime $timestamp;
```

The `$mon` is a month number, ranging from 0 to 11, which is handy as an index into an array of month names. The `$year` is the number of years since 1900, oddly enough, so add 1900 to get the real year number. The `$wday` ranges from 0 (for Sunday) through 6 (for Saturday), and the `$yday` is the day-of-the-year (ranging from 0 for January 1, through 364 or 365 for December 31).

There are two related functions that you'll also find useful. The `gmtime` function is just the same as `localtime`, except that it returns the time in Universal Time (what we once called Greenwich Mean Time). If you need the current timestamp number from the system clock, just use the `time` function. Both `localtime` and `gmtime` default to using the current `time` value if you don't supply a parameter:

```
my $now = gmtime;  # Get the current universal timestamp as a string
```

For more information on manipulating date and time information, see the information about some useful modules in Appendix B.

Bitwise Operators

When you need to work with numbers bit-by-bit, as when working with the mode bits returned by `stat`, you'll need to use the bitwise operators. The bitwise-and operator (&) reports which bits are set in the left argument *and* in the right argument. For example, the expression 10 & 12 has the value 8. The bitwise-and needs to have a one-bit in both operands to produce a one-bit in the result. That means that the logical-and operation on ten (which is 1010 in binary) and twelve (which is 1100) gives eight (which is 1000, with a one-bit only where the left operand has a one-bit *and* the right operand also has a one-bit). See Figure 11-1.

```
1010
& 1100
1000
```

Figure 11-1. Bitwise-and addition

The different bitwise operators and their meanings are shown in this table:

Expression	Meaning
10 & 12	Bitwise-and—which bits are true in both operands (this gives 8)
10 | 12	Bitwise-or—which bits are true in one operand or the other (this gives 14)
10 ^ 12	Bitwise-xor—which bits are true in one operand or the other but not both (this gives 6)
6 << 2	Bitwise shift left—shift the left operand the number of bits shown by the right operand, adding zero-bits at the least-significant places (this gives 24)
25 >> 2	Bitwise shift right—shift the left operand the number of bits shown by the right operand, discarding the least-significant bits (this gives 6)
~ 10	Bitwise negation, also called unary bit complement—return the number with the opposite bit for each bit in the operand (this gives 0xFFFFFFF5, but see the text)

So, here's an example of some things you could do with the $mode returned by stat. The results of these bit manipulations could be useful with chmod, which we'll see in Chapter 13, *Manipulating Files and Directories*:

```
# $mode is the mode value returned from a stat of CONFIG
warn "Hey, the configuration file is world-writable!\n"
  if $mode & 0002;                          # configuration security problem
my $classical_mode = 0777 & $mode;          # mask off extra high-bits
my $u_plus_x = $classical_mode | 0100;      # turn one bit on
my $go_minus_r = $classical_mode & (~ 0044); # turn two bits off
```

Using Bitstrings

All of the bitwise operators can work with bitstrings, as well as with integers. If the operands are integers, the result will be an integer. (The integer will be at least a 32-bit integer, but may be larger if your machine supports that. That is, if you have a 64-bit machine, ~10 may give the 64-bit result 0xFFFFFFFFFFFFFFF5, rather than the 32-bit result 0xFFFFFFF5.)

But if any operand of a bitwise operator is a string, Perl will perform the operation on that bitstring. That is, "\xAA" | "\x55" will give the string "\xFF". Note that these values are single-byte strings; the result is a byte with all eight bits set. Bitstrings may be arbitrarily long.

This is one of the very few places where Perl distinguishes between strings and numbers. See the *perlop* manpage for more information on using bitwise operators on strings.

Using the Special Underscore Filehandle

Every time you use `stat`, `lstat`, or a file test in a program, Perl has to go out to the system to ask for a stat buffer on the file (that is, the return buffer from the stat system call). That means if you want to know whether a file is both readable and writable, you've essentially asked the system twice for the same information (which isn't likely to change in a fairly nonhostile environment).

This looks like a waste of time,[*] and in fact, it can be avoided. Doing a file test, `stat`, or `lstat` on the special _ filehandle (that is, the operand is nothing but a single underscore) tells Perl to use whatever happened to be lounging around in memory from the previous file test, `stat`, or `lstat` function, rather than going out to the operating system again. Sometimes this is dangerous: a subroutine call can invoke `stat` without your knowledge, blowing your buffer away. But if you're careful, you can save yourself a few unneeded system calls, thereby making your program considerably faster. Here's that example of finding files to put on the backup tapes again, using the new tricks we've learned:

```
my @original_files = qw/ fred barney betty wilma pebbles dino bamm-bamm /;
my @big_old_files;                       # The ones we want to put on backup tapes
foreach (@original_files) {
  push @big_old_files, $_
    if (-s) > 100_000 and -A _ > 90;     # More efficient than before
}
```

Note that we used the default of `$_` for the first test—this is no more efficient (except perhaps for the programmer), but it gets the data from the operating system. The second test uses the magic _ filehandle; for this test, the data left around after getting the file's size is used, which is exactly what we want.

Note that testing the _ filehandle is not the same as allowing the operand of a file test, `stat`, or `lstat` to default to testing `$_`; using `$_` would be a fresh test each time on the current file named by the contents of `$_`, but using _ saves the trouble of calling the system again. Here is another case where similar names were chosen for radically different functions. By now, you are probably used to it.

---

[*] Because it is. Asking the system for information is relatively slow.

Exercises

See Appendix A for answers to the following exercises:

1. [20] Make a program which asks the user for a source file name, a destination file name, a search pattern, and a replacement string. (Be sure to ask the user interactively for these; don't get them from the command-line arguments.) Your program should read the source file and write it out as the destination file, replacing the search pattern with the replacement string wherever it appears. That is, the destination file will be a modified duplicate of the source file. Can you overwrite an existing file (not the same as the input file)? Can you use regular expression metacharacters in the search pattern? (That is, can you enter `(fred|wilma) flintstone` to search for either name?) Can you use the memory variables and backslash escapes in the replacement string? (That is, can you use `\u\L$1\E Flintstone` as the replacement string to properly capitalize the names of Fred and Wilma?) Don't worry if you can't accomplish each of these things; it's more important simply to see what happens when you try.

2. [15] Make a program which takes a list of files named on the command line and reports for each one whether it's readable, writable, executable, or doesn't exist. (Hint: It may be helpful to have a function which will do all of the file tests for one file at a time.) What does it report about a file which has been *chmod*'ed to 0? (That is, if you're on a Unix system, use the command *chmod 0 some_file* to mark that file as neither being readable, writable, nor executable.) In most shells, use a star as the argument to mean all of the normal files in the current directory. That is, you could type something like `./ex11-2 *` to ask the program for the attributes of many files at once.

3. [10] Make a program to identify the oldest file named on the command line and report its age in days. What does it do if the list is empty? (That is, if no files are mentioned on the command line.)

12

Directory Operations

The files we created in the previous chapter were generally in the same place as our program. But modern operating systems let us organize files into directories, allowing us to keep our Beatles MP3s away from our important Llama book chapter sources so that we don't accidentally send an MP3 file to the publisher. Perl lets you manipulate these directories directly, in ways that are even fairly portable from one operating system to another.

Moving Around the Directory Tree

Your program runs with a "working directory," which is the starting point for relative pathnames. That is, if you refer to the file **fred**, that means "**fred** in the current working directory."

The **chdir** operator changes the working directory. It's just like the Unix shell's *cd* command:

```
chdir "/etc" or die "cannot chdir to /etc: $!";
```

Because this is a system request, the value of **$!** will be set if an error occurs. You should normally check **$!** when a false value is returned from **chdir**, since that indicates that something has not gone as requested.

The working directory is inherited by all processes that Perl starts (we'll talk more about that in Chapter 14). However, the change in working directory cannot affect the process that invoked Perl, such as the shell.* So you can't make a Perl program to replace your shell's *cd* command.

---

* This isn't a limitation on Perl's part; it's actually a feature of Unix, Windows, and other systems. If you really need to change the shell's working directory, see the documentation of your shell.

If you omit the parameter, Perl determines your home directory as best as possible and attempts to set the working directory to your home directory, similar to using the *cd* command at the shell without a parameter. This is one of the few places where omitting the parameter doesn't use $_.

Some shells permit you to use a tilde-prefixed path with *cd* to use another user's home directory as a starting point (like cd ~merlyn). This is a function of the shell, not the operating system, and Perl is calling the operating system directly. Thus, a tilde-prefix will not work with chdir.

Globbing

Normally, the shell expands any filename patterns on each command line into the matching filenames. This is called *globbing*. For example, if you give a filename pattern of *.pm to the *echo* command, the shell expands this list to a list of names that match:

```
$ echo *.pm
barney.pm dino.pm fred.pm wilma.pm
$
```

The *echo* command doesn't have to know anything about expanding *.pm, because the shell has already expanded it. This works even for your Perl programs:

```
$ cat >show-args
foreach $arg (@ARGV) {
  print "one arg is $arg\n";
}
^D
$ perl show-args *.pm
one arg is barney.pm
one arg is dino.pm
one arg is fred.pm
one arg is wilma.pm
$
```

Note that *show-args* didn't need to know anything about globbing—the names were already expanded in @ARGV.

But sometimes we end up with a pattern like *.pm inside our Perl program. Can we expand this pattern into the matching filenames without working very hard? Sure—just use the glob operator:

```
my @all_files = glob "*";
my @pm_files = glob "*.pm";
```

Here, @all_files gets all the files in the current directory, alphabetically sorted, and not including the files beginning with a period, just like the shell. And @pm_files gets the same list as we got before by using *.pm on the command line.

In fact, anything you can say on the command line, you can also put as the (single) argument to `glob`, including multiple patterns separated by spaces:

```
my @all_files_including_dot = glob ".* *";
```

Here, we've included an additional "dot star" parameter to get the filenames that begin with a dot as well as the ones that don't. Please note that the space between these two items inside the quoted string is significant, as it separates two different items to be globbed.*

The reason this works exactly as the shell works is that prior to Perl Version 5.6, the `glob` operator simply called */bin/csh*† behind the scenes to perform the expansion. Because of this, globs were time-consuming and could break in large directories, or in some other cases. Conscientious Perl hackers avoided globbing in favor of directory handles, which will be discussed in "Directory Handles" later in this chapter. However, if you're using a modern version of Perl, you should no longer be concerned about such things.

An Alternate Syntax for Globbing

Although we use the term globbing freely, and we talk about the `glob` operator, you might not see the word `glob` in very many of the programs that use globbing. Why not? Well, most legacy code was written before the `glob` operator was given a name. Instead, it was called up by the angle-bracket syntax, similar to reading from a filehandle:

```
my @all_files = <*>; ## exactly the same as my @all_files = glob "*";
```

The value between the angle brackets is interpolated similar to a double-quoted string, which means that Perl variables are expanded to their current Perl values before being globbed:

```
my $dir = "/etc";
my @dir_files = <$dir/* $dir/.*>;
```

Here, we've fetched all the non-dot and dot files from the designated directory, because `$dir` has been expanded to its current value.

So, if using angle brackets means both filehandle reading and globbing, how does Perl decide which of the two operators to use? Well, a filehandle has to be a Perl

---

* Windows users may be accustomed to using a glob of *.* to mean "all files". But that actually means "all files with a dot in their names," even in Perl on Windows.

† Or it will call a valid substitute if a C-shell wasn't available.

identifier. So if the item between the angle brackets is strictly a Perl identifier, it's a filehandle read; otherwise, it's a globbing operation. For example:

```
my @files = <FRED/*>;   ## a glob
my @lines = <FRED>;     ## a filehandle read
my $name = "FRED";
my @files = <$name/*>; ## a glob
```

The one exception is if the contents are a simple scalar variable (not an element of a hash or array), then it's an *indirect filehandle read,** where the variable contents give the name of the filehandle to be read:

```
my $name = "FRED";
my @lines = <$name>; ## an indirect filehandle read of FRED handle
```

Determining whether it's a glob or a filehandle read is made at compile time, and thus it is independent of the content of the variables.

If you want, you can get the operation of an indirect filehandle read using the `readline` operator,† which also makes it clearer:

```
my $name = "FRED";
my @lines = readline FRED;  ## read from FRED
my @lines = readline $name; ## read from FRED
```

But the `readline` operator is rarely used, as indirect filehandle reads are uncommon and are generally performed against a simple scalar variable anyway.

Directory Handles

Another way to get a list of names from a given directory is with a *directory handle*. A directory handle looks and acts like a filehandle. You open it (with `opendir` instead of `open`), you read from it (with `readdir` instead of `readline`), and you close it (with `closedir` instead of `close`). But instead of reading the contents of a file, you're reading the *names* of files (and other things) in a directory. For example:

```
my $dir_to_process = "/etc";
opendir DH, $dir or die "Cannot open $dir: $!";
foreach $file (readdir DH) {
  print "one file in $dir is $file\n";
}
closedir DH;
```

---

* If the indirect handle is a text string, then it's subject to the "symbolic reference" test that is forbidden under `use strict`. However, the indirect handle might also be a typeglob or reference to an IO object, and then it would work even under `use strict`.

† If you're using Perl 5.005 or later.

Like filehandles, directory handles are automatically closed at the end of the program or if the directory handle is reopened onto another directory.

Unlike globbing, which in older versions of Perl fired off a separate process, a directory handle never fires off another process. So it makes them more efficient for applications that demand every ounce of power from the machine. However, it's also a lower-level operation, meaning that we have to do more of the work ourselves.

For example, the names are returned in no particular order.* And the list includes all files, not just those matching a particular pattern (like `*.pm` from our globbing examples). And the list includes all files, especially the dot files, and particularly the dot and dot-dot entries.†

So, if we wanted only the *pm*-ending files, we could use a skip-over function inside the loop:

```
while ($name = readdir DIR) {
  next unless $name =~ /\.pm$/;
  ... more processing ...
}
```

Note here that the syntax is that of a regular expression, not a glob. And if we wanted all the non-dot files, we could say that:

```
next if $name =~ /^\./;
```

Or if we wanted everything but the common dot (current directory) and dot-dot (parent directory) entries, we could explicitly say that:

```
next if $name eq "." or $name eq "..";
```

Now we'll look at the part that gets most people mixed up, so pay close attention. The filenames returned by the **readdir** operator have *no* pathname component. It's just the *name* within the directory. So, we're not looking at */etc/passwd*, we're just looking at *passwd*. (And because this is another difference from the globbing operation, it's easy to see how people get confused.)

So you'll need to patch up the name to get the full name:

```
opendir SOMEDIR, $dirname or die "Cannot open $dirname: $!";
while (my $name = readdir SOMEDIR) {
  next if $name =~ /^\./; # skip over dot files
  $name = "$dirname/$name"; # patch up the path
  next unless -f $name and -r $name; # only readable files
  ...
}
```

---

* It's actually the unsorted order of the directory entries, similar to the order you get from *ls -f* or *find*.

† Do not make the mistake of many old Unix programs and presume that dot and dot-dot are always returned as the first two entries (sorted or not). If that hadn't even occurred to you, pretend we never said it, because it's a false presumption. In fact, we're now sorry for even bringing it up.

Without the patch, the file tests would have been checking files in the current directory, rather than in the directory named in `$dirname`. This is the single most-common mistake when using directory handles.

Recursive Directory Listing

You probably won't need recursive directory access for the first few dozen hours of your Perl programming career. So rather than distract you with the possibility of replacing all those ugly *find* scripts with Perl right now, we'll simply entice you by saying that Perl comes with a nice library called `File::Find`, which you can use for nifty recursive directory processing. We're also saying this to keep you from writing your own routines, which everyone seems to want to do after those first few dozen hours of programming, and then getting puzzled about things like "local directory handles" and "how do I change my directory back?" So, when you're ready, the knowledge will come, but stay with us to learn about Manipulating Files and Directories (in the next chapter) instead, right after you finish these exercises.

Exercises

See Appendix A for answers to the following exercises.

1. [12] Write a program to ask the user for a directory name, then change to that directory. If the user enters a line with nothing but whitespace, change to his or her home directory as a default. After changing, list the ordinary directory contents (not the items whose names begin with a dot) in alphabetical order. (Hint: Will that be easier to do with a directory handle or with a glob?) If the directory change doesn't succeed, just alert the user—but don't try show the contents.

2. [4] Modify the program to include all files, not just the ones that don't begin with a dot.

3. [5] If you used a directory handle for the previous exercise, rewrite it to use a glob. Or if you used a glob, try it now with a directory handle.

13

Manipulating Files and Directories

Perl is commonly used to wrangle files and directories. Because Perl grew up in a Unix environment and still spends most of its time there, most of the description in this chapter may seem Unix-centric. But the nice thing is that to whatever degree possible, Perl works exactly the same way on non-Unix systems.

And now a word of warning—some cultures consider the number "13" to be very unlucky. We deliberately placed this material as Chapter 13 of this book, since we're about to do some pretty dangerous things if bugs creep into the code (like remove files without a chance of recovery), so be very careful when you're playing with the exercises.

Removing Files

Most of the time, we make files so that the data can stay around for a while. But when the data has outlived its life, it's time to make the file go away. At the Unix shell level, we'd type an *rm* command to remove a file or files:

```
$ rm slate bedrock lava
```

In Perl, we use the `unlink` operator:

```
unlink "slate", "bedrock", "lava";
```

This sends the three named files away to bit heaven, never to be seen again.

Now, since `unlink` takes a list, and the `glob` function (described in Chapter 12) returns a list, we can combine the two to delete many files at once:

```
unlink glob "*.o";
```

This is similar to `rm *.o` at the shell, except that we didn't have to fire off a separate *rm* process. So we can make those important files go away that much faster!

The return value from **unlink** tells us how many files have been successfully deleted. So, back to the first example, we can check its success:

```
my $successful = unlink "slate", "bedrock", "lava";
print "I deleted $successful file(s) just now\n";
```

Sure, if this number is 3, we know it removed all of the files, and if it's 0, then we removed none of them. But what if it's 1 or 2? Well, there's no clue which ones were removed. If you need to know, do them one at a time in a loop:

```
foreach my $file (qw(slate bedrock lava)) {
  unlink $file or warn "failed on $file: $!\n";
}
```

Here, each file being deleted one at a time means the return value will be 0 (failed) or 1 (succeeded), which happens to look like a nice Boolean value, controlling the execution of **warn**. Using **or warn** is similar to **or die**, except that it's not fatal, of course (as we said back in Chapter 11). In this case, we put the newline on the end of the message to warn, because it's not a bug in *our* program that causes the message.

When a particular **unlink** fails, the **$!** variable is set to something related to the operating system error, which we've included in the message. This makes sense to use only when doing one filename at a time, because the next operating system failed request resets the variable. You can't remove a directory with **unlink** (just like you can't remove a directory with the simple *rm* invocation either). Look for the **rmdir** function coming up shortly for that.

Now, here's a little-known Unix fact. It turns out that you can have a file that you can't read, you can't write, you can't execute, maybe you don't even own the file—that is, it's somebody else's file altogether—but you can still delete the file. That's because the permission to unlink a file doesn't depend upon the permission bits on the file itself; it's the permission bits on the directory that contains the file that matter.

We mention this because it's normal for a beginning Perl programmer, in the course of trying out **unlink**, to make a file, to *chmod* it to 0 (so that it's not readable or writable), and then to see whether this makes **unlink** fail. But instead it vanishes without so much as a whimper.* If you really want to see a failed **unlink**, though, just try to remove */etc/passwd* or a similar system file. Since that's a file controlled by the system administrator, you won't be able to remove it.†

---

* Some of these folks know that *rm* would generally ask before deleting such a file. But *rm* is a command, and **unlink** is a system call. System calls never ask permission, and they never say they're sorry.

† Of course, if you're silly enough to try this kind of thing when you are logged in as the system administrator, you deserve what you get.

Renaming Files

Giving an existing file a new name is simple with the **rename** function:

```
rename "old", "new";
```

This is similar to the Unix *mv* command, taking a file named *old* and giving it the name *new* in the same directory. You can even move things around:

```
rename "over_there/some/place/some_file", "some_file";
```

This moves a file called **some_file** from another directory into the current directory, provided the user running the program has the appropriate permissions.[*]

Like most functions that request something of the operating system, **rename** returns false if it fails, and sets **$!** with the operating system error, so you can (and often should) use **or die** (or **or warn**) to report this to the user.

One frequent[†] question in the Unix shell-usage newsgroups is how to rename everything that ends with "**.old**" to the same name with "**.new**". Here's how to do it in Perl nicely:

```
foreach my $file (glob "*.old") {
  my $newfile = $file;
  $newfile =~ s/\.old$/.new/;
  if (-e $newfile) {
    warn "can't rename $file to $newfile: $newfile exists\n";
  } elsif (rename $file, $newfile) {
    ## success, do nothing
  } else {
    warn "rename $file to $newfile failed: $!\n";
  }
}
```

The check for the existence of **$newfile** is needed because **rename** will happily rename a file right over the top of an existing file, presuming the user has permission to remove the destination filename. We put the check in so that it's less likely that we'll lose information this way. Of course, if you *wanted* to replace existing files like *wilma.new*, you wouldn't bother testing with **-e** first.

---

[*] And the files must reside on the same filesystem. We'll see why this rule exists a little later in this chapter.

[†] This isn't just any old frequent question; the question of renaming a batch of files at once is the *most-*frequent question asked in these newsgroups. And that's why it's the *first* question answered in the FAQs for those newsgroups. And yet, it stays in first place. Hmmm.

Those first two lines inside the loop can be combined (and often are) to simply be:

```
(my $newfile = $file) =~ s/\.old$/.new/;
```

This works to declare `$newfile`, copy its initial value from `$file`, then select `$newfile` to be modified by the substitution. You can read this as "transform `$file` to `$newfile` using this replacement on the right." And yes, because of precedence, those parentheses are required.

Also, some programmers seeing this substitution for the first time wonder why the backslash is needed on the left, but not on the right. The two sides aren't symmetrical: the left part of a substitution is a regular expression, and the right part is a double-quotish string. So we use the pattern `/\.old$/` to mean ".old anchored at the end of the string" (anchored at the end, because we don't want to rename the *first* occurrance of `.old` in a file called *betty.old.old*), but on the right we can simply write `.new` to make the replacement.

Links and Files

To understand more about what's going on with files and directories, it helps to understand the Unix model of files and directories, even if your non-Unix system doesn't work in exactly this way. As usual, there's more to the story than we're able to explain here, so check any good book on Unix internal details if you need the full story.

A *mounted volume* is a hard disk drive (or something else that works more-or-less like that, such as a disk partition, a floppy disk, a CD-ROM, or a DVD-ROM). It may contain any number of files and directories. Each file is stored in a numbered *inode*, which we can think of as a particular piece of disk real estate. One file might be stored in inode 613, while another is in inode 7033.

To locate a particular file, though, we'll have to look it up in a directory. A directory is a special kind of file, maintained by the system. Essentially, it is a table of filenames and their inode numbers.* Along with the other things in the directory, there are always two special directory entries. One is `.` (called "dot"), which is the name of that very directory; and the other is `..` ("dot-dot"), which is the directory one step higher in the hierarchy (i.e., the directory's parent directory).†

---

* On Unix systems (others don't generally have inodes, hard links, and such), you can use the *ls* command's *-i* option to see files' inode numbers. Try a command like *ls -ail*. When two or more inode numbers are the same for multiple items on a given filesystem, there's really just one file involved, one piece of the disk.

† The Unix system *root* directory has no parent. In that directory, `..` is the same directory as `.`, which is the system *root* directory itself.

Figure 13-1 provides an illustration of two inodes. One is for a file called *chicken*, and the other is Barney's directory of poems, */home/barney/poems*, which contains that file. The file is stored in inode 613, while the directory is stored in inode 919. (The directory's own name, *poems*, doesn't appear in the illustration, because that's stored in another directory.) The directory contains entries for three files (including *chicken*) and two directories (one of which is the reference back to the directory itself, in inode 919), along with each item's inode number.

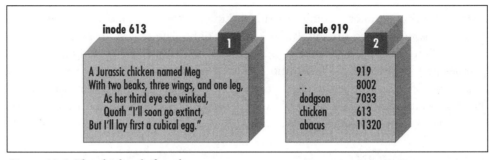

Figure 13-1. The chicken before the egg

When it's time to make a new file in a given directory, the system adds an entry with the file's name and the number of a new inode. How can the system tell that a particular inode is available, though? Each inode holds a number called its *link count*. The link count is always zero if the inode isn't listed in any directory, so any inode with a link count of zero is available for new file storage. When the inode is added to a directory, the link count is incremented; when the listing is removed, the link count is decremented. For the file *chicken* as illustrated above, the inode count of 1 is shown in the box above the inode's data.

But some inodes have more than one listing. For example, we've already seen that each directory entry includes **.**, which points back to that directory's own inode. So the link count for a directory should always be at least two: its listing in its parent directory and its listing in itself. In addition, if it has subdirectories, each of those will add a link, since each will contain **...**.* In Figure 13-1, the directory's inode count of 2 is shown in the box above its data. A link count is the number of true names for the inode.†

---

* This implies that the link count of a directory is always equal to two plus the number of directories it contains. On some systems that's true, in fact, but some other systems work differently.

† In the traditional output of *ls -l*, the number of hard links to the item appears just to the right of the permission flags (like "`-rwxr-xr-x`"). Now you know why this number is more than one for directories and nearly always 1 for ordinary files.

Could an ordinary file inode have more than one listing in the directory? It certainly could. Suppose that, working in the directory shown above, Barney uses the Perl's `link` function to create a new link:

```
link "chicken", "egg"
    or warn "can't link chicken to egg: $!";
```

This is similar to typing "`ln chicken egg`" at the Unix shell prompt. If `link` succeeds, it returns true. If it fails, it returns false and sets `$!`, which Barney is checking in the error message. After this runs, the name *egg* is another name for the file *chicken*, and vice versa; neither name is "more real" than the other, and (as you may have guessed) it would take some detective work to find out which came first. Figure 13-2 shows a picture of the new situation, where there are two links to inode 613.

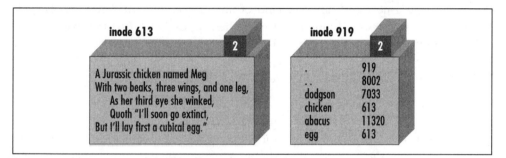

Figure 13-2. The egg is linked to the chicken

These two filenames are thus talking about the same place on the disk. If the file *chicken* holds 200 bytes of data, *egg* holds the same 200 bytes, for a total of 200 bytes (since it's really just one file with two names). If Barney appends a new line of text to file *egg*, that line will also appear at the end of *chicken*.*

Now, if Barney were to accidentally (or intentionally) delete *chicken*, that data will not be lost—it's still available under the name *egg*. And vice versa: if he were to delete *egg*, he'd still have *chicken*. Of course, if he deletes both of them, the data will be lost.†

There's another rule about the links in directory listings: the inode numbers in a given directory listing all refer to inodes on that same mounted volume.‡ This rule

---

* If you experiment with making links and changing text files, be aware that most text editors don't edit the file "in place" but instead save a modified copy. If Barney were to edit *egg* with a text editor, he'd most likely end up with a new file called *egg* and the old file called *chicken*—two separate files, rather than two links to the same file.

† Although the system won't necessarily overwrite this inode right away, there's no easy way in general to get the data back once the link count has gone to zero. Have you made a backup recently?

‡ The one exception is the special `..` entry in the volume's *root* directory, which refers to the directory in which that volume is mounted.

ensures that if the physical medium (the diskette, perhaps) is moved to another machine, all of the directories stick together with their files. That's why you can use **rename** to move a file from one directory to another, but only if both directories are on the same filesystem (mounted volume). If they were on different disks, the inode's data would have to be relocated, which is too complex an operation for a simple system call.

And yet another restriction on links is that they can't make new names for directories. That's because the directories are arranged in a hierarchy. If you were able to change that, utility programs like *find* and *pwd* could easily become lost trying to find their way around the filesystem.

So, links can't be added to directories, and they can't cross from one mounted volume to another. Fortunately, there's a way to get around these restrictions on links, by using a new and different kind of link: a *symbolic link.** A symbolic link (also called a *soft link* to distinguish it from the true or *hard links* that we've been talking about up to now) is a special entry in a directory that tells the system to look elsewhere. Let's say that Barney (working in the same directory of poems as before) creates a symbolic link with Perl's **symlink** function, like this:

```
symlink "dodgson", "carroll"
    or warn "can't symlink dodgson to carroll: $!";
```

This is similar to what would happen if Barney used the command "*ln -s dodgson carroll*" from the shell. Figure 13-3 shows a picture of the result, including the poem in inode 7033.

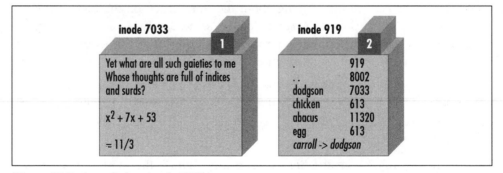

Figure 13-3. A symlink to inode 7033

Now if Barney chooses to read */home/barney/poems/carroll*, he gets the same data as if he had opened */home/barney/poems/dodgson*, because the system follows the symbolic link automatically. But that new name isn't the "real" name of the file, because (as you can see in the diagram) the link count on inode 7033 is still just

---

* Some very old Unix systems don't support symlinks, but those are pretty rare nowadays.

one. That's because the symbolic link simply tells the system, "If you got here looking for *carroll*, now you want to go off to find something called *dodgson* instead."

A symbolic link can freely cross mounted filesystems or provide a new name for a directory, unlike a hard link. In fact, a symbolic link could point to any filename, one in this directory or in another one—or even to a file that doesn't exist! But that also means that a soft link can't keep data from being lost as a hard link can, since the symlink doesn't contribute to the link count. If Barney were to delete *dodgson*, the system would no longer be able to follow the soft link.* Even though there would still be an entry called *carroll*, trying to read from it would give an error like `file not found`. The file test `-l 'carroll'` would report true, but `-e 'carroll'` would be false: it's a symlink, but it doesn't exist.

Since a soft link could point to a file that doesn't yet exist, it could be used when creating a file as well. Barney has most of his files in his home directory, */home/barney*, but he also needs frequent access to a directory with a long name that is difficult to type: */usr/local/opt/system/httpd/root-dev/users/staging/barney/cgi-bin*. So he sets up a symlink named */home/barney/my_stuff*, which points to that long name, and now it's easy for him to get to it. If he creates a file (from his home directory) called *my_stuff/bowling*, that file's real name is */usr/local/opt/system/httpd/root-dev/users/staging/barney/cgi-bin/bowling*. Next week, when the system administrator moves these files of Barney's to */usr/local/opt/internal/httpd/www-dev/users/staging/barney/cgi-bin*, Barney just repoints the one symlink, and now he and all of his programs can still find his files with ease.

It's normal for either */usr/bin/perl* or */usr/local/bin/perl* (or both) to be symbolic links to the true Perl binary on your system. This makes it easy to switch to a new version of Perl. Say you're the system administrator, and you've built the new Perl. Of course, your older version is still running, and you don't want to disrupt anything. When you're ready for the switch, you simply move a symlink or two, and now every program that begins with `#!/usr/bin/perl` will automatically use the new version. In the unlikely case that there's some problem, it's a simple thing to replace the old symlinks and have the older Perl running the show again. (But, like any good admin, you notified your users to test their code with the new */usr/bin/perl-7.2* well in advance of the switch, and you told them that they can keep using the older one during the next month's grace period by changing their programs' first lines to `#!/usr/bin/perl-6.1`, if they need to.)

Perhaps suprisingly, both hard and soft links are very useful. Many non-Unix operating systems have neither, and the lack is sorely felt. On some non-Unix systems,

---

* Deleting *carroll* would merely remove the symlink, of course.

symbolic links may be implemented as a "shortcut" or an "alias"—check the *perlport* manpage for the latest details.

To find out where a symbolic link is pointing, use the `readlink` function. This will tell you where the symlink leads, or it will return `undef` if its argument wasn't a symlink:

```
my $where = readlink "carroll";           # Gives "dodgson"

my $perl = readlink "/usr/local/bin/perl";  # Maybe tells where perl is
```

You can remove either kind of link with `unlink`—and now you see where that operation gets its name. `unlink` simply removes the directory entry associated with the given filename, decrementing the link count and thus possibly freeing the inode.

Making and Removing Directories

Making a directory inside an existing directory is easy. Just invoke the `mkdir` function:

```
mkdir "fred", 0755 or warn "Cannot make fred directory: $!";
```

Again, true means success, and `$!` is set on failure.

But what's that second parameter, 0755? That's the initial permission setting[*] on the newly created directory (you can always change it later). The value here is specified as an octal value because the value will be interpreted as a Unix permission value, which has a meaning based on groups of three bits each, and octal values represent that nicely. Yes, even on Windows or MacPerl, you still need to know a little about Unix permissions values to use the `mkdir` function. Mode 0755 is a good one to use, because it gives you full permission, but lets everyone else have read access but no permission to change anything.

The `mkdir` function doesn't require you to specify this value in octal—it's just looking for a numeric value (either a literal or a calculation). But unless you can quickly can figure that 0755 octal is 493 decimal in your head, it's probably easier to let Perl calculate that. And if you accidentally leave off the leading zero, you get 755 decimal, which is 1363 octal, a strange permission combination indeed.

---

[*] The permission value is modified by the umask value in the usual way. See umask(2) for further information.

As we saw earlier (in Chapter 2), a string value being used as a number is never interpreted as octal, even if it starts with a leading 0. So this doesn't work:

```
my $name = "fred";
my $permissions = "0755";  # danger... this isn't working
mkdir $name, $permissions;
```

Oops, we just created a directory with that bizarre 01363 permissions, because 0755 was treated as decimal. To fix that, use the oct function, which forces octal interpretation of a string whether or not there's a leading zero:

```
mkdir $name, oct($permissions);
```

Of course, if you are specifying the permission value directly within the program, just use a number instead of a string. The need for the extra oct function shows up most often when the value comes from user input. For example, suppose we take the arguments from the command line:

```
my ($name, $perm) = @ARGV;  # first two args are name, permissions
mkdir $name, oct($perm) or die "cannot create $name: $!";
```

The value here for $perm is interpreted as a string initially, and thus the oct function interprets the common octal representation properly.

To remove empty directories, use the rmdir function in a manner similar to the unlink function:

```
rmdir glob "fred/*";  # remove all empty directories below fred/

foreach my $dir (qw(fred barney betty)) {
  rmdir $dir or warn "cannot rmdir $dir: $!\n";
}
```

As with unlink, rmdir returns the number of directories removed, and if invoked with a single name, sets $! in a reasonable manner on a failure.

The rmdir operator fails for non-empty directories. As a first pass, you can attempt to delete the contents of the directory with unlink, then try to remove what should now be an empty directory. For example, suppose we need a place to write many temporary files during the execution of a program:

```
my $temp_dir = "/tmp/scratch_$$";        # based on process ID; see the text
mkdir $temp_dir, 0700 or die "cannot create $temp_dir: $!";
...
# use $temp_dir as location of all temporary files
...
unlink glob "$temp_dir/* $temp_dir/.*"; # delete contents of $temp_dir
rmdir $temp_dir;                         # delete now-empty directory
```

The initial temporary directory name includes the current process ID, which is unique for every running process and is accessed with the $$ variable (similar to the shell). We do this to avoid colliding with any other processes, as long as they also include their process ID as part of their pathname as well. (In fact, it's common to use the program's name as well as the process ID, so if the program is called quarry, the directory would probably be something like /tmp/quarry_$$.)

At the end of the program, that last unlink should remove all the files in this temporary directory, and then the rmdir function can delete the then-empty directory. However, if we've created subdirectories under that directory, the unlink operator fails on those, and the rmdir also fails. For a more robust solution, check out the rmtree function provided by the File::Path module of the standard distribution.

Modifying Permissions

The Unix *chmod* command changes the permissions on a file or directory. Similarly, Perl has the chmod function to perform this task:

```
chmod 0755, "fred", "barney";
```

As with many of the operating system interface functions, chmod returns the number of items successfully altered, and when used with a single argument, sets $! in a sensible way for error messages when it fails. The first parameter is the Unix permission value (even for non-Unix versions of Perl). For the same reasons we presented earlier in describing mkdir, this value is usually specified in octal.

Symbolic permissions (like *+x* or *go=u-w*) accepted by the Unix *chmod* command are not valid for the chmod function.*

Changing Ownership

If the operating system permits it, you may change the ownership and group membership of a list of files with the chown function. The user and group are both changed at once, and both have to be the numeric user-ID and group-ID values. For example:

```
my $user = 1004;
my $group = 100;
chown $user, $group, glob "*.o";
```

What if you have a username like merlyn instead of the number? Simple. Just call the getpwnam function to translate the name into a number, and the corresponding getgrnam† to translate the group name into its number:

---

* Unless you've installed and invoke the File::chmod module from CPAN, which can apparently upgrade the chmod operator to understand symbolic mode values.

† These two are among the ugliest function names known to mankind. But don't blame Larry for them; he's just giving them the same names that the folks at Berkeley did.

```
defined(my $user = getpwnam "merlyn") or die "bad user";
defined(my $group = getgrnam "users") or die "bad group";
chown $user, $group, glob "/home/merlyn/*";
```

The **defined** function verifies that the return value is not **undef**, which will be returned if the requested user or group is not valid.

The **chown** function returns the number of files affected, and it sets $! on error.

Changing Timestamps

In those rare cases when you want to lie to other programs about when a file was most recently modified or accessed, you can use the **utime** function to fudge the books a bit. The first two arguments give the new access time and modification time, while the remaining arguments are the list of filenames to alter to those timestamps. The times are specified in internal timestamp format (the same type of values returned from the **stat** function that we mentioned in Chapter 12).

One convenient value to use for the timestamps is "right now", returned in the proper format by the **time** function. So to update all the files in the current directory to look like they were modified a day ago, but accessed just now, we could simply do this:

```
my $now = time;
my $ago = $now - 24 * 60 * 60;  # seconds per day
utime $now, $ago, glob "*";     # set access to now, mod to a day ago
```

Of course, nothing stops you from creating a file that is arbitrarily stamped far in the future or past (within the limits of the Unix timestamp values of 1970 to 2038, or whatever your non-Unix system uses, until we get 64-bit timestamps). Maybe you could use this to create a directory where you keep your notes for that time-travel novel you're writing.

The third timestamp (the ctime value) is always set to "now" whenever anything alters a file, so there's no way to set it (it would have to be reset to "now" after you set it) with the **utime** function. That's because it's primary purpose is for incremental backups: if the file's ctime is newer than the date on the backup tape, it's time to back it up again.

Using Simple Modules

Suppose that you've got a long filename like */usr/local/bin/perl* in your program, and you need to find out the *basename*. That's easy enough, since the basename is everything after the last slash (it's just "*perl*" in this case):

```
my $name = "/usr/local/bin/perl";
(my $basename = $name) =~ s#.*/##;  # Oops!
```

As we saw earlier, first Perl will do the assignment inside the parentheses, then it will do the substitution. The substitution is supposed to replace any string ending with a slash (that is, the directory name portion) with an empty string, leaving just the basename.

And if you try this, it seems to work. Well, it *seems* to, but actually, there are three problems.

First, a Unix file or directory name could contain a newline character. (It's not something that's likely to happen by accident, but it's permitted.) So, since the regular expression dot (".") can't match a newline, a filename like the string `"/home/fred/flintstone\n/brontosaurus"` won't work right—that code would think the basename is `"flintstone\n/brontosaurus"`. You could fix that with the `/s` option to the pattern (if you remembered about this subtle and infrequent case), making the substitution look like this: `s#.*/##s`

The second problem is that this is Unix-specific. It assumes that the forward slash will always be the directory separator, as it is on Unix, and not the backslash or colon that some systems use.

And the third (and biggest) problem with this is that we're trying to solve a problem that someone else has already solved. Perl comes with a number of *modules*, which are smart extensions to Perl that add to its functionality. And if those aren't enough, there are many other useful modules available on CPAN, with new ones being added every week. You (or, better yet, your system administrator) can install them if you need their functionality.

In the rest of this section, we'll show you how to use some of the features of a couple of simple modules that come with Perl. (There's more that these modules can do; this is just an overview to illustrate the general principles of how to use a simple module.)

Alas, we can't show you everything you'd need to know about using modules in general, since you'd have to understand advanced topics like references and objects in order to use some modules.* But this section should prepare you for using many simple modules. Further information on some interesting and useful modules is included in Appendix B.

The File::Basename Module

In the previous example, we found the basename of a filename in a way that's not portable. We showed that something that seemed straightforward was susceptible

---

* As we'll see in the next few pages, though, you may be able to use a module that uses objects and references without having to understand those advanced topics.

to subtle mistaken assumptions (here, the assumption was that newlines would never appear in file or directory names). And we were re-inventing the wheel, solving a problem that others have solved (and debugged) many times before us.

Here's a better way to extract the basename of a filename. Perl comes with a module called `File::Basename`. With the command *perldoc File::Basename*, or with your system's documentation system, you can read about what it does. That's the first step when using a new module. (It's often the third and fifth step, as well.)

Soon you're ready to use it, so you declare it with a **use** directive near the top of your program:[*]

```
use File::Basename;
```

During compilation, Perl sees that line and loads up the module. Now, it's as if Perl has some new functions that you may use in the remainder of your program.[†] The one we wanted in the earlier example is the **basename** function itself:

```
my $name = "/usr/local/bin/perl";
my $basename = basename $name;  # gives 'perl'
```

Well, that worked for Unix. What if our program were running on MacPerl or Windows or VMS, to name a few? There's no problem—this module can tell which kind of machine you're using, and it uses that machine's filename rules by default. (Of course, you'd have that machine's kind of filename string in `$name`, in that case.)

There are some related functions also provided by this module. One is the **dirname** function, which pulls the directory name from a full filename. The module also lets you separate a filename from its extension, or change the default set of filename rules.[‡]

Using Only Some Functions from a Module

Suppose you discovered that when you went to add the `File::Basename` module to your existing program, you already have a subroutine called **&dirname**—that is,

---

[*] It's traditional to declare modules near the top of the file, since that makes it easy for the maintenance programmer to see which modules you'll be using. That greatly simplifies matters when it's time to install your program on a new machine, for example.

[†] You guessed it: there's more to the story, having to do with packages and fully qualified names. When your programs are growing beyond a few hundred lines in the main program (not counting code in modules), which is quite large in Perl, you should probably read up about these advanced features. Start with the *perlmod* manpage.

[‡] You might need to change the filename rules if you were trying to work with a Unix machine's filenames from a Windows machine—perhaps while sending commands over an FTP connection, for example.

you already have a subroutine with the same name as one of the module's functions.* Now there's trouble, because the new dirname is *also* implemented as a
Perl subroutine (inside the module). What do you do?

Simply give File::Basename, in your use declaration, an *import list* showing
exactly which function names it should give you, and it'll supply those and no
others. Here, we'll get nothing but basename:

```
use File::Basename qw/ basename /;
```

And here, we'll ask for no new functions at all:

```
use File::Basename qw/ /;
```

Why would you want to do that? Well, this directive tells Perl to load up File::
Basename, just as before, but not to *import* any function names. Importing lets us
use the short, simple function names like basename and dirname. But even if we
don't import those names, we can still use the functions. When they're not
imported, though, we have to call them by their full names:

```
use File::Basename qw/ /;                      # import no function names

my $betty = &dirname($wilma);                  # uses our own subroutine &dirname
(not shown)

my $name = "/usr/local/bin/perl";
my $dirname = File::Basename::dirname $name;   # dirname from the module
```

As you see, the full name of the dirname function from the module is File::
Basename::dirname. We can always use the function's full name (once we've
loaded the module) whether we've imported the short name dirname or not.

Most of the time, you'll want to use a module's default import list. But you can
always override that with a list of your own, if you want to leave out some of the
default items. Another reason to supply your own list would be if you wanted to
import some function not on the default list, since most modules include some
(infrequently needed) functions that are not on the default import list.

As you'd guess, some modules will, by default, import more symbols than others.
Each module's documentation should make it clear which symbols it imports, if
any, but you are always free to override the default import list by specifying one
of your own, just as we did with File::Basename. Supplying an empty list
imports no symbols.

---

* Well, it's not likely that you would already have a &dirname subroutine that you use for another purpose, but this is just an example. Some modules offer hundreds (really!) of new functions, making a
  name collision that much more frequent.

The File::Spec Module

Now you can find out a file's basename. That's useful, but you'll often want to put that together with a directory name to get a full filename. For example, here we want to take a filename like */home/rootbeer/ice-2.1.txt* and add a prefix to the basename:

```
use File::Basename;

print "Please enter a filename: ";
chomp(my $old_name = <STDIN>);

my $dirname = dirname $old_name;
my $basename = basename $old_name;

$basename =~ s/^/not/;   # Add a prefix to the basename
my $new_name = "$dirname/$basename";

rename($old_name, $new_name)
   or warn "Can't rename '$old_name' to '$new_name': $!";
```

Do you see the problem here? Once again, we're making the assumption that file-names will follow the Unix conventions and use a forward slash between the directory name and the basename. Fortunately, Perl comes with a module to help with this problem, too.

The `File::Spec` module is used for manipulating *file specifications*, which are the names of files, directories, and the other things that are stored on filesystems. Like `File::Basename`, it understands what kind of system it's running on, and it chooses the right set of rules every time. But unlike `File::Basename`, `File::Spec` is an object-oriented (often abbreviated "OO") module.

If you've never caught the fever of OO, don't let that bother you. If you under-stand objects, that's great; you can use this OO module. If you don't understand objects, that's okay, too. You just type the symbols as we show you, and it works just as if you knew what you were doing.

In this case, we learn from reading the documentation for `File::Spec` that we want to use a *method* called `catfile`. What's a method? It's just a different kind of function, as far as we're concerned here. The difference is that you'll always call the methods from `File::Spec` with their full names, like this:

```
use File::Spec;

.
.    # Get the values for $dirname and $basename as above
.
```

```
my $new_name = File::Spec->catfile($dirname, $basename);

rename($old_name, $new_name)
  or warn "Can't rename '$old_name' to '$new_name': $!";
```

As you can see, the full name of a method is the name of the module (called a *class*, here), a small arrow, and the short name of the method. It is important to use the small arrow, rather than the double-colon that we used with `File::Basename`.

Since we're calling the method by its full name, though, what symbols does the module import? None of them. That's normal for OO modules. So you don't have to worry about having a subroutine with the same name as one of the many methods of `File::Spec`.

Should you bother using modules like these? It's up to you, as always. If you're sure your program will never be run anywhere but on a Unix machine, say, and you're sure you completely understand the rules for filenames on Unix,* then you may prefer to hardcode your assumptions into your programs. But these modules give you an easy way to make your programs more robust in less time—and more portable at no extra charge.

Exercises

The programs here are potentially dangerous! Be careful to test them in a mostly empty directory to make it difficult to accidentally delete something useful.

See Appendix A for answers to the following exercises.

1. [6] Write a program that works like *rm*, deleting any files named on the command line. (You don't need to handle any of the options of *rm*.)

2. [10] Write a program that works like *mv*, renaming the first command-line argument to the second command-line argument. (You don't need to handle any of the options of *mv* or additional arguments.) Remember to allow for the destination to be a directory; if it is, use the same original basename in the new directory.

3. [7] If your operating system supports it, write a program that works like *ln*, making a hard link from the first command-line argument to the second. (You don't need to handle options of *ln* or more arguments.) If your system doesn't have hard links, just print out a message telling what operation you would perform if it were available. Hint: This program has something in common with the previous one—recognizing that could save you time in coding.

---

* If you didn't know that filenames and directory names could contain newline characters, as we mentioned earlier in this section, then you *don't* know all the rules, do you?

4. [7] If your operating system supports it, fix up the program from the previous exercise to allow an optional *-s* switch before the other arguments to indicate that you want to make a soft link instead of a hard link. (Even if you don't have hard links, see whether you can at least make soft links with this program.)

5. [7] If your operating system supports it, write a program to find any symbolic links in the current directory and print out their values (like *ls -l* would: `name -> value`).

14

Process Management

One of the best parts of being a programmer is launching someone else's code so that you don't have to write it yourself. It's time to learn how to manage your children* by launching other programs directly from Perl.

And like everything else in Perl, There's More Than One Way To Do It, with lots of overlap, variations, and special features. So if you don't like the first way, just read on for another page or two for a solution more to your liking.

Perl is very portable; most of the rest of this book doesn't need many notes saying that it works this way on Unix systems and that way on Windows and the other way on VMS. But when you're starting other programs on your machine, different programs are available on a Macintosh than you'll likely find on a Cray. The examples in this chapter are primarily Unix-based; if you have a non-Unix system, you can expect to see some differences.

The system Function

The simplest way to launch a child process in Perl to run a program is the `system` function. For example, to invoke the Unix *date* command from within Perl, it looks like:

```
system "date";
```

The child process runs the *date* command, which inherits Perl's standard input, standard output, and standard error. This mean that the normal short date-and-time string generated by *date* ends up wherever Perl's STDOUT was already going.

---

* Child processes, that is.

The parameter to the system function is generally whatever you'd normally type at the shell. So if it were a more complicated command, like "*ls -l $HOME*", we'd just have put all that into the parameter:

```
system 'ls -l $HOME';
```

Note that we had to switch here from double quotes to single quotes, since $HOME is the shell's variable. Otherwise, the shell would never have seen the dollar sign, since that's also an indicator for Perl to interpolate. Alternatively, we could write:

```
system "ls -l \$HOME";
```

But that can get quickly unwieldly.

Now, the *date* command is output-only, but let's say it had been a chatty command, asking first "for which time zone do you want the time?"[*] That'll end up on standard output, and then the program will listen on standard input (inherited from Perl's STDIN) for the response. You'll see the question, and type in the answer (like "Zimbabwe time"), and then *date* will finish its duty.

While the child process is running, Perl is patiently waiting for it to finish. So if the *date* command took 37 seconds, then Perl is paused for those 37 seconds. You can use the shell's facility to launch a background process,[†] however:

```
system "long_running_command with parameters &";
```

Here, the shell gets launched, which then notices the ampersand at the end of the command line, causing the *long_running_command* to be made into a background process. And then the shell exits rather quickly, which Perl notices and moves on. In this case, the *long_running_command* is really a grandchild of the Perl process, to which Perl really has no direct access or knowledge.

When the command is "simple enough," no shell gets involved, so for the *date* and *ls* commands earlier, the requested command is launched directly by Perl, which searches the inherited PATH[‡] to find the command, if necessary. But if there's anything weird in the string (such as shell metacharacters like the dollar sign, semicolon, or vertical bar), then the standard Bourne Shell (*/bin/sh*[§]) gets invoked to work through the complicated stuff. In that case, the shell is the child

---

[*] As far as we know, no one has made a *date* command that works like this.

[†] See what we mean about this depending upon your system? The Unix shell (*/bin/sh*) lets you use the ampersand on this kind of command to make a background process. If your non-Unix system doesn't support this way to launch a background process, then you can't do it this way, that's all.

[‡] The PATH can be changed by adjusting $ENV{'PATH'} at any time. Initially, this is the environment variable inherited from the parent process (usually the shell). Changing this value affects new child processes, but cannot affect any preceding parent processes. The PATH is the list of directories where executable programs (commands) are found, even on some non-Unix systems.

[§] Or whatever was determined when Perl was built. Practically always, this is just */bin/sh* on Unix-like systems.

process, and the requested commands are grandchildren (or further offspring). For example, you can write an entire little shell script in the argument:

```
system 'for in *; do echo == $i ==; cat $i; done';
```

Here again, we're using single quotes, because the dollar signs here are meant for the shell and not for Perl. Double quotes would have permitted Perl to expand $i to its current Perl value, and not let the shell expand it to its own value.* By the way, that little shell script goes through all of the normal files in the current directory, printing out each one's name and contents; you can try it out yourself if you don't believe us.

Avoiding the Shell

The system operator may also be invoked with more than one argument,† in which case a shell doesn't get involved, no matter how complicated the text:

```
my $tarfile = "something*wicked.tar";
my @dirs = qw(fred|flintstone <barney&rubble> betty );
system "tar", "cvf", $tarfile, @dirs;
```

In this case, the first parameter ("tar" here) gives the name of a command found in the normal PATH-searching way, while the remaining arguments are passed, one by one, directly to that command. Even if the arguments have shell-significant characters, such as the name in $tarfile or the directory names in @dirs, the shell never gets a chance to mangle the string. So that tar command will get precisely five parameters. Compare this with:

```
system "tar cvf $tarfile @dirs";  # Oops!
```

Here, we've now piped a bunch of stuff into a *flintstone* command and put it into the background, and opened *betty* for output.

And that's a bit scary,‡ especially if those variables are from user input—such as from a web form or something. So, if you *can* arrange things so that you can use the multiple-argument version of system, you probably should use that way to launch your subprocess. (You'll have to give up the ability to have the shell do the work for you to set up I/O redirection, background processes, and the like, though. There's no such thing as a free launch.)

---

* Of course, if you set $i = '$i', then it would work anyway, until a maintenance programmer came along and "fixed" that line out of existence.

† Or with a parameter in the indirect-object slot, like system { 'fred' } 'barney';, which runs the program barney, but lies to it so it thinks that it's called 'fred'. See the *perlfunc* manpage.

‡ Unless you're using taint checking and have done all the right things to prescan your data to ensure that the user isn't trying to pull a fast one on you.

Note that redundantly, a single argument invocation of **system** is nearly equivalent to the proper multiple-argument version of **system**:

```
system $command_line;
system "/bin/sh", "-c", $command_line;
```

But nobody writes the latter, unless you want things to be processed by a different shell, like the C-shell:

```
system "/bin/csh", "-fc", $command_line;
```

Even this is pretty rare, since the One True Shell* seems to have a lot more flexibility, especially for scripted items.

The return value of the system operator is based upon the exit status of the child command†. In Unix, an exit value of 0 means that everything is OK, and a nonzero exit value usually indicates that something went wrong:

```
unless (system "date") {
  # Return was zero - meaning success
  print "We gave you a date, OK!\n";
}
```

Note that this is backward from the normal "true is good—false is bad" strategy for most of the operators, so to write a typical "do this or die" style, we'll need to flip false and true. The easiest way is to simply prefix the **system** operator with a bang (the logical not operator):

```
!system "rm -rf files_to_delete" or die "something went wrong";
```

In this case, including $! in the error message would not be appropriate, because the failure is most likely somewhere within the experience of the *rm* command, and it's not a system-call related error within Perl that $! can reveal.

The exec Function

Everything we've just said about **system** syntax and semantics is also true about the **exec** function, except for one (very important) thing. The **system** function creates a child process, which then scurries off to perform the requested action while Perl naps. The **exec** function causes the Perl process *itself* to perform the requested action. Think of it as more like a "goto" than a subroutine call.

---

* That's */bin/sh*, or whatever your Unix system has installed as the most Bourne-like shell. If you don't have a One True Shell, Perl figures out how to invoke some other command-line interpreter, with notable consequences—noted, that is, in the documentation for that Perl port.

† It's actually the "wait" status, which is the child exit code times 256, plus 128 if core was dumped, plus the signal number triggering termination, if any. But we rarely check the specifics of that, and a simple true/false value suffices for nearly all applications.

For example, suppose we wanted to run the *bedrock* command in the */tmp* directory, passing it arguments of *-o args1* followed by whatever arguments our own program was invoked with. That'd look like this:

```
chdir "/tmp" or die "Cannot chdir /tmp: $!";
exec "bedrock", "-o", "args1", @ARGV;
```

When we reach the `exec` operation, Perl locates *bedrock*, and "jumps into it." At that point, there is no Perl process any more,* just the process running the *bedrock* command. When *bedrock* is finished, there's no Perl to come back to, so we'd get a prompt back if we invoked this program from the command line.

Why is this useful? Well, if the purpose of this Perl program were to set up a particular environment to run another program, the purpose is fulfilled as soon as the other program has started. If we'd used `system` instead of `exec`, we'd have a Perl program just standing around tapping its toes waiting for the other program to complete, just so Perl could finally immediately exit as well, and that's a wasted resource.

Having said that, it's actually quite rare to use `exec`, except in combination with `fork` (which we'll see later). If you are puzzling over `system` versus `exec`, just pick `system`, and nearly all of the time, you'll be just fine.

Because Perl is no longer in control once the requested command has started, it doesn't make any sense to have any Perl code following the `exec`, except for handling the error when the requested command cannot be started:

```
exec "date";
die "date couldn't run: $!";
```

In fact, if you have warnings turned on, and if you have any code after the `exec` other than a `die`,† you'll get notified.

The Environment Variables

When you're starting another process (with any of the methods discussed here), you may need to set up its environment in one way or another. As we mentioned earlier, you could start the process with a certain working directory, which it inherits from your process. Another common configuration detail is the environment variables.

The best-known environment variable is `PATH`. (If you've never heard of it, you probably haven't used a system that has environment variables.) On Unix and

---

* Actually, it's the same process, having performed the Unix `exec(2)` system call (or equivalent). The process ID remains the same.

† Or exit. Or if it's at the end of a block. This may change in a new release of Perl, too.

similar systems, PATH is a colon-separated list of directories that may hold programs. When you type a command like *rm fred*, the system will look for the *rm* command in that list of directories, in order. Perl (or your system) will use PATH whenever it needs to find the program to run. If the program in turn runs other programs, those may also be found along the PATH. (Of course, if you give a complete name for a command, such as */bin/echo*, there's no need to search PATH. But that's generally much less convenient.)

In Perl, the environment variables are available via the special %ENV hash; each key in this hash represents one environment variable. At the start of your program's execution, %ENV holds values it has inherited from its parent process (generally the shell). Modifying this hash changes the environment variables, which will then be inherited by new processes and possibly used by Perl as well. For example, suppose you wished to run the system's **make** utility (which typically runs other programs), and you want to use a private directory as the first place to look for commands (including **make** itself). And let's say that you don't want the IFS environment variable to be set when you run the command, because that might cause *make* or some subcommand do the wrong thing. Here we go:

```
$ENV{'PATH'} = "/home/rootbeer/bin:$ENV{'PATH'}";
delete $ENV{'IFS'};
my $make_result = system "make";
```

Newly created processes will generally inherit from their parent the environment variables, the current working directory, the standard input, output, and error streams, and a few more-esoteric items. See the documentation about programming on your system for more details. (But your program can't change the environment for the shell or other parent process that started it, on most systems.)

Using Backquotes to Capture Output

With both **system** and **exec**, the output of the launched command ends up wherever Perl's standard output is going. Sometimes, it's interesting to capture that output as a string value to perform further processing. And that's done simply by creating a string using backquotes instead of single or double quotes:

```
my $now = `date`;               # grab the output of date
print "The time is now $now";   # newline already present
```

Normally, this *date* command spits out a string approximately 30 characters long to its standard output, giving the current date and time followed by a newline. When we've placed *date* between backquotes, Perl executes the *date* command, arranging for its standard output to be captured as a string value, and in this case assigned to the $now variable.

This is very similar to the Unix shell's meaning for backquotes. However, the shell also performs the additional job of ripping off the final end-of-line to make it easier to use the value as part of other things. Perl is honest; it gives the real output. To get the same result in Perl, we can simply add an additional chomp operation on the result:

```
chomp(my $no_newline_now = `date`);
print "A moment ago, it was $no_newline_now, I think.\n";
```

The value beween backquotes is just like the single-argument form of system,* and is interpreted as a double-quoted string, meaning that backslash-escapes and variables are expanded appropriately.† For example, to fetch the Perl documentation on a list of Perl functions, we might invoke the *perldoc* command repeatedly, each time with a different argument:

```
my @functions = qw{ int rand sleep length hex eof not exit sqrt umask };
my %about;

foreach (@functions) {
  $about{$_} = `perldoc -t -f $_`;
}
```

Note that $_ will be a different value for each invocation, letting us grab the output of a different command varying only in one of its parameters. Also note that if you haven't seen some of these functions yet, it might be useful to look them up in the documentation to see what they do!

There's no easy equivalent of single quotes for backquotes‡; variable references and backslash items are always expanded. Also, there's no easy equivalent of the multiple-argument version of system (where a shell is never involved). If the command inside the backquotes is complex enough, a Unix Bourne Shell (or whatever your system uses instead) is invoked to interpret the command automatically.

At the risk of actually introducing the behavior by demonstrating how *not* to do it, we'd also like to suggest that you avoid using backquotes in a place where the value isn't being captured.§ For example:

```
print "Starting the frobnitzigator:\n";
`frobnitz -enable`; # please don't do this!
print "Done!\n";
```

---

* That is, it's also always interpreted by the One True Shell (*/bin/sh*) or alternative, as with system.

† So, if you want to pass a real backslash to the shell, you'll need to use two. If you need to pass two (which happens frequently on Windows systems), you'll need to use four.

‡ For a couple of harder ways, you can place your string inside qx'...'delimiters, or you can put it all in a variable using a single-quoted string, then interpolate *that* string into a backquoted string, since the interpolation will be only one level.

§ This is called a "void" context.

The problem is that Perl has to work a bit harder to capture the output of this command, even when you're just throwing it away, and then you also lose the option to use multiple arguments to **system** to precisely control the argument list. So from both a security standpoint and an efficiency viewpoint, just use **system** instead, please.

Standard error of a backquoted command is inherited from Perl's current standard error output. If the command spits out error messages to standard error, you'll probably see them on the terminal, which could be confusing to the user who hasn't personally invoked the *frobnitz* command. If you want to capture error messages with standard output, you can use the shell's normal "merge standard error to the current standard output," which is spelled 2>&1 in the normal Unix shell:

```
my $output_with_errors = `frobnitz -enable 2>&1`;
```

Note that this will make the standard error output intermingled with the standard output, much as it appears on the terminal (although possibly in a slightly different sequence because of buffering). If you need the output and the error output separated, there are many harder-to-type solutions.*

Similarly, standard input is inherited from Perl's current standard input. Most commands we typically use with backquotes do not read standard input, so that's rarely a problem. However, let's say the *date* command asked which time zone (as we imagined earlier). That'll be a problem, because the prompt for "which time zone" will be sent to standard output, which is being captured as part of the value, and then the *date* command will start trying to read from standard input. But since the user has never seen the prompt, he or she doesn't know to be typing anything! Pretty soon, the user calls you up and tells you that your program is stuck.

So, stay away from commands that read standard input. If you're not sure whether something reads from standard input, then add a redirection from */dev/null* for input, like this:

```
my $result = `some_questionable_command arg arg argh </dev/null`;
```

Then the child shell will redirect input from */dev/null*, and the grandchild questionable command will at worst try to read and immediately get an end of file.

Using Backquotes in a List Context

If the output from a command has multiple lines, the scalar use of backquotes returns it as a single long string containing newline characters. However, using the same backquoted string in a list context yields a list containing one line of output per element.

---

* Such as IPC::Open3 in the standard Perl library, or writing your own forking code, as we will see later.

For example, the Unix *who* command normally spits out a line of text for each
current login on the system as follows:

```
merlyn      tty/42     Dec 7  19:41
rootbeer    console    Dec 2  14:15
rootbeer    tty/12     Dec 6  23:00
```

The left column is the username, the middle column is the tty name (that is, the
name of the user's connection to the machine), and the rest of the line is the date
and time of login (and possibly remote login information, but not in this example).
In a scalar context, we get all that at once, which we would then need to split up:

```
my $who_text = `who`;
```

But in a list context, we automatically get the data broken up by lines:

```
my @who_lines = `who`;
```

We'll have a number of separate elements in **@who_lines**, each one terminated by
a newline. Of course, adding a **chomp** around the outside of that will rip off those
newlines, but let's go a different direction. If we put that as part of the value for a
foreach, we'll iterate over the lines automatically, placing each one in $_:

```
foreach (`who`) {
  my($user, $tty, $date) = /(\S+)\s+(\S+)\s+(.*)/;
  $ttys{$user} .= "$tty at $date\n";
}
```

This loop will iterate three times for the data above. (Your system will probably
have more than three active logins at any given time.) Notice that we've got a regular expression match, and in the absence of the binding operator ("=~"), that's
matching against $_, which is good because that's where the data is.

Also notice the regular expression is looking for a nonblank word, some
whitespace, a nonblank word, some whitespace, and then the rest of the line up
to, but not including, the newline (since dot doesn't match newline by default).*
That's also good, because that's what the data looks like each time in $_. That'll
make $1 be "**merlyn**", $2 be "**tty/42**", and $3 be "**Dec 7 19:41**", as a suc-
cessful match on the first time through the loop.

However, this regular expression match is in a list context, so instead of returning
back a true/false value (as when you have a regular expression match in a scalar
context), we take the memory variables and bundle them up in sequence as a list.
In this case, the right side of that assignment is thus a three-element list, which
happens to correspond to the three elements of the literal list on the left, and we

---

* Now you can see *why* dot doesn't match newline by default. It makes it easy to write patterns like this
  one, in which we don't have to worry about a newline at the end of the string.

get those nice corresponding assignments. So, `$user` ends up being `"merlyn"`, and so on.

The second statement inside the loop simply stores away the tty and date information, appending to a (possibly `undef`) value in the hash, because a user might be logged in more than once, as user `"rootbeer"` was in our example.

Processes as Filehandles

So far, we've been looking at ways to deal with synchronous processes, where Perl stays in charge, launches a command, (usually) waits for it to finish, then possibly grabs its output. But Perl can also launch a child process that stays alive, communicating* to Perl on an ongoing basis until the task is complete.

The syntax for launching a concurrent (parallel) child process is to put the command as the "filename" for an **open** call, and either precede the command or follow the command with a vertical bar, which is the "pipe" character. For that reason, this is often called a *piped open*:

```
open DATE, "date|" or die "cannot pipe from date: $!";
open MAIL, "|mail merlyn" or die "cannot pipe to mail: $!";
```

In the first example, with the vertical bar on the right, the command is launched with its standard output connected to the **DATE** filehandle opened for reading, similar to the way that the command *date | your_program* would work from the shell. In the second example, with the vertical bar on the left, the command's standard input is connected to the **MAIL** filehandle opened for writing, similar to what happens with the command *your_program | mail merlyn*. In either case, the command is now launched and continues independently of the Perl process.†

The open fails if the child process cannot be created. If the command itself does not exist or exits erroneously, this will (generally) not be seen as an error when opening, but as an error when closing. We'll get to that in a moment.

For all intents and purposes, the rest of the program doesn't know, doesn't care, and would have to work pretty hard to figure out that this is a filehandle opened on a process rather than on a file. So, to get data from a filehandle opened for reading, we'll just do the normal read:

```
my $now = <DATE>;
```

---

* Via pipes, or whatever your operating system provides for simple interprocess communication.

† If the Perl process exits before the command is complete, a command that's been reading will see end-of-file, while a command that's been writing will get a "broken pipe" error signal on the next write, by default.

And to send data to the mail process (waiting for the body of a message to deliver to *merlyn* on standard input), a simple print-with-a-filehandle will do:

```
print MAIL "The time is now $now"; # presume $now ends in newline
```

In short, you can pretend that these filehandles are hooked up to magical files, one that contains the output of the *date* command, and one that will automatically be mailed by the *mail* command.

If a process is connected to a filehandle that is open for reading, and then exits, the filehandle returns end-of-file, just like reading up to the end of a normal file. When you close a filehandle open for writing to a process, the process will see end-of-file. So, to finish sending the email, close the handle:

```
close MAIL;
die "mail: non-zero exit of $?" if $?;
```

Closing a filehandle attached to a process waits for the process to complete, so that Perl can get the process's exit status. The exit status is then available in the $? variable (reminiscent of the same variable in the Bourne Shell), and is the same kind of number as the value returned by the **system** function: zero for success, nonzero for failure. Each new exited process overwrites the previous value though, so save it quickly if you want it. (The $? variable also holds the exit status of the most recent **system** or backquoted command, if you're curious.)

The processes are synchronized just like a pipelined command. If you try to read and no data is available, the process is suspended (without consuming additional CPU time) until the sending program has started speaking again. Similarly, if a writing process gets ahead of the reading process, the writing process is slowed down until the reader starts to catch up. There's a buffer (usually 4K bytes or so) in between so they don't have to stay precisely in lock step.

Why use processes as filehandles? Well, it's the only easy way to write to a process based on the results of a computation. But if you're just reading, backquotes are often much easier to manage, unless you want to have the results as they come in.

For example, the Unix *find* command locates files based on their attributes, and it can take quite a while if used on a fairly large number of files (such as starting from the *root* directory). You can put a *find* command inside backquotes, but it's often nicer to see the results as they are found:

```
open F, "find / -atime +90 -size +1000 -print|" or die "fork: $!";
while (<F>) {
  chomp;
  printf "%s size %dK last accessed on %s\n",
    $_, (1023 + -s $_)/1024, -A $_;
}
```

The *find* command here is looking for all the files that were not accessed within the past 90 days and that are larger than 1000 blocks. (These are good candidates to be moved off to longer-term storage.) While *find* is searching and searching, Perl can wait. As each file is found, Perl responds to the incoming name and displays some information about that file for further research. Had this been written with backquotes, we'd not see any output until the *find* commmand had finished, and it's comforting to see that it's actually doing the job even before it's done.

Getting Down and Dirty with Fork

In addition to the high-level interfaces already described, Perl provides nearly direct access to the low-level process management system calls of Unix and some other systems. If you've never done this before,* you will probably want to skip this section. While it's a bit much to cover all that stuff in a chapter like this, let's at least look at a quick reimplementation of this:

```
system "date";
```

Let's look at how that would be done using the low-level system calls:

```
defined(my $pid = fork) or die "Cannot fork: $!";
unless ($pid) {
  # Child process is here
  exec "date";
  die "cannot exec date: $!";
}
# Parent process is here
waitpid($pid, 0);
```

Here, we've checked the return value from **fork**, which will be **undcf** if it failed. Usually it will succeed, causing two separate processes to continue to the next line, but only the parent process has a nonzero value in **$pid**, so only the child process executes the **exec** function. The parent process skips over that and executes the **waitpid** function, waiting for that particular child to finish (if others finish in the meantime, they are ignored). If that all sounds like gobbledygook, just remember that you can continue to use the **system** function without being laughed at by your friends.

When you go to this extra trouble, you also have full control over arbitrary pipe creation, rearranging filehandles, and noticing your process ID and your parent's process ID (if knowable). But again, that's all a bit complicated for this chapter, so see the details in the *perlipc* manpage (and in any good book on application programming on your system) for further information.

---

* Or you're not running on a system that has support for forking. But the Perl developers are working hard to add forking even on systems whose underlying process model is very different than the one in Unix.

Sending and Receiving Signals

A Unix signal is a tiny message sent to a process. It can't say much; it's like a car horn honking—does that honk you hear mean "look out—the bridge collapsed" or "the light has changed—get going" or "stop driving—you've got a baby on the roof" or "hello, world"? Well, fortunately, Unix signals are a little easier to interpret than that, because there's a different one for each of these situations.*

Different signals are identified by a name (such as SIGINT, meaning "interrupt signal") and a corresponding small integer (in the range from 1 to 16, 1 to 32, or 1 to 63, depending on your Unix flavor). Signals are typically sent when a significant event happens, such as pressing the interrupt character (typically Control-C) on the terminal, which sends a SIGINT to all the processes attached to that terminal.† Some signals are sent automatically by the system, but they can also come from another process.

You can send signals from your Perl process to another process, but you have to know the target's process ID number. How to figure that out is a bit complicated,‡ but let's say you know that you want to send a SIGINT to process 4201. That's easy enough:

```
kill 2, 4201 or die "Cannot signal 4201 with SIGINT: $!";
```

It's named "kill" because one of the primary purposes of signals is to stop a process that's gone on long enough. You can also use the string 'INT' in place of the 2 there, because signal number 2 is SIGINT. If the process no longer exists,§ you'll get a false return value, so you can also use this technique to see whether a process is still alive. A special signal number of 0 says "just check to see whether I *could* send a signal if I wanted to, but I don't want to, so don't actually send anything." So a process probe might look like:

```
unless (kill 0, $pid) {
  warn "$pid has gone away!";
}
```

---

* Well, not exactly these situations, but analogous Unix-like ones. For these, the signals are SIGHUP, SIGCONT, SIGINT, and the fake SIGZERO (signal number zero).

† And you thought that pressing Control-C stopped your program. Actually, it simply sends the SIGINT signal, and that stops the program by default. As we'll see later in this chapter, you can make a program that does something different when SIGINT comes in, rather than stopping at once.

‡ Usually you have the process ID because it's a child process you produced with fork, or you found it in a file or from an external program. Using an external program can be difficult and problematic, which is why many long-running programs save their own current process ID into a file, usually described in the program's documentation.

§ Sending a signal will also fail if you're not the superuser and it's someone else's process. It would be rude to send SIGINT to someone else's programs, anyway.

Perhaps a little more interesting than sending signals is catching signals. Why might you want to do this? Well, suppose you have a program that creates files in */tmp*, and you normally delete those files at the end of the program. If someone presses Control-C during the execution, that leaves trash in */tmp*, a very unpolite thing to do. To fix this, create a signal handler that takes care of the cleanup:

```
my $temp_directory = "/tmp/myprog.$$"; # create files below here
mkdir $temp_directory, 0700 or die "Cannot create $temp_directory: $!";

sub clean_up {
  unlink glob "$temp_directory/*";
  rmdir $temp_directory;
}

sub my_int_handler {
  &clean_up;
  die "interrupted, exiting...\n";
}

$SIG{'INT'} = 'my_int_handler';

.
.   # Time passes, the program runs, creates some temporary
.   # files in the temp directory, maybe somone presses Control-C
.

# Now it's the end of normal execution
&clean_up;
```

The assignment into the special **%SIG** hash activates the handler (until revoked). The key is the name of the signal (without the constant SIG prefix), and the value is a string* naming the subroutine, without the ampersand. From then on, if a **SIGINT** comes along, Perl stops whatever it's doing and jumps immediately to the subroutine. Our subroutine cleans up the temp files and then exits. (And if nobody presses Control-C, we'll still call **&clean_up** at the end of normal execution.)

If the subroutine returns rather than exiting, execution resumes right where it was interrupted. This can be useful if the interrupt needs to actually interrupt something rather than causing it to stop. For example, suppose processing each line of a file takes a few seconds, which is pretty slow, and you want to abort the overall processing when an interrupt is processed, but not in the middle of processing a line. Just set a flag in the interrupt procedure, and check it at the end of each line's processing:

```
my $int_count;
sub my_int_handler { $int_count++ }
$SIG{'INT'} = 'my_int_handler';
...
$int_count = 0;
```

---

* The value can also be a subroutine reference, but we're not doing those here.

```
while (<SOMEFILE>) {
  ... some processing that takes a few seconds ...
  if ($int_count) {
    # interrupt was seen!
    print "[processing interrupted...]\n";
    last;
  }
}
```

Now as each line is processed, the value of $int_count will be 0 if no one has pressed Control-C, and so the loop continues to the next item. However, if an interrupt comes in, the interrupt handler increments the $int_count flag, breaking out of the loop when checked at the end.

So, you can either set a flag or break out of the program, and that covers most of what you'll need from catching signals. The current implementation of signal handlers is not entirely without faults,* however, so keep the stuff you're doing in there to an absolute minimum, or your program may end up blowing up sometime when you least expect it.

Exercises

See Appendix A for answers to the following exercises:

1. [6] Write a program that changes to some particular (hardcoded) directory, like the system's *root* directory, then executes the *ls -l* command to get a long-format directory listing in that directory. (If you use a non-Unix system, use your own system's command to get a detailed directory listing.)

2. [10] Modify the previous program to send the output of the command to a file called *ls.out* in the current directory. The error output should go to a file called *ls.err*. (You don't need to do anything special about the fact that either of these files may end up being empty.)

3. [8] Write a program to parse the output of the *date* command to determine the current day of the week. If the day of the week is a weekday, print get to work, otherwise print go play. The output of the *date* command begins with Mon on a Monday.† If you don't have a *date* command on your

---

* This is one of the top items on the Perl developers' list of things to be fixed, so we expect reliable signal handling to be one of the first items on the new feature list for Perl 6. The problem is that a signal may come in at any time, even when Perl isn't ready for one. If Perl is (for example) in the middle of allocating some memory when a signal comes in, the signal handler can accidentally try to allocate some memory and—your program is dead. You can't control when your Perl code will allocate memory, but XSUB code (usually written in C) can safely handle signals. See the Perl documentation for more information about this advanced topic.

† At least when the days of the week are being given in English. You might have to adjust accordingly if that's not the case on your system.

non-Unix system, make a fake little program that simply prints a string like
date might print. We'll even give you this two-line program if you promise not
to ask us how it works:

```
#!/usr/bin/perl
print localtime() . "\n";
```

15

Strings and Sorting

As we mentioned near the beginning of this book, Perl is designed to be good at solving programming problems that are about 90% working with text and 10% everything else. So it's no surprise that Perl has strong text processing abilities, including all that we've done with regular expressions. But sometimes the regular expression engine is too fancy, and you'll need a simpler way of working with a string, as we'll see in this chapter.

Finding a Substring with index

Finding a substring depends on where you have lost it. If you happen to have lost it within a bigger string, you're in luck, because the **index** function can help you out. Here's how it looks:

```
$where = index($big, $small);
```

Perl locates the first occurrence of the small string within the big string, returning an integer location of the first character. The character position returned is a zero-based value—if the substring is found at the very beginning of the string, **index** returns 0. If it's one character later, the return value is 1, and so on. If the substring can't be found at all, the return value is −1 to indicate that.[*] In this example, **$where** gets 6:

```
my $stuff = "Howdy world!";
my $where = index($stuff, "wor");
```

---

[*] Former C programmers will recognize this as being like C's index function. Current C programmers ought to recognize it as well—but by this point in the book, you should really be a *former* C programmer.

Another way you could think of the position number is the number of characters to skip over before getting to the substring. Since $where is 6, we know that we have to skip over the first six characters of $stuff before we find **wor**.

The **index** function will always report the location of the *first found* occurrence of the substring. But you can tell it to start searching at a later point than the start of the string by using the optional third parameter, which tells **index** to start at that position:

```
my $stuff  = "Howdy world!";
my $where1 = index($stuff, "w");            # $where1 gets 2
my $where2 = index($stuff, "w", $where1 + 1);  # $where2 gets 6
my $where3 = index($stuff, "w", $where2 + 1);  # $where3 gets -1 (not found)
```

(Of course, you wouldn't normally search repeatedly for a substring without using a loop.) That third parameter is effectively giving a minimum value for the return value; if the substring can't be found at that position or later, the return value will be **-1**.

Once in a while, you might prefer to have the *last found* occurrence of the substring.* You can get that with the **rindex** function. In this example, we can find the last slash, which turns out to be at position 4 in a string:

```
my $last_slash = rindex("/etc/passwd", "/");  # value is 4
```

The **rindex** function also has an optional third parameter, but in this case it effectively gives the *maximum* permitted return value:

```
my $fred = "Yabba dabba doo!";
my $where1 = rindex($fred, "abba");  # $where1 gets 7
my $where2 = rindex($fred, "abba", $where1 - 1);  # $where2 gets 1
my $where3 = rindex($fred, "abba", $where2 - 1);  # $where3 gets -1
```

Manipulating a Substring with substr

The **substr** operator works with only a part of a larger string. It looks like this:

```
$part = substr($string, $initial_position, $length);
```

It takes three arguments: a string value, a zero-based initial position (like the return value of **index**), and a length for the substring. The return value is the substring:

```
my $mineral = substr("Fred J. Flintstone", 8, 5);  # gets "Flint"
my $rock = substr "Fred J. Flintstone", 13, 1000;  # gets "stone"
```

---

* Well, it's not really the last one found—Perl cleverly starts searching from the other end of the string, and then returns the first location it finds, which amounts to the same result. Of course, the return value is the same zero-based number as we always use for describing locations of substrings.

As you may have noticed in the previous example, if the requested length (1000 characters, in this case) would go past the end of the string, there's no complaint from Perl, but you simply get a shorter string than you might have. But if you want to be sure to go to the end of the string, however long or short it may be, just omit that third parameter (the length), like this:

```
my $pebble = substr "Fred J. Flintstone", 13;  # gets "stone"
```

The initial position of the substring in the larger string can be negative, counting from the end of the string (that is, position −1 is the last character).[*] In this example, position −3 is three characters from the end of the string, which is the location of the letter i:

```
my $out = substr("some very long string", -3, 2);  # $out gets "in"
```

As you might expect, **index** and **substr** work well together. In this example, we can extract a substring that starts at the location of the letter l:

```
my $long = "some very very long string";
my $right = substr($long, index($long, "l") );
```

Now here's something really cool: The selected portion of the string can be changed if the string is a variable:[†]

```
my $string = "Hello, world!";
substr($string, 0, 5) = "Goodbye";  # $string is now "Goodbye, world!"
```

As you see, the assigned (sub)string doesn't have to be the same length as the substring it's replacing. The string's length is adjusted to fit. Or if that wasn't cool enough to impress you, you could use the binding operator (=~) to restrict an operation to work with just part of a string. This example replaces **fred** with **barney** wherever possible within just the last twenty characters of a string:

```
substr($string, -20) =~ s/fred/barney/g;
```

To be completely honest, we've never actually needed that functionality in any of our own code, and chances are that you'll never need it either. But it's nice to know that Perl can do more than you'll ever need, isn't it?

Much of the work that **substr** and **index** do could be done with regular expressions. Use those where they're appropriate. But **substr** and **index** can often be faster, since they don't have the overhead of the regular expression engine: they're

---

[*] This is analogous to what we saw with array indices in Chapter 3. Just as arrays may be indexed either from 0 (the first element) upwards or from −1 (the last element) downwards, substring locations may be indexed from position 0 (at the first character) upwards or from position −1 (at the last character) downwards.

[†] Well, technically, it can be any *lvalue*. What that term means precisely is beyond the scope of this book, but you can think of it as anything that can be put on the left side of the equals sign (=) in a scalar assignment. That's usually a variable, but it can (as you see here) even be an invocation of the **substr** operator.

never case-insensitive, they have no metacharacters to worry about, and they don't set any of the memory variables.

Besides assigning to the `substr` function (which looks a little weird at first glance, perhaps), you can also use `substr` in a slightly more traditional manner* with the four-argument version, in which the fourth argument is the replacement substring:

```
my $previous_value = substr($string, 0, 5, "Goodbye");
```

The previous value comes back as the return value, although as always, you can use this function in a void context to simply discard it.

Formatting Data with sprintf

The `sprintf` function takes the same arguments as `printf` (except for the optional filehandle, of course), but it returns the requested string instead of printing it. This is handy if you want to store a formatted string into a variable for later use, or if you want more control over the result than `printf` alone would provide:

```
my $date_tag = sprintf
  "%4d/%02d/%02d %2d:%02d:%02d",
  $yr, $mo, $da, $h, $m, $s;
```

In that example, `$date_tag` gets something like `"2038/01/19  3:00:08"`. The format string (the first argument to `sprintf`) used a leading zero on some of the format number, which we didn't mention when we talked about `printf` formats in Chapter 6. The leading zero on the format number means to use leading zeroes as needed to make the number as wide as requested. Without a leading zero in the formats, the resulting date-and-time string would have unwanted leading spaces instead of zeroes, looking like `"2038/ 1/19  3: 0: 8"`.

Using sprintf with "Money Numbers"

One popular use for `sprintf` is when a number needs to be rendered with a certain number of places after the decimal point, such as when an amount of money needs to be shown as `2.50` and not `2.5`—and certainly not as `2.49997`! That's easy to accomplish with the `"%.2f"` format:

```
my $money = sprintf "%.2f", 2.49997;
```

The full implications of rounding are numerous and subtle, but in most cases you should keep numbers in memory with all of the available accuracy, rounding off only for output.

---

* By traditional we mean in the "function invocation" sense, but not the "Perl" sense, since this feature was introduced to Perl relatively recently.

If you have a "money number" that may be large enough to need commas to show its size, you might find it handy to use a subroutine like this one.*

```
sub big_money {
  my $number = sprintf "%.2f", shift @_;
  # Add one comma each time through the do-nothing loop
  1 while $number =~ s/^(-?\d+)(\d\d\d)/$1,$2/;
  # Put the dollar sign in the right place
  $number =~ s/^(-?)/$1\$/;
  $number;
}
```

This subroutine uses some techniques you haven't seen yet, but they logically follow from what we've shown you. The first line of the subroutine formats the first (and only) parameter to have exactly two digits after the decimal point. That is, if the parameter were the number `12345678.9`, now our $number is the string `"12345678.90"`.

The next line of code uses a **while** modifier. As we mentioned when we covered that modifier in Chapter 10, that can always be rewritten as a traditional **while** loop:

```
while ($number =~ s/^(-?\d+)(\d\d\d)/$1,$2/) {
  1;
}
```

What does that say to do? It says that, as long as the substitution returns a true value (signifying success), the loop body should run. But the loop body does nothing! That's okay with Perl, but it tells us that the purpose of that statement is to do the conditional expression (the substitution), rather than the useless loop body. The value `1` is traditionally used as this kind of a placeholder, although any other value would be equally useful.† This works just as well as the loop above:

```
'keep looping' while $number =~ s/^(-?\d+)(\d\d\d)/$1,$2/;
```

So, now we know that the substitution is the real purpose of the loop. But what is the substitution doing? Remember that $number will be some string like `"12345678.90"` at this point. The pattern will match the first part of the string, but it can't get past the decimal point. (Do you see why it can't?) Memory $1 will get `"12345"`, and $2 will get `"678"`, so the substitution will make $number into `"12345,678.90"` (remember, it couldn't match the decimal point, so the last part of the string is left untouched).

---

* Yes, we know that not everywhere in the world are commas used to separate groups of digits, not everywhere are the digits grouped by threes, and not everywhere the currency symbol appears as it does for U.S. dollars. But this is a good example anyway, so there!

† Which is to say, useless. By the way, in case you're wondering, Perl optimizes away the constant expression so it doesn't even take up any runtime.

Do you see what the dash is doing near the start of that pattern? (Hint: The dash is allowed at only one place in the string.) We'll tell you at the end of this section, in case you haven't figured it out.

We're not done with that substitution statement yet. Since the substitution succeeded, the do-nothing loop goes back to try again. This time, the pattern can't match anything from the comma onward, so $number becomes "12,345,678. 90". The substitution thus adds a comma to the number each time through the loop.

Speaking of the loop, it's still not done. Since the previous substitution was a success, we're back around the loop to try again. But this time, the pattern can't match at all, since it has to match at least four digits at the start of the string, so now that is the end of the loop.

Why couldn't we have simply used the /g modifier to do a "global" search-and-replace, to save the trouble and confusion of the 1 while? We couldn't use that because we're working backwards from the decimal point, rather than forward from the start of the string. Putting the commas in a number like this can't be done simply with the s///g substitution alone.*

So, did you figure out the dash? It's allowing for a possible minus-sign at the start of the string. The next line of code makes the same allowance, putting the dollar-sign in the right place so that $number is something like "$12,345,678.90", or perhaps "-$12,345,678.90" if it's negative. Note that the dollar sign isn't necessarily the first character in the string, or that line would be a lot simpler. Finally, the last line of code returns our nicely formatted "money number," ready to be printed in the annual report.

Advanced Sorting

Earlier, in Chapter 3, we showed that you could sort a list in ascending ASCIIbetical order by using the builtin **sort** operator. What if you want a numeric sort? Or a case-insensitive sort? Or maybe you want to sort items according to information stored in a hash. Well, Perl lets you sort a list in whatever order you'd need; we'll see all of those examples by the end of the chapter.

You'll tell Perl what order you want by making a *sort-definition subroutine*, or *sort subroutine* for short. Now, when you first hear the term "sort subroutine," if you've been through any computer science courses, visions of bubble sort and shell sort and quick sort race through your head, and you say, "No, never again!"

---

* At least, it can't be done without some more-advanced regular expression techniques than we've shown you so far. Those darn Perl developers keep making it harder and harder to write Perl books that use the word "can't."

Don't worry; it's not that bad. In fact, it's pretty simple. Perl already knows how to sort a list of items; it merely doesn't know which order you want. So the sort-definition subroutine simply tells it the order.

Why is this necessary? Well, if you think about it, sorting is putting a bunch of things in order by comparing them all. Since you can't compare them all at once, you need to compare two at a time, eventually using what you find out about each pair's order to put the whole kit'n'caboodle in line. Perl already understands all of those steps *except* for the part about how you'd like to compare the items, so that's all you have to write.

This means that the sort subroutine doesn't need to sort many items after all. It merely has to be able to compare two items. If it can put two items in the proper order, Perl will be able to tell (by repeatedly consulting the sort subroutine) what order you want for your data.

The sort subroutine is defined like an ordinary subroutine (well, almost). This routine will be called repeatedly, each time checking on a pair of elements from the list to be sorted.

Now, if you were writing a subroutine that's expecting to get two parameters that need sorting, you might write something like this to start:

```
sub any_sort_sub {  # It doesn't really work this way
    my($a, $b) = @_;  # Get and name the two parameters
    # start comparing $a and $b here
    ...
}
```

But the sort subroutine will be called again and again, often hundreds or thousands of times. Declaring the variables $a and $b and assigning them values at the top of the subroutine will take just a little time, but multiply that by the thousands of times that the routine will be called, and you can see that it contributes significantly to the overall execution speed.

We don't do it like that. (In fact, if you did it that way, it wouldn't work.) Instead, it is as if Perl has done this for us, before our subroutine's code has even started.[*] You'll really write a sort subroutine without that first line; both $a and $b have

---

[*] To be honest, it's closer to being as if Perl has used local($a, $b) in a private block around the sort invocation, because these variables are really globals rather than lexical variables. (Unless you do something unusual, though, you can't tell the difference inside the sort subroutine; you can pretend these are my variables. use strict makes a special exception for these two globals, so you don't need to declare them in any way.) This means that if your program already has its own $a or $b, you won't be able to access those while Perl is sorting the list. Also, be sure to note that the two items to be sorted are *not* passed in via @_ (unless you use a subroutine prototype, which we won't cover in this book, but see the documentation for the full details). Inside the sort subroutine, just use $a and $b, and try not to worry too much about where they came from. And as if that wasn't enough, if there's a lexical $a or $b somewhere in scope, the subroutine definition doesn't work either. Whew!

been assigned for you. When the sort subroutine starts running, $a and $b are two elements from the original list.

The subroutine returns a coded value describing how the elements compare (like C's qsort(3) does, but it's Perl's own internal sort implementation). If $a should appear before $b in the final list, the sort subroutine returns –1 to say so. If $b should appear before $a, it returns 1.

If the order of $a and $b doesn't matter, the subroutine returns 0. Why would it not matter? Perhaps you're doing a case-insensitive sort and the two strings are fred and Fred. Or perhaps you're doing a numeric sort, and the two numbers are equal.

We could now write a numeric sort subroutine like this:

```
sub by_number {
  # a sort subroutine, expect $a and $b
  if ($a < $b) { -1 } elsif ($a > $b) { 1 } else { 0 }
}
```

To use the sort subroutine, just put its name (without an ampersand) between the keyword **sort** and the list to be sorted. This example puts a numerically sorted list of numbers into @result:

```
my @result = sort by_number @some_numbers;
```

We called the subroutine **by_number** because that describes how it's sorting. But more importantly, you can read the line of code that uses it with sort as saying "sort by number," as you would in English. Many sort subroutine names begin with **by_** to describe how they sort. Or we could have called this one **numerically**, for a similar reason, but that's more typing and more chance to mess something up.

Notice that we don't have to do anything in the sort subroutine to declare $a and $b, and to set their values—and if we did, the subroutine wouldn't work right. We just let Perl set up $a and $b for us, and so all we need to write is the comparison.

In fact, we can make it even simpler (and more efficient). Since this kind of three-way comparison is frequent, Perl has a convenient shortcut to use to write it. In this case, we use the spaceship operator (<=>).* This operator compares two numbers and returns –1, 0, or 1 as needed to sort them numerically. So we could have written that sort subroutine better, like this:

```
sub by_number { $a <=> $b }
```

---

* We call it that because it looks like one of the Tie-fighters from *Star Wars*. Well, it looks like that to us, anyway.

Since the spaceship compares numbers, you may have guessed that there's a corresponding three-way string-comparison operator: `cmp`. These two are easy to remember and keep straight. The spaceship has a family resemblance to the numeric comparison operators like `>=`, but it's three characters long instead of two because it has three possible return values instead of two. And `cmp` has a family resemblance to the string comparison operators like `ge`, but it's three characters long instead of two because it *also* has three possible return values instead of two.[*]

Of course, `cmp` by itself provides the same order as the default sort. You'd never need to write this subroutine, which yields merely the default sort order:[†]

```
sub ASCIIbetically { $a cmp $b }
my @strings = sort ASCIIbetically @any_strings;
```

But you can use `cmp` to build a more complex sort order, like a case-insensitive sort:

```
sub case_insensitive { "\L$a" cmp "\L$b" }
```

In this case, we're comparing the string from `$a` (forced to lowercase) against the string from `$b` (forced to lowercase), giving a case-insensitive sort order.

Note that we're not modifying the elements themselves; we're merely using their values. That's actually important: for efficiency reasons, `$a` and `$b` aren't copies of the data items. They're actually new, temporary aliases for elements of the original list, so if we changed them we'd be mangling the original data. Don't do that—it's neither supported nor recommended.

When your sort subroutine is as simple as the ones we show here (and most of the time, it is), you can make the code even simpler yet, by replacing the name of the sort routine with the entire sort routine "in line," like so:

```
my @numbers = sort { $a <=> $b } @some_numbers;
```

In fact, in modern Perl, you'll hardly ever see a separate sort subroutine; you'll frequently find sort routines written inline as we've done here.

Suppose you want to sort in descending numeric order. That's easy enough to do with the help of **reverse**:

```
my @descending = reverse sort { $a <=> $b } @some_numbers;
```

But here's a neat trick. The comparison operators (`<=>` and `cmp`) are very nearsighted; that is, they can't see which operand is `$a` and which is `$b`, but only which *value* is on the left and which is on the right. So if `$a` and `$b` were to swap

---

[*] This is no accident. Larry does things like this on purpose, to make Perl easier to learn and remember. Remember, he's a linguist at heart, so he's studied how people think of languages.

[†] You'd never need to write this unless, of course, you were writing an introductory Perl book and needed it for an example.

places, the comparison operator would get the results backwards every time. That means that this is another way to get a reversed numeric sort:

```
my @descending = sort { $b <=> $a } @some_numbers;
```

You can (with a little practice) read this at a glance. It's a descending-order comparison (because $b comes before $a, which is descending order), and it's a numeric comparison (because it uses the spaceship instead of cmp). So, it's sorting numbers in reverse order.

Sorting a Hash by Value

Once you've been sorting lists happily for a while you'll run into a situation where you want to sort a hash by value. For example, three of our characters went out bowling last night, and we've got their bowling scores in the following hash. We want to be able to print out the list in the proper order, with the game winner at the top, so we want to sort the hash by score:

```
my %score = ("barney" => 195, "fred" => 205, "dino" => 30);
my @winners = sort by_score keys %score;
```

Of course, we aren't really going to be able to sort the hash by score; that's just a verbal shortcut. You can't sort a hash! But when we've used **sort** with hashes before now, we've been sorting the keys of the hash (in ASCIIbetical order). Now, we're still going to be sorting the keys of the hash, but the order is now defined by their corresponding values from the hash. In this case, the result should be a list of our three characters' names, in order according to their bowling scores.

Writing this sort subroutine is fairly easy. What we want is to use a numeric comparison on the scores, rather than the names. That is, instead of comparing $a and $b (the players' names), we want to compare $score{$a} and $score{$b} (their scores). If you think of it that way, it almost writes itself, as in:

```
sub by_score { $score{$b} <=> $score{$a} }
```

Let's step through this and see how it works. Let's imagine that the first time it's called, Perl has set $a to **barney** and $b to **fred**. So the comparison is $score{"fred"} <=> $score{"barney"}, which (as we can see by consulting the hash) is 205 <=> 195. Remember, now, the spaceship is nearsighted, so when it sees 205 before 195, it says, in effect: "No, that's not the right numeric order; $b should come before $a." So it tells Perl that **fred** should come before **barney**.

Maybe the next time the routine is called, $a is **barney** again but $b is now **dino**. The nearsighted numeric comparison sees 30 <=> 195 this time, so it reports that that they're in the right order; $a does indeed sort in front of $b. That is, **barney** comes before dino. At this point, Perl has enough information to put the list in order: fred is the winner, then barney in second place, then dino.

Why did the comparison use the $score{$b} before the $score{$a}, instead of the other way around? That's because we want bowling scores arranged in *descending* order, from the highest score of the winner down. So you can (again, after a little practice) read this one at sight as well: $score{$b} <=> $score{$a} means to sort according to the scores, in reversed numeric order.

Sorting by Multiple Keys

We forgot to mention that there was a fourth player bowling last night with the other three, so the hash really looked like this:

```
my %score = (
  "barney" => 195, "fred" => 205,
  "dino" => 30, "bamm-bamm" => 195,
);
```

Now, as you can see, bamm-bamm has the same score as barney. So which one will be first in the sorted list of players? There's no telling, because the comparison operator (seeing the same score on both sides) will have to return zero when checking those two.

Maybe that doesn't matter, but we generally prefer to have a well-defined sort. If several players have the same score, we want them to be together in the list, of course. But within that group, the names should be in ASCIIbetical order. But how can we write the sort subroutine to say that? Again, this turns out to be pretty easy:

```
my @winners = sort by_score_and_name keys %score;

sub by_score_and_name {
  $score{$b} <=> $score{$a}   # by descending numeric score
    or
  $a cmp $b                    # ASCIIbetically by name
}
```

How does this work? Well, if the spaceship sees two different scores, that's the comparison we want to use. It returns −1 or 1, a true value, so the low-precedence short-circuit or will mean that the rest of the expression will be skipped, and the comparison we want is returned. (Remember, the short-circuit or returns the last expression evaluated.) But if the spaceship sees two identical scores, it returns 0, a false value, and thus the cmp operator gets its turn at bat, returning an appropriate ordering value considering the keys as strings. That is, if the scores are the same, the string-order comparison breaks the tie.

We know that when we use the **by_score_and_name** sort subroutine like this, it will never return 0. (Do you see why it won't? The answer is in the footnote.*) So we know that the sort order is always well-defined; that is, we know that the result today will be the same as the result with the same data tomorrow.

There's no reason that your sort subroutine has to be limited to two levels of sorting, of course. Here the Bedrock library program puts a list of patron ID numbers in order according to a five-level sort.† This example sorts according to the amount of each patron's outstanding fines (as calculated by a subroutine **&fines**, not shown here), the number of items they currently have checked out (from **%items**), their name (in order by family name, then by personal name, both from hashes), and finally by the patron's ID number, in case everything else is the same:

```
@patron_IDs = sort {
  &fines($b) <=> &fines($a) or
  $items{$b} <=> $items{$a} or
  $family_name{$a} cmp $family_name{$a} or
  $personal_name{$a} cmp $family_name{$b} or
  $a <=> $b
} @patron_IDs;
```

Exercises

See Appendix A for answers to the following exercises:

1. [10] Write a program to read in a list of numbers and sort them numerically, printing out the resulting list in a right-justified column. Try it out on this sample data, or use the file *numbers*, from the O'Reilly web site (see the Preface):

   ```
   17 1000 04 1.50 3.14159 -10 1.5 4 2001 90210 666
   ```

2. [15] Make a program that will print the following hash's data sorted in case-insensitive alphabetical order by last name. When the last names are the same, sort those by first name (again, without regard for case). That is, the first name in the output should be Fred's, while the last one should be Betty's. All of the people with the same family name should be grouped together. Don't alter the data. The names should be printed with the same capitalization as shown here. (You can find the source code to create a hash like this in the file *sortable_hash* with the other downloaded files.)

---

* The only way it could return 0 would be if the two strings were identical, and (since the strings are keys of a hash) we already know that they're different. Of course, if you passed a list with duplicate (identical) strings to **sort**, it would return 0 when comparing those, but we're passing a list of hash keys.

† It's not unusual in the modern world to need a five-level sort like this, although it was quite infrequent in prehistoric times.

```
my %last_name = qw{
    fred flintstone Wilma Flintstone Barney Rubble
    betty rubble Bamm-Bamm Rubble PEBBLES FLINTSTONE
};
```

3. [15] Make a program that looks through a given string for every occurrence of a given substring, printing out the positions where the substring is found. For example, given the input string `"This is a test."` and the substring `"is"`, it should report positions 2 and 5. If the substring were `"a"`, it should report 8. What does it report if the substring is `"t"`?

16

Simple Databases

Databases permit us to allow data to persist beyond the end of our program. The kinds of databases we're talking about in this chapter are merely simple ones; how to use full-featured database implementations (Oracle, Sybase, Informix, mySQL, and others) is a topic that could fill an entire book, and usually does. The databases in this chapter are those that are simple enough to implement that you don't need to know about modules to use them.[*]

DBM Files and DBM Hashes

Every system thas has Perl also has a simple database already available in the form of DBM files. This lets your program store data for quick lookup in a file or in a pair of files. When two files are used, one holds the data and the other holds a table of contents, but you don't need to know that in order to use DBM files. We're intentionally being a little vague about the exact implementation, because that will vary depending upon your machine and configuration; see the `AnyDBM_file` manpage for more information. Also, among the downloadable files from the O'Reilly website is a utility called *which_dbm,* which tries to tell you which implementation you're using, how many files there are, and what extensions they use, if any.

Some DBM file implementations (we'll call it "a file," even though it may be two actual files) have a limit of around 1000 bytes for each key and value in the file. Your actual limit may be larger or smaller than this number, but as long as you aren't trying to store gigantic text strings in the file, it shouldn't be a problem.

---

[*] To be sure, on some of these, the core of Perl will load a module for you. But you don't need to know anything about modules to use these databases.

There's no limit to the number of individual data items in the file, as long as you have enough disk space.

In Perl, we can access the DBM file as a special kind of hash called a DBM hash. This is a powerful concept, as we'll see.

Opening and Closing DBM Hashes

To associate a DBM database with a DBM hash (that is, to open it), use the **dbmopen** function,[*] which looks similar to **open**, in a way:

```
dbmopen(%DATA, "my_database", 0644)
    or die "Cannot create my_database: $!";
```

The first parameter is the name of a Perl hash. (If this hash already has values, the values are inaccessible while the DBM file is open.) This hash becomes connected to the DBM database whose name was given as the second parameter, often stored on disk as a pair of files with the extensions *.dir* and *.pag*. (The filename as given in the second parameter shouldn't include either extension, though; the extensions will be automatically added as needed.) In this case, the files might be called *my_database.dir* and *my_database.pag*.

Any legal hash name may be used as the name of the DBM hash, although upper-case-only hash names are traditional because their resemblance to filehandles reminds us that the hash is connected to a file. The hash name isn't stored anywhere in the file, so you can call it whatever you'd like.

If the file doesn't exist, it will be created and given a permission mode based upon the value in the third parameter.[†] The number is typically specified in octal; the frequently used value of 0644 gives read-only permission to everyone but the owner, who gets read/write permission. If you're trying to open an existing file, you'd probably rather have the **dbmopen** fail if the file isn't found, so just use **undef** as the third parameter.

The return value from the **dbmopen** is true if the database could be opened or created, and false otherwise, just like **open**. You should generally use **or die** in the same spirit as **open**.

The DBM hash typically stays open throughout the program. When the program terminates, the association is terminated. You can also break the association in a manner similar to closing a filehandle, by using **dbmclose**:

---

[*] Here we depart from other beginner documentation, which claims that **dbmopen** is deprecated and suggests that you use the more complicated **tie** interface instead. We disagree, since **dbmopen** works just fine, and it keeps you from having to think harder about what you're doing. Keep the common tasks simple!

[†] The actual mode will be modified by the **umask**; see the *perlfunc* manpage for more information.

```
dbmclose(%DATA);
```

Using a DBM Hash

Here's the beauty of the DBM hash: it works just like the hashes you already understand! To read from the file, look at an element of the hash. To write to the file, store something into the hash. In short, it's like any other hash, but instead of being stored in memory, it's stored on disk. And thus, when your program opens it up again, the hash is already stuffed full of the data from the previous invocation.

All of the normal hash operations are available:

```
$DATA{"fred"} = "bedrock";       # create (or update) an element
delete $DATA{"barney"};          # remove an element of the database

foreach my $key (keys %DATA) {   # step through all values
  print "$key has value of $DATA{$key}\n";
}
```

That last loop could have a problem, since **keys** has to traverse the entire hash, possibly producing a very large list of keys. If you are scanning through a DBM hash, it's generally more memory-efficient to use the **each** function:

```
while (my($key, $value) = each(%DATA)) {
  print "$key has value of $value\n";
}
```

If you are accessing DBM files that are maintained by C programs, you should be aware that C programs generally tack on a trailing NUL (`"\0"`) character to the end of their strings, for reasons known only to Kernighan and Ritchie.[*] The DBM library routines do not need this NUL (they handle binary data using a byte count, not a NUL-terminated string), and so the NUL is stored as part of the data.

To cooperate with these programs, you must therefore append a NUL character to the end of your keys and values, and discard the NUL from the end of the returned values to have the data make sense. For example, to look up **merlyn** in the sendmail aliases database on a Unix system, you might do something like this:

```
dbmopen(my %ALI, "/etc/aliases", undef) or die "no aliases?";
my $value = $ALI{"merlyn\0"};                # note appended NUL
$value =~ s/\0$//;                           # remove trailing NUL
print "Randal's mail is headed for: $value\n"; # show result
```

If your DBM files may be concurrently accessed by more than one process (for example if they're being updated over the Web), you'll generally need to use an

---

[*] Well, they're not the only ones: it's because C uses the NUL byte as the end-of-string marker.

auxiliary lock file. The details of this are beyond the scope of this book; see *The Perl Cookbook* by Tom Chrisitansen and Nathan Torkington (O'Reilly & Associates, Inc.).

Manipulating Data with pack and unpack

When storing data into a DBM file (or in one of the other types of databases we'll see in this chapter), you may need to store more than one item under a single key. And sometimes you'll need to be able to prepare some information to be sent over a network connection or to a system-level function, or to decode it upon arrival. That's why Perl has the **pack** and **unpack** functions.

The **pack** function takes a format string and a list of arguments and packs the arguments together to make a string. Here, we can pack three numbers of varying sizes into a seven-byte string using the formats **c**, **s**, and **l** (these might remind some folks of the words "char", "short", and "long"). The first number gets packed into one byte, the second into two bytes, and the third into four bytes, which explains why we say this is a seven-byte string:

```
my $buffer = pack("c s l", 31, 4159, 265359);
```

When you want the original list of items back, you can use the same format string with the **unpack** function:

```
my($char, $short, $long) = unpack("c s l", $buffer);
```

There are many different format letters available; some of these are the same on every machine (so they're useful for sending data over a network), while others depend upon how your machine likes to work with data (these are useful for interacting with your system's own data). See the **perlfunc** manpage for the latest list of format letters, as new ones are being added in every new version of Perl.

Whitespace may be used at will in a format string to improve readability, as we did in the previous example. For most format letters, you can follow the format letter with a number to indicate a number of times; that is, a format of `"ccccccc"` may be written more compactly as `"c7"`. Instead of a number, you may follow the last format letter with a star (*), which means to use that format as many times as needed to use up the remaining items in the list (in **pack**) or to use up the rest of the string (in **unpack**). So a format of `"c*"` will either unpack a string into a list of small integers, or pack up those small integers to make a string. For some format letters, such as **a**, the number is not a repeat count; `"a20"` is a twenty-character ASCII string, padded with NUL characters as needed.

Fixed-length Random-access Databases

Another form of persistent data is the fixed-length, record-oriented disk file.* In this scheme, the data consists of a number of records of identical length. The numbering of the records is either not important or determined by some indexing scheme.

For example, we might want to store some information about each bowler at Bedrock Lanes. Let's say we decide to have a series of records, one per bowler, in which the data holds the player's name, age, last five bowling scores, and the time and date of his last game.

We need to decide upon a suitable format for this data. Let's say that after studying the available formats in the documentation for **pack**, we decide to use 40 characters for the player's name, a one-byte integer for his age,† five two-byte integers for his last five scores,‡ and a four-byte integer for the timestamp of his most-recent game,§ giving a format string of `"a40 C I5 L"`. Each record is thus 55 bytes long. If we were reading all of the data in the database, we'd read chunks of 55 bytes until we got to the end. If we wanted to go to the fifth record, we'd skip ahead 4 × 55 bytes (220 bytes) and read the fifth record directly.

Perl supports programs that use such a disk file. In order to do so, however, you need to learn a few more things, including how to:

1. Open a disk file for both reading and writing

2. Move around in this file to an arbitrary position

3. Fetch data by a length rather than up to the next newline

4. Write data down in fixed-length blocks

The **open** function has an additional mode we haven't shown yet. If you use `"+<"` at the front of the filename parameter's string, that is similar to using `"<"` to open the existing file for reading, except that it also asks for write permission on the file. Thus you can have read/write access to the file:

---

* By "fixed-length," we don't mean that the file itself is of a fixed length; it's each individual record that is of a fixed length. In this section, we'll use an example file in which every record is 55 bytes long.

† Since one byte may have 256 different values, this will hold ages from 0 to 255 with ease. If Methuselah comes to bowl in Bedrock, we'll have to redesign the database.

‡ We can't use one-byte integers for the scores, because a bowling score can be as high as 300. Two-byte integers can hold values from 0 to 65535 (if unsigned) or –32768 to 32767 (if signed). We can use some of these extra values as special codes; for example, if a player has only three games on record, the other scores could be set to 9999 to indicate this.

§ The standard Unix timestamp format (and the time value used by many other systems) is a 32-bit integer, which fits into four bytes, of course. You'll probably find it handy to use a module to manipulate time and date formats.

```
open(FRED, "<fred");  # open file fred for reading (error if file absent)
open(FRED, "+<fred"); # open file fred read/write (error if file absent)
```

Similarly, `"+>"` says to create a new file (as `">"` would), but to have read access to it as well, thus also giving read/write access:

```
open(WILMA, ">wilma");  # make new file wilma (wiping out existing file)
open(WILMA, "+>wilma"); # make new file wilma, but also with read access
```

Do you see the important difference between the two new modes? Both give read/write access to a file. But `"+<"` lets you work with an existing file; it doesn't create it. The second mode, `"+>"` isn't often useful, because it gives read/write access to a new, empty file that it has just created. That's mostly used for temporary (scratch) files.

Once we've got the file open, we need to move around in it. You do this with the **seek** function:

```
seek(FRED, 55 * $n, 0);  # seek to start of record $n
```

The first parameter to **seek** is a filehandle, the second parameter gives the offset in bytes from the start of the file, and the third parameter is zero.* To get to a certain record in our file of bowling data, you'll need to skip over some other records. Since each record is 55 bytes long, we'll multiply $n times 55 to find out which byte position we want. (Note that the record numbers are thus zero-based; record zero is at the beginning of the file.)

Once the file pointer has been positioned with **seek**, the next input or output operation will start at that position.

When we're ready to read from the file, we can't use the ordinary line-input operator because that's made to read lines, not 55-byte records. There may not be a newline character in this entire file, or it may appear in packed data in the middle of a record. Instead, we'll use the **read** function:

```
my $buf;  # The input buffer variable
my $number_read = read(FRED, $buf, 55);
```

As you can see, the first parameter to **read** is the filehandle. The second parameter is a buffer variable; the data read will be placed into this variable. (Yes, this is an odd way to get the result.) The third parameter is the number of bytes to read; here we've asked for 55 bytes, since that's the size of our record. Normally, you can expect the length of $buf to be the specified number of bytes, and you can expect that the return value (in $number_read) to be the same. But if your

---

* Actually, the third parameter is the "whence" parameter. You can use a different value than zero if you want to seek to a position relative to the current position, or relative to the end of the file; see the *perl-func* manpage for more information. Most people will simply want to use zero here.

current position in the file is only five bytes from the end when you request 55 bytes, you'll get only five. Under normal circumstances, you'll get as many bytes as you ask for.

Once you've got those 55 bytes, what can you do with them? You can unpack them (using the format we previously designed) to get the bowler's name and other information, of course:

```
my($name, $age, $score_1, $score_2, $score_3, $score_4, $score_5, $when)
    = unpack "a40 C I5 L", $buf;
```

Since we can read the information from the file with **read**, can you guess how we can write it back into the file? Sorry, it's not **write**; that was a trick question.* You already know the correct function, which is **print**. But you have to be sure that the data string is exactly the right size; if it's too large, you'll overwrite the next record's data, but if it's too small, leftover data in the current record may be mixed with the new data. To ensure that the length is correct, we'll use **pack**. Let's say that Wilma has just bowled a game and her new score is in $new_score. That will be the first of the five most-recent scores we keep for her ($score_5, as the oldest one, will be discarded), and in place of $when (the timestamp of her previous game), we'll store the current time from the **time** function:

```
print FRED pack("a40 C I5 L",
    $name, $age,
    $new_score, $score_1, $score_2, $score_3, $score_4,
    time);
```

On some systems, you'll have to use **seek** whenever you switch from reading to writing, even if the current position in the file is already correct. It's not a bad idea, then, to always use **seek** right before reading or printing.

Rather than use the two constant values **"a40 C I5 L"** and 55 throughout the program, as we've done here, it would generally be better to define them just once near the top of the code. That way, if we ever need to change the database format, we don't have to go searching through our code for places where the number 55 appears. Here's one way you might define both of those values, using the **length** function to determine the length of a string so you won't have to count bytes:

```
my $pack_format = "a40 C I5 L";
my $pack_length = length pack($pack_format, "dummy data",
    0, 1, 2, 3, 4, 5, 6);
```

---

* Perl actually does have a **write** function, but that is used with formats, which are beyond the scope of this book. See the *perlform* manpage.

Variable-length (Text) Databases

Many simple databases are merely text files written in a format that allows a program to read and maintain them. For example, a configuration file for some program might be a text file, with one configuration parameter being set on each line. Or maybe the file is a mailing list, with one name and address on each line (probably with the components of the name and address separated by tab characters).

Updating text files is more difficult than it probably seems at first. But that's only because we're used to seeing text files rendered as pages (or screens) of text. If you could see the file as it is written in the filesystem, the difficulty is more apparent. Since we can't show you the file as it's actually written without opening up a disk drive, here's our rendition of a piece of a text file[*]:

```
He had bought a large map representing the sea,\n  Without the l
east vestige of land:\nAnd the crew were much pleased when they
found it to be\n  A map they could all understand.\n\n"What's th
e good of Mercator's North Poles and Equators,\n  Tropics, Zones
, and Meridian Lines?"\nSo the Bellman would cry: and the crew w
ould reply\n  "They are merely conventional signs!\n\n"Other map
s are such shapes, with their islands and capes!\n  But we've go
t our brave Captain to thank:"\n(So the crew would protest) "tha
t he's bought us the best-\n  A perfect and absolute blank!"\n\n
```

If you had this file open in your text editor, it would be easy to change a word, add a comma, or fix a misspelling. If your editor is powerful enough, in fact, you could change the indentation of each line with a single command. But the text file is a stream of bytes; if you wanted to add even a single comma, the remainder of the text file (possibly thousands or millions of bytes) would have to move over to make room. Nearly every tiny change would mean lots of slow copying operations on the file. So how can we edit the file efficiently?

The most common way of programmatically updating a text file is by writing an entirely new file that looks similar to the old one, but making whatever changes we need as we go along. As you'll see, this technique gives nearly the same result as updating the file itself, but it has some beneficial side effects as well.

In this example, we've got hundreds of files with a similar format. One of them is *fred03.dat*, and it's full of lines like these:

```
Program name: granite
Author: Gilbert Bates
Company: RockSoft
Department: R&D
Phone: +1 503 555-0095
```

---

[*] Of course, the real file wouldn't have lines at all; it's one long stream of text. And the newline character should really be a single-character code. But these differences don't hurt this as an example.

```
Date: Tues March 9, 1999
Version: 2.1
Size: 21k
Status: Final beta
```

We need to fix this file so that it has some different information. Here's roughly what this one should look like when we're done:

```
Program name: granite
Author: Randal L. Schwartz
Company: RockSoft
Department: R&D
Date: June 12, 2002 6:38 pm
Version: 2.1
Size: 21k
Status: Final beta
```

In short, we need to make three changes. The name of the **Author** should be changed; the **Date** should be updated to today's date, and the **Phone** should be removed completely. And we have to make these changes in hundreds of similar files as well.

Perl supports a way of in-place editing of files with a little extra help from the diamond operator ("<>"). Here's a program to do what we want, although it may not be obvious how it works at first. This program's only new feature is the special variable $^I; ignore that for now, and we'll come back to it:

```
#!/usr/bin/perl -w

use strict;

chomp(my $date = `date`);
@ARGV = glob "fred*.dat" or die "no files found";
$^I = ".bak";

while (<>) {
  s/^Author:.*/Author: Randal L. Schwartz/;
  s/^Phone:.*\n//;
  s/^Date:.*/Date: $date/;
  print;
}
```

Since we need today's date, the program starts by using the system *date* command. A better way to get the date (in a slightly different format) would almost surely be to use Perl's own **localtime** function in a scalar context:

```
my $date = localtime;
```

To get the list of files for the diamond operator, we read them from a glob. The next line sets $^I, but keep ignoring that for the moment.

The main loop reads, updates, and prints one line at a time. (With what you know so far, that means that all of the files' newly modified contents will be dumped to your terminal, scrolling furiously past your eyes, without the files being changed at all. But stick with us.) Note that the second substitution can replace the entire line containing the phone number with an empty string—leaving not even a newline— so when that's printed, nothing comes out, and it's as if the **Phone** never existed. Most input lines won't match any of the three patterns, and those will be unchanged in the output.

So this result is close to what we want, except that we haven't shown you how the updated information gets back out on to the disk. The answer is in the variable `$^I`. By default it's **undef**, and everything is normal. But when it's set to some string, it makes the diamond operator ("<>") even more magical than usual.

We already know about much of the diamond's magic—it will automatically open and close a series of files for you, or read from the standard-input stream if there aren't any filenames given. But when there's a string in `$^I`, that string is used as a backup filename's extension. Let's see that in action.

Let's say it's time for the diamond to open our file *fred03.dat*. It opens it like before, but now it renames it, calling it *fred03.dat.bak*.* We've still got the same file open, but now it has a different name on the disk. Next, the diamond creates a new file and gives it the name *fred03.dat*. That's okay; we weren't using that name any more. And now the diamond selects the new file as the default for output, so that anything that we print will go into that file.†

So now the `while` loop will read a line from the old file, update that, and print it out to the new file. This program can update hundreds of files in a few seconds on a typical machine. Pretty powerful, huh?

Once the program has finished, what does the user see? The user says, "Ah, I see what happened! Perl edited my file *fred03.dat*, making the changes I needed, and saved me a copy of the original in the backup file *fred03.dat.bak* just to be helpful!" But we now know the truth: Perl didn't really edit any file. It made a modified copy, said "Abracadabra!", and switched the files around while we were watching sparks come out of the magic wand. Tricky.

Some folks use a tilde ("~") as the value for `$^I`, since that resembles what *emacs* does for backup files. Another possible value for `$^I` is the empty string. This enables in-place editing, but doesn't save the original data in a backup file. But since a small typo in your pattern could wipe out all of the old data, using the empty string is recommended only if you want to find out how good your backup

---

* Some of the details of this procedure will vary on non-Unix systems, but the end result should be nearly the same. See the release notes for your port of Perl.

† The diamond also tries to duplicate the original file's permission and ownership settings as much as possible; for example, if the old one was world-readable, the new one should be, as well.

tapes are. It's easy enough to delete the backup files when you're done. And when something goes wrong and you need to rename the backup files to their original names, you'll be glad that you know how to use Perl to do that (see the multiple-file rename example in Chapter 13).

In-place Editing from the Command Line

A program like the example from the previous section is fairly easy to write. But Larry decided it wasn't easy enough.

Imagine that you need to update hundreds of files that have the misspelling `Randall` instead of the one-l name `Randal`. You could write a program like the one in the previous section. Or you could do it all with a one-line program, right on the command line:

```
$ perl -p -i.bak -w -e 's/Randall/Randal/g' fred*.dat
```

Perl has a whole slew of command-line options that can be used to build a complete program in a few keystrokes.[*] Let's see what these few do.

Starting the command with `perl` does something like putting `#!/usr/bin/perl` at the top of a file does: it says to use the program *perl* to process what follows.

The `-p` option tells Perl to write a program for you. It's not much of a program, though; it looks something like this.[†]

```
while (<>) { print; }.
```

If you want even less, you could use `-n` instead; that leaves out the `print` statement. (Fans of *awk* will recognize -p and -n.) Again, it's not much of a program, but it's pretty good for the price of a few keystrokes.

The next option is `-i.bak`, which you might have guessed sets `$^I` to `".bak"` before the program starts. If you don't want a backup file, you can use `-i` alone, with no extension.

We've seen `-w` before—it turns on warnings.

The `-e` option says "executable code follows." That means that the `s/Randall/Randal/g` string is treated as Perl code. Since we've already got a `while` loop (from the `-p` option), this code is put inside the loop, before the `print`. For technical reasons, the last semicolon in the `-e` code is optional. But if you have more than one `-e`, and thus more than one chunk of code, only the semicolon at the end of the last one may safely be omitted.

---

[*] See the *perlrun* manpage for the complete list.

[†] Actually, the `print` occurs in a `continue` block. See the *perlsyn* and *perlrun* manpages for more information.

The last command-line parameter is `fred*.dat`, which says that `@ARGV` should hold the list of filenames that match that glob. Put the pieces all together, and it's as if we had written a program like this:

```
#!/usr/bin/perl -w

@ARGV = glob "fred*.dat";
$^I = ".bak";

while (<>) {
  s/Randall/Randal/g;
  print;
}
```

Compare this program to the one we used in the previous section. It's pretty similar. These command-line options are pretty handy, aren't they?

Exercises

These exercises are all related; it may be helpful to see what the second and third should do before starting on the first. See Appendix A for answers.

1. [15] Make a program that will read through the *perlfunc.pod* file looking for identifier names on `=item` lines (as in the similar exercise at the end of Chapter 9). The program should write a database showing the *first* line number on which each identifier appears. That is, if `fred` was mentioned on lines 23, 29, and 54, the value stored under the key `fred` would be 23. (Hint: the special `$.` variable gives the line number of the line that was just read.)

2. [10] Make a program that will take a Perl function name on the command line, and report what `=item` line of the *perlfunc.pod* file first mentions that function. Your program should not have to read through a long file to get this answer. What should your program do if the function name isn't found?

3. [10] (Extra credit exercise.) Modify the program from the previous exercise so that when the function is found in the database, your program will launch your favorite pager program to view the *perlfunc.pod* file at that line. (Hint: many programs that can be used for viewing text files work like *less* does, with a command line like `less +1234 filename` to start viewing the file at line 1234. Your favorite text editor may also support this convention, which is also used by *more, pico, vi, emacs,* and *view*.)

17

Some Advanced Perl Techniques

What we've put in the rest of this book is the core of Perl, the part that every Perl user should understand. But there are a few other techniques that, while not obligatory, are still valuable tools to have in your toolbox. We've gathered the most important of those for this chapter.

Don't be misled by the title of the chapter, though; the techniques here aren't especially more difficult to understand than what we have elsewhere. They are "advanced" merely in the sense that they aren't necessary for beginners. The first time you read this book, you may want to skip (or skim) this chapter so you can get right to using Perl. Come back to it a month or two later, when you're ready to get even more out of Perl. Consider this entire chapter a huge footnote*.

Trapping Errors with eval

Sometimes, your ordinary, everyday code can cause a fatal error in your program. Each of these typical statements could crash a program:

```
$barney = $fred / $dino;         # divide-by-zero error?

print "match\n" if /^($wilma)/;  # illegal regular expression error?

open CAVEMAN, $fred              # user-generated error from die?
  or die "Can't open file '$fred' for input: $!";
```

You could go to some trouble to catch some of these, but it's hard to get them all. (How could you check the string $wilma from that example to ensure that it makes a valid regular expression?) Fortunately, Perl provides a simple way to catch fatal errors: wrap the code in an **eval** block:

---

* We contemplated doing that in one of the drafts, but got firmly rejected by O'Reilly's editors.

```
eval { $barney = $fred / $dino } ;
```

Now, even if **$dino** is zero, that line won't crash the program. The **eval** is actually an expression (not a control structure, like **while** or **foreach**) so that semicolon is required at the end of the block.

When a normally fatal error happens during the execution of an **eval** block, the block is done running, but the program doesn't crash. So that means that right after an **eval** finishes, you'll be wanting to know whether it exited normally or whether it caught a fatal error for you. The answer is in the special **$@** variable. If the **eval** caught a fatal error, **$@** will hold what would have been the program's dying words, perhaps something like: Illegal division by zero at my_ program line 12. If there was no error, **$@** will be empty. Of course, that means that **$@** is a useful Boolean (true/false) value, true if there was an error, so you'll sometimes see code like this after an **eval** block:

```
print "An error occurred: $@" if $@;
```

The **eval** block is a true block, so it makes a new scope for lexical (**my**) variables. This piece of a program shows an **eval** block hard at work:

```
foreach my $person (qw/ fred wilma betty barney dino pebbles /) {
  eval {
    open FILE, "<$person"
      or die "Can't open file '$person': $!";

    my($total, $count);

    while (<FILE>) {
      $total += $_;
      $count++;
    }

    my $average = $total/$count;
    print "Average for file $person was $average\n";

    &do_something($person, $average);
  };

  if ($@) {
    print "An error occurred ($@), continuing\n";
  }
}
```

How many possible fatal errors are being trapped here? If there is an error in opening the file, that error is trapped. Calculating the average may divide by zero, so that error is trapped. Even the call to the mysteriously named **&do_something** subroutine will be protected against fatal errors, because an **eval** block traps any otherwise-fatal errors that occur during the time that it's active. (This feature is handy if you have to call a subroutine written by someone else, and you don't know whether they've coded defensively enough to avoid crashing your program.)

If an error occurs during the processing of one of the files, we'll get an error message, but the program will go on to the next file without further complaint.

You can nest **eval** blocks inside other **eval** blocks. The inner one traps errors while it runs, keeping them from reaching the outer blocks. (Of course, after the inner **eval** finishes, if it caught an error, you may wish to re-post the error by using **die**, thereby letting the outer **eval** catch it.) An **eval** block traps any errors that occur during its execution, including errors that happen during subroutine calls (as we saw in the example earlier).

We mentioned earlier that the **eval** is an expression, which is why the trailing semicolon is needed after the closing curly brace. But since it's an expression, it has a return value. If there's no error, it's like a subroutine: the return value is the last expression evaluated, or it's returned early with an optional **return** keyword. Here's another way to do the math without having to worry about divide-by-zero:

```
my $barney = eval { $fred / $dino };
```

If the **eval** traps a fatal error, the return value is either **undef** or an empty list, depending upon the context. So in the previous example, **$barney** is either the correct result from dividing, or it's **undef**; we don't really need to check **$@** (although it's probably a good idea to check **defined($barney)** before we use it further).

There are four kinds of problems that **eval** can't trap. The first group are the very serious errors that crash Perl itself, such as running out of memory or getting an untrapped signal. Since Perl itself isn't running, there's no way it can trap these errors.[*]

Of course, syntax errors inside the **eval** block are caught at compile time—they're never returned in **$@**.

The **exit** operator terminates the program at once, even if it's called from a subroutine inside an **eval** block. (This correctly implies that when writing a subroutine, you should use **die** rather than **exit** to signal when something goes wrong.)

The fourth and final kind of problem that an **eval** block can't trap are warnings, either user-generated ones (from **warn**) or Perl's internally generated warnings (requested with the **-w** command-line option or the **use warnings** pragma). There's a separate mechanism from **eval** for trapping warnings; see the discussion of the **__WARN__** pseudosignal in the Perl documentation for the details.

---

[*] Some of these errors are listed with an (**X**) code on the *perldiag* manpage, if you're curious.

We should also mention that there's another form of eval that can be dangerous if it's mishandled. In fact, you'll sometimes run across someone who will say that you shouldn't use eval in your code for security reasons. They're (mostly) right that eval should be used only with great care, but they're talking about the *other* form of eval, sometimes called "eval of a string". If the keyword eval is followed directly by a block of code in curly braces, as we're doing here, there's no need to worry—that's the safe kind of eval.

Picking Items from a List with grep

Sometimes you'll want only certain items from a list. Maybe it's only the odd numbers selected from a list of numbers, or maybe it's only the lines mentioning Fred from a file of text. As we'll see in this section, picking some items from a list can be done simply with the grep operator.

Let's try that first one and get the odd numbers from a large list of numbers. We don't need anything new to do that:

```
my @odd_numbers;

foreach (1..1000) {
  push @odd_numbers, $_ if $_ % 2;
}
```

That code uses the modulus operator (%), which we saw in Chapter 2. If a number is even, that number "mod two" gives zero, which is false. But an odd number will give one; since that's true, only the odd numbers will be pushed onto the array.

Now, there's nothing wrong with that code as it stands—except that it's a little longer to write and slower to run than it might be, since Perl provides the grep operator:

```
my @odd_numbers = grep { $_ % 2 } 1..1000;
```

That line gets a list of 500 odd numbers in one quick line of code. How does it work? The first argument to grep is a block that uses $_ as a placeholder for each item in the list, and returns a Boolean (true/false) value. The remaining arguments are the list of items to search through. The grep operator will evaluate the expression once for each item in the list, much as our original foreach loop did. For the ones where the last expression of the block returns a true value, that element is included in the list that results from grep.

While the grep is running, $_ is aliased to one element of the list after another. We've seen this behavior before, in the foreach loop. It's generally a bad idea to modify $_ inside the grep expression, because this will damage the original data.

The `grep` operator shares its name with a classic Unix utility that picks matching lines from a file by using regular expressions. We can do that with Perl's `grep`, which is much more powerful. Here we pull only the lines mentioning `fred` from a file:

```
my @matching_lines = grep { /\bfred\b/i } <FILE>;
```

There's a simpler syntax for `grep`, too. If all you need for the selector is a simple expression (rather than a whole block), you can just use that expression, followed by a comma, in place of the block. Here's the simpler way to write that latest example:

```
my @matching_lines = grep /\bfred\b/i, <FILE>;
```

Transforming Items from a List with map

Another common task is transforming items from a list. For example, suppose you have a list of numbers that should be formatted as "money numbers" for output, as with the subroutine `&big_money` (from Chapter 15). But we don't want to modify the original data; we need a modified copy of the list just for output. Here's one way to do that:

```
my @data = (4.75, 1.5, 2, 1234, 6.9456, 12345678.9, 29.95);
my @formatted_data;

foreach (@data) {
  push @formatted_data, &big_money($_);
}
```

That looks similar in form to the example code used at the beginning of the section on `grep`, doesn't it? So it may not surprise you that the replacement code resembles the first `grep` example:

```
my @data = (4.75, 1.5, 2, 1234, 6.9456, 12345678.9, 29.95);

my @formatted_data = map { &big_money($_) } @data;
```

The `map` operator looks much like `grep` because it has the same kind of arguments: a block that uses `$_`, and a list of items to process. And it operates in a similar way, evaluating the block once for each item in the list, with `$_` aliased to a different original list element each time. But the last expression of the block is used differently; instead of giving a Boolean value, the final value actually becomes part of the resulting list.[*]

---

[*] One other important difference is that the expression used by `map` is evaluated in a list context and may return any number of items, not necessarily one each time.

Any `grep` or `map` statement could be rewritten as a `foreach` loop pushing items onto a temporary array. But the shorter way is typically more efficient and more convenient. Since the result of `map` or `grep` is a list, it can be passed directly to another function. Here we can print that list of formatted "money numbers" as an indented list under a heading:

```
print "The money numbers are:\n",
    map { sprintf("%25s\n", $_) } @formatted_data;
```

Of course, we could have done that processing all at once, without even the temporary array `@formatted_data`:

```
my @data = (4.75, 1.5, 2, 1234, 6.9456, 12345678.9, 29.95);
print "The money numbers are:\n",
    map { sprintf("%25s\n", &big_money($_) ) } @data;
```

As we saw with `grep`, there's also a simpler syntax for `map`. If all you need for the selector is a simple expression (rather than a whole block), you can just use that expression, followed by a comma, in place of the block:

```
print "Some powers of two are:\n",
    map "\t" . ( 2 ** $_ ) . "\n", 0..15;
```

Unquoted Hash Keys

Perl offers many shortcuts that can help the programmer. Here's a handy one: you may omit the quote marks on some hash keys.

Of course, you can't omit the quote marks on just *any* key, since a hash key may be any arbitrary string. But keys are often simple. If the hash key is made up of nothing but letters, digits, and underscores without starting with a digit, you *may* be able to omit the quote marks. This kind of simple string without quote marks is called a *bareword*, since it stands alone without quotes.

One place you are permitted to use this shortcut is the most common place a hash key appears: in the curly braces of a hash element reference. For example, instead of `$score{"fred"}`, you could write simply `$score{fred}`. Since many hash keys are simple like this, not using quotes is a real convenience. But beware; if there's anything inside the curly braces besides a bareword, Perl will interpret it as an expression.

Another place where hash keys appear is when assigning an entire hash using a list of key-value pairs. The big arrow (=>) is especially useful between a key and a value, because (again, only if the key is a bareword) the big arrow quotes it for you:

```
# Hash containing bowling scores
my %score = (
  barney    => 195,
  fred      => 205,
```

```
    dino    => 30,
  );
```

This is the one important difference between the big arrow and a comma; a bareword to the left of the big arrow is implicitly quoted. (Whatever is on the right is left alone, though.) This feature of the big arrow doesn't have to be used only for hashes, although that's the most frequent use.

More Powerful Regular Expressions

After already reading three chapters about regular expressions, you know that they're a powerful feature in the core of Perl. But there are even more features that the Perl developers have added; we'll see some of the most important ones in this section. At the same time, you'll see a little more about the internal operation of the regular expression engine.

Non-greedy Quantifiers

The four quantifiers we've already seen (in Chapter 8) are all *greedy*. That means that they match as much as they can, only to reluctantly give some back if that's necessary to allow the overall pattern to succeed. Here's an example: Suppose you're using the pattern /fred.+barney/ on the string fred and barney went bowling last night. Of course, we know that the regular expression will match that string, but let's see how it goes about it.*

First, of course, the subpattern fred matches the identical literal string. The next part of the pattern is the .+, which matches any character except newline, at least one time. But the plus quantifier is greedy; it prefers to match as much as possible. So it immediately matches all of the rest of the string, including the word night. (This may surprise you, but the story isn't over yet.)

Now the subpattern barney would like to match, but it can't—we're at the end of the string. But since the .+ could still be successful even if it matched one fewer character, it reluctantly gives back the letter t at the end of the string. (It's greedy, but it wants the whole pattern to succeed even more than it wants to match everything all by itself.)

The subpattern barney tries again to match, and still can't. So the .+ gives back the letter h and lets it try again. One character after another, the .+ gives back

---

* The regular expression engine makes a few optimizations that make the true story different than we tell it here, and those optimizations change from one release of Perl to the next. You shouldn't be able to tell from the functionality that it's not doing as we say, though. If you want to know how it really works, you should read the latest source code. Be sure to submit patches for any bugs you find.

what it matched until finally it gives up all of the letters of **barney**. Now, finally, the subpattern **barney** can match, and the overall match succeeds.

Regular expression engines do a lot of backtracking like that, trying every different way of fitting the pattern to the string until one of them succeeds, or until none of them has.* But as you could see from this example, that can involve a lot of backtracking, as the quantifier gobbles up too much of the string and has to be forced to return some of it.

For each of the greedy quantifiers, though, there's also a non-greedy quantifier available. Instead of the plus (+), we can use the non-greedy quantifier +?, which matches one or more times (just as the plus does), except that it prefers to match as few times as possible, rather than as many as possible. Let's see how that new quantifier works when the pattern is rewritten as /fred.+?barney/.

Once again, **fred** matches right at the start. But this time the next part of the pattern is .+?, which would prefer to match no more than one character, so it matches just the space after **fred**. The next subpattern is **barney**, but that can't match here (since the string at the current position begins with **and barney**...). So the .+? reluctantly matches the **a** and lets the rest of the pattern try again. Once again, **barney** can't match, so the .+? accepts the letter **n** and so on. Once the .+? has matched five characters, **barney** can match, and the pattern is a success.

There was still some backtracking, but since the engine had to go back and try again just a few times, it should be a big improvement in speed. Well, it's an improvement if you'll generally find **barney** near **fred**. If your data often had **fred** near the start of the string and **barney** only at the end, the greedy quantifier might be a faster choice. In the end, the speed of the regular expression depends upon the data.

But the non-greedy quantifiers aren't just about efficiency. Although they'll always match (or fail to match) the same strings as their greedy counterparts, they may match different amounts of the strings. For example, suppose you had some HTML-like† text, and you want to remove all of the tags <BOLD> and </BOLD>, leaving their contents intact. Here's the text:

```
I'm talking about the cartoon with Fred and <BOLD>Wilma</BOLD>!
```

---

* In fact, some regular expression engines try every different way, even continuing on *after* they find one that fits. But Perl's regular expression engine is primarily interested in whether the pattern can or cannot match, so finding even one match means that the engine's work is done. Again, see Jeffrey Friedl's *Mastering Regular Expressions*.

† Once again, we aren't using real HTML because you can't correctly parse HTML with simple regular expressions. If you really need to work with HTML or a similar markup language, use a module that's made to handle the complexities.

And here's a substitution to remove those tags. But what's wrong with it?

```
s#<BOLD>(.*)</BOLD>#$1#g;
```

The problem is that the star is greedy.* What if the text had said this instead?

```
I thought you said Fred and <BOLD>Velma</BOLD>, not <BOLD>Wilma</BOLD>
```

In that case, the pattern would match from the first `<BOLD>` to the last `</BOLD>`, leaving intact the ones in the middle of the line. Oops! Instead, we want a non-greedy quantifier. The non-greedy form of star is `*?`, so the substitution now looks like this:

```
s#<BOLD>(.*?)</BOLD>#$1#g;
```

And it does the right thing.

Since the non-greedy form of the plus was `+?` and the non-greedy form of the star was `*?`, you've probably realized that the other two quantifiers look similar. The non-greedy form of any curly-brace quantifier looks the same, but with a question mark after the closing brace, like `{5,10}?` or `{8,}?`.† And even the question-mark quantifier has a non-greedy form: `??`. That matches either once or not at all, but it prefers not to match anything.

Matching Multiple-line Text

Classic regular expressions were used to match just single lines of text. But since Perl can work with strings of any length, Perl's patterns can match multiple lines of text as easily as single lines. Of course, you have to include an expression that holds more than one line of text. Here's a string that's four lines long:

```
$_ = "I'm much better\nthan Barney is\nat bowling,\nWilma.\n";
```

Now, the anchors `^` and `$` are normally anchors for the start and end of the whole string (see "Anchors" in Chapter 8). But the `/m` regular expression option lets them match at internal newlines as well (think `m` for multiple lines). This makes them anchors for the start and end of each *line*, rather than the whole string. So this pattern can match:

```
print "Found 'wilma' at start of line\n" if /^wilma\b/im;
```

---

* There's another possible problem: we should have used the `/s` modifier as well, since the end tag may be on a different line than the start tag. It's a good thing that this is just an example; if we were writing something like this for real, we would have taken our own advice and used a well-written module.

† In theory, there's also a non-greedy quantifier form that specifies an exact number, like `{3}?`. But since that says to match exactly three of the preceding item, it has no flexibility to be either greedy or non-greedy.

Similarly, you could do a substitution on each line in a multiline string. Here, we read an entire file into one variable,* then add the file's name as a prefix at the start of each line:

```
open FILE, $filename
  or die "Can't open '$filename': $!";
my $lines = join '', <FILE>;
$lines =~ s/^/$filename: /gm;
```

Slices

It often happens that we need to work with only a few elements from a given list. For example, the Bedrock Library keeps information about their patrons in a large file.† Each line in the file describes one patron with six colon-separated fields: a person's name, library card number, home address, home phone number, work phone number, and number of items currently checked out. A little bit of the file looks something like this:

```
fred flintstone:2168:301 Cobblestone Way:555-1212:555-2121:3
barney rubble:709918:3128 Granite Blvd:555-3333:555-3438:0
```

One of the library's applications needs only the card numbers and number of items checked out; it doesn't use any of the other data. It could use code something like this to get only the fields it needs:

```
while (<FILE>) {
  chomp;
  my @items = split /:/;
  my($card_num, $count) = ($items[1], $items[5]);
  ...  # now work with those two variables
}
```

But the array **@items** isn't needed for anything else; it seems like a waste.‡ Maybe it would be better to assign the result of **split** to a list of scalars, like this:

```
my($name, $card_num, $addr, $home, $work, $count) = split /:/;
```

Well, that avoids the unneeded array **@items**—but now we have four scalar variables that we didn't really need. For this situation, some people used to make up a number of dummy variable names, like **$dummy_1**, that showed that they really didn't care about that element from the **split**. But Larry thought that that was too much trouble, so he added a special use of **undef**. If an item in a list being

---

* Hope it's a small one. The file, that is, not the variable.

† It should really be a full-featured database rather than a flat file. They plan to upgrade their system, right after the next Ice Age.

‡ It's not much of a waste, really. But stay with us. All of these techniques are used by programmers who don't understand slices, so it's worthwhile to see all of them here.

assigned to is **undef**, that means simply to ignore the corresponding element of the source list:

```
my(undef, $card_num, undef, undef, undef, $count) = split /:/;
```

Is this any better? Well, it has an advantage that there aren't any unneeded variables. But it has the disadvantage that you have to count **undef**s to tell which element is **$count**. And this becomes quite unwieldy if there are more elements in the list. For example, some people who wanted just the mtime value from **stat** were writing code like this:

```
my(undef, undef, undef, undef, undef, undef, undef,
   undef, undef, $mtime) = stat $some_file;
```

If you use the wrong number of **undef**s, you'll get the atime or ctime by mistake, and that's a tough one to debug. There's a better way: Perl can index into a list as if it were an array. This is a *list slice*. Here, since the mtime is item 9 in the list returned by **stat**,* we can get it with a subscript:

```
my $mtime = (stat $some_file)[9];
```

Those parentheses are required around the list of items (in this case, the return value from **stat**). If you wrote it like this, it wouldn't work:

```
my $mtime = stat($some_file)[9];  # Syntax error!
```

A list slice has to have a subscript expression in square brackets after a list in parentheses. The parentheses holding the arguments to a function call don't count.

Going back to the Bedrock Library, the list we're working with is the return value from **split**. We can now use a slice to pull out item 1 and item 5 with subscripts:

```
my $card_num = (split /:/)[1];
my $count = (split /:/)[5];
```

Using a scalar-context slice like this (pulling just a single element from the list) isn't bad, but it would be more efficient and simpler if we didn't have to do the **split** twice. So let's not do it twice; let's get both values at once by using a list slice in list context:

```
my($card_num, $count) = (split /:/)[1, 5];
```

The indices pull out element 1 and element 5 from the list, returning those as a two-element list. When that's assigned to the two **my** variables, we get exactly what we wanted. We do the **slice** just once, and we set the two variables with a simple notation.

---

* It's the tenth item, but the index number is 9, since the first item is at index 0. This is the same kind of zero-based indexing that we've used already with arrays.

A slice is often the simplest way to pull a few items from a list. Here, we can pull just the first and last items from a list, using the fact that index −1 means the last element:[*]

```
my($first, $last) = (sort @names)[0, -1];
```

The subscripts of a slice may be in any order and may even repeat values. This example pulls five items from a list of ten:

```
my @names = qw{ zero one two three four five six seven eight nine };
my @numbers = ( @names )[ 9, 0, 2, 1, 0 ];
print "Bedrock @numbers\n";   # says Bedrock nine zero two one zero
```

Array Slice

That previous example could be made even simpler. When slicing elements from an array (as opposed to a list), the parentheses aren't needed. So we could have done the slice like this:

```
my @numbers = @names[ 9, 0, 2, 1, 0 ];
```

This isn't merely a matter of omitting the parentheses; this is actually a different notation for accessing array elements: an *array slice*. Earlier (in Chapter 3), we said that the at-sign on **@names** meant "all of the elements." Actually, in a linguistic sense, it's more like a plural marker, much like the letter "s" in words like "cats" and "dogs." In Perl, the dollar sign means there's just one of something, but the at-sign means there's a list of items.

A slice is always a list, so the array slice notation uses an at-sign to indicate that. When you see something like **@names[** ... **]** in a Perl program, you'll need to do just as Perl does and look at the at-sign at the beginning as well as the square brackets at the end. The square brackets mean that you're indexing into an array, and the at-sign means that you're getting a whole list[†] of elements, not just a single one (which is what the dollar sign would mean). See Figure 17-1.

The punctuation mark at the front of the variable reference (either the dollar sign or at-sign) determines the context of the subscript expression. If there's a dollar sign in front, the subscript expression is evaluated in a scalar context to get an index. But if there's an at-sign in front, the subscript expression is evaluated in a list context to get a list of indices.

---

[*] Sorting a list merely to find the extreme elements isn't likely to be the most efficient way. But Perl's sort is fast enough that this is generally acceptable, as long as the list doesn't have more than a few hundred elements.

[†] Of course, when we say "a whole list," that doesn't necessarily mean more elements than one—the list could be empty, after all.

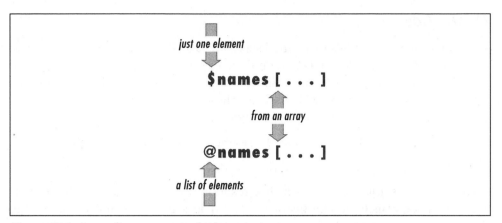

Figure 17-1. Array slices versus single elements

So we see that `@names[ 2, 5 ]` means the same list as (`$names[2]`, `$names[5]`) does. If you want that list of values, you can simply use the array slice notation. Any place you might want to write the list, you can instead use the simpler array slice.

But the slice can be used in one place where the list can't: a slice may be interpolated directly into a string:

```
my @names = qw{ zero one two three four five six seven eight nine };
print "Bedrock @names[ 9, 0, 2, 1, 0 ]\n";
```

If we were to interpolate `@names`, that would give all of the items from the array, separated by spaces. If instead we interpolate `@names[ 9, 0, 2, 1, 0 ]`, that gives just those items from the array, separated by spaces.*

Let's go back to the Bedrock Library for a moment. Maybe now our program is updating Mr. Slate's address and phone number in the patron file, because he just moved into a large new place in the Hollyrock hills. If we've got a list of information about him in `@items`, we could do something like this to update just those two elements of the array:

```
my $new_home_phone = "555-6099";
my $new_address = "99380 Red Rock West";
@items[2, 3] = ($new_address, $new_home_phone);
```

Once again, the array slice makes a more compact notation for a list of elements. In this case, that last line is the same as an assignment to (`$items[2]`, `$items[3]`), but more compact and efficient.

---

* More accurately, the items of the list are separated by the contents of Perl's `$"` variable, whose default is a space. This should not normally be changed. When interpolating a list of values, Perl internally does `join $", @list`, where `@list` stands in for the list expression.

Hash Slice

In a way exactly analogous to an array slice, we can also slice some elements from a hash in a *hash slice*. Remember when three of our characters went bowling, and we kept their bowling scores in the %score hash? We could pull those scores with a list of hash elements or with a slice. These two techniques are equivalent, although the second is more concise and efficient:

```
my @three_scores = ($score{"barney"}, $score{"fred"}, $score{"dino"});

my @three_scores = @score{ qw/ barney fred dino/ };
```

A slice is always a list, so the hash slice notation uses an at-sign to indicate that.* When you see something like @score{ ... } in a Perl program, you'll need to do just as Perl does and look at the at-sign at the beginning as well as the curly braces at the end. The curly braces mean that you're indexing into a hash; the at-sign means that you're getting a whole list of elements, not just a single one (which is what the dollar sign would mean). See Figure 17-2.

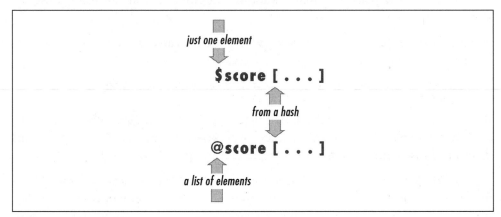

Figure 17-2. Hash slices versus single elements

As we saw with the array slice, the punctuation mark at the front of the variable reference (either the dollar sign or at-sign) determines the context of the subscript expression. If there's a dollar sign in front, the subscript expression is evaluated in a scalar context to get a single key.† But if there's an at-sign in front, the subscript expression is evaluated in a list context to get a list of keys.

---

* If it sounds as if we're repeating ourselves here, it's because we want to emphasize that hash slices are analogous to array slices. If it sounds as if we're not repeating ourselves here, it's because we want to emphasize that hash slices are analogous to array slices.

† There's an exception you're not likely to run across, since it isn't used much in modern Perl code. See the entry for $; in the *perlvar* manpage.

It's normal at this point to wonder why there's no percent sign ("%") here, when we're talking about a hash. That's the marker that means there's a whole hash; a hash slice (like any other slice) is always a *list*, not a hash.* In Perl, the dollar sign means there's just one of something, but the at-sign means there's a list of items, and the percent sign means there's an entire hash.

As we saw with array slices, a hash slice may be used instead of the corresponding list of elements from the hash, anywhere within Perl. So we can set our friends' bowling scores in the hash (without disturbing any other elements in the hash) in this simple way:

```
my @players = qw/ barney fred dino /;
my @bowling_scores = (195, 205, 30);
@score{ @players } = @bowling_scores;
```

That last line does the same thing as if we had assigned to the three-element list (`$score{"barney"}`, `$score{"fred"}`, `$score{"dino"}`).

A hash slice may be interpolated, too. Here, we print out the scores for our favorite bowlers:

```
print "Tonight's players were: @players\n";
print "Their scores were: @score{@players}\n";
```

Exercise

See Appendix A for an answer to the following exercise:

1. [30] Make a program that reads a list of strings from a file, one string per line, and then lets the user interactively enter patterns that may match some of the strings. For each pattern, the program should tell how many strings from the file matched, then which ones those were. Don't re-read the file for each new pattern; keep the strings in memory. The filename may be hard-coded in the file. If a pattern is invalid (for example, if it has unmatched parentheses), the program should simply report that error and let the user continue trying patterns. When the user enters a blank line instead of a pattern, the program should quit. (If you need a file full of interesting strings to try matching, try the file *sample_text* in the files you've surely downloaded by now from the O'Reilly website; see the Preface.)

---

* A hash slice is a slice (not a hash) in the same way that a house fire is a fire (not a house), while a fire house is a house (not a fire). More or less.

A

Exercise Answers

This appendix contains the answers to the excerses that appear throughout the book.

Answers to Chapter 2 Exercises

1. Here's one way to do it:

```
#!/usr/bin/perl -w
$pi = 3.141592654;
$circ = 2 * $pi * 12.5;
print "The circumference of a circle of radius 12.5 is $circ.\n";
```

As you see, we started this program with a typical #! line; your path to Perl may vary. We also turned on warnings.

The first real line of code sets the value of $pi to our value of π. There are several reasons a good programmer will prefer to use a constant* value like this: it takes time to type 3.141592654 into your program if you ever need it more than once. It may be a mathematical bug if you accidentally used 3.141592654 in one place and 3.14159 in another. There's only one line to check on to make sure you didn't accidentally type 3.141952654 and send your space probe to the wrong planet. It's easier to type $pi than π, especially if you don't have Unicode. And it will be easy to maintain the program in case the value of π ever changes.†

Next we calculate the circumference, storing it into $circ, and we print it out in a nice message. The message ends with a newline character, because every

---

* If you'd prefer a more formal sort of constants, the constant pragma may be what you're looking for.

† It nearly did change by a legislative act in the state of Indiana. *http://www.urbanlegends.com/legal/pi_indiana.html*

line of a good program's output should end with a newline. Without it, you might end up with output looking something like this, depending upon your shell's prompt:

```
The circumference of a circle of radius 12.5 is 78.53981635.bash-2.01$ █
```

The box represents the input cursor, blinking at the end of the line, and that's the shell's prompt at the end of the message.* Since the circumference isn't really 78.53981635.bash-2.01$, this should probably be construed as a bug. So use \n at the end of each line of output.

2. Here's one way to do it:

```
#!/usr/bin/perl -w
$pi = 3.141592654;
print "What is the radius? ";
chomp($radius = <STDIN>);
$circ = 2 * $pi * $radius;
print "The circumference of a circle of radius $radius is $circ.\n";
```

This is just like the last one, except that now we ask the user for the radius, and then we use $radius in every place where we previously used the hard-coded value 12.5. If we had written the first program with more foresight, in fact, we would have had a variable named $radius in that one as well. Note that we chomped the line of input. If we hadn't, the mathematical formula would still have worked, because a string like "12.5\n" is converted to the number 12.5 without any problem. But when we print out the message, it would look like this:

```
The circumference of a circle of radius 12.5
 is 78.53981635.
```

Notice that the newline character is still in $radius, even though we've used that variable as a number. Since we had a space between $radius and the word "is" in the print statement, there's a space at the beginning of the second line of output. The moral of the story is: chomp your input unless you have a reason not to do that.

3. Here's one way to do it:

```
#!/usr/bin/perl -w
$pi = 3.141592654;
print "What is the radius? ";
chomp($radius = <STDIN>);
$circ = 2 * $pi * $radius;
if ($radius < 0) {
  $circ = 0;
}
print "The circumference of a circle of radius $radius is $circ.\n";
```

---

* We asked O'Reilly to spend the extra money to print the input cursor with blinking ink, but they wouldn't do it for us.

Here we added the check for a bogus radius. Even if the given radius was impossible, the returned circumference will at least be nonnegative. You could have changed the given radius to be zero, and then calculated the circumference, too; there's more than one way to do it. In fact, that's the Perl motto: There Is More Than One Way To Do It. And that's why each exercise answer starts with "Here's one way to do it."

4. Here's one way to do it:

```
print "Enter first number: ";
chomp($one = <STDIN>);
print "Enter second number: ";
chomp($two = <STDIN>);
$result = $one * $two;
print "The result is $result.\n";
```

Notice that we've left off the #! line for this answer. In fact, from here on, we'll assume that you know it's there, so you don't need to read it each time.

Perhaps those are poor choices for variable names. In a large program, a maintenance programmer might think that $two should have the value of 2. In this short program, it probably doesn't matter, but in a large one we could have called them something more descriptive, with names like $first_response.

In this program, it wouldn't make any difference if we forgot to **chomp** the two variables $one and $two, since we never use them as strings once they've been set. But if next week our maintenance programmer edits the program to print a message like: **The result of multiplying $one by $two is $result.\n**, those pesky newlines will come back to haunt us. Once again, **chomp** unless you have a reason not to **chomp**[*]—like in the next exercise.

5. Here's one way to do it:

```
print "Enter a string: ";
$str = <STDIN>;
print "Enter a number of times: ";
chomp($num = <STDIN>);
$result = $str x $num;
print "The result is:\n$result";
```

This program is almost the same as the last one, in a sense. We're "multiplying" a string by a number of times. So we've kept the structure of the previous exercise. In this case, though, we didn't want to **chomp** the first input item—the string—because the exercise asked for the strings to appear on separate lines. So, if the user entered **fred** and a newline for the string, and 3 for the number, we'd get a newline after each **fred** just as we wanted.

---

[*] Chomping is like chewing—not always needed, but most of the time it doesn't hurt.

In the `print` statement at the end, we put the newline before `$result` because we wanted to have the first `fred`, printed on a line of its own. That is, we didn't want output like this, with only two of the three `fred`s aligned in a column:

```
The result is: fred
fred
fred
```

At the same time, we didn't need to put another newline at the end of the `print` output because `$result` should already end with a newline.

In most cases, Perl won't mind where you put spaces in your program; you can put in spaces or leave them out. But it's important not to accidentally spell the wrong thing! If the `x` runs up against the preceding variable name `$str`, Perl will see `$strx`, which won't work.

Answers to Chapter 3 Exercises

1. Here's one way to do it:

   ```
   print "Enter some lines, then press Ctrl-D:\n"; # or maybe Ctrl-Z
   @lines = <STDIN>;
   @reverse_lines = reverse @lines;
   print @reverse_lines;
   ```

   ...or, even more simply:

   ```
   print "Enter some lines, then press Ctrl-D:\n";
   print reverse <STDIN>;
   ```

   Most Perl programmers would prefer the second one, as long as you don't need to keep the list of lines around for later use.

2. Here's one way to do it:

   ```
   @names = qw/ fred betty barney dino wilma pebbles bamm-bamm /;
   print "Enter some numbers from 1 to 7, one per line, then press Ctrl-D:\n";
   chomp(@numbers = <STDIN>);
   foreach (@numbers) {
     print "$names[ $_ - 1 ]\n";
   }
   ```

   We have to subtract one from the index number so that the user can count from 1 to 7 even though the array is indexed from 0 to 6. Another way to accomplish this would be to have a dummy item in the `@names` array, like this:

   ```
   @names = qw/ dummy_item fred betty barney dino wilma pebbles bamm-bamm /;
   ```

   Give yourself extra credit if you checked to make sure that the user's choice of index was in fact in the range 1 to 7.

3. Here's one way to do it, if you want the output all on one line:

```
chomp(@lines = <STDIN>);
@sorted = sort @lines;
print "@sorted\n";
```

...or, to get the output on separate lines:

```
print sort <STDIN>;
```

Answers to Chapter 4 Exercises

1. Here's one way to do it:

```
sub total {
  my $sum;  # private variable
  foreach (@_) {
    $sum += $_;
  }
  $sum;
}
```

This subroutine uses $sum to keep a running total. At the start of the subroutine, $sum is undef, since it's a new variable. Then, the foreach loop steps through the parameter list (from @_), using $_ as the control variable. (Note: once again, there's no automatic connection between @_, the parameter array, and $_, the default variable for the foreach loop.)

The first time through the foreach loop, the first number (in $_) is added to $sum. Of course, $sum is undef, since nothing has been stored in there. But since we're using it as a number, which Perl sees because of the numeric operator +=, Perl acts as if it's already initialized to 0. Perl thus adds the first parameter to 0, and puts the total back into $sum.

Next time through the loop, the next parameter is added to $sum, which is no longer undef. The sum is placed back into $sum, and on through the rest of the parameters. Finally, the last line returns $sum to the caller.

There's a potential bug in this subroutine, depending upon how you think of things. Suppose that this subroutine was called with an empty parameter list (as we considered with the rewritten subroutine &max in the chapter text). In that case, $sum would be undef, and that would be the return value. But in this subroutine, it would probably be "more correct" to return 0 as the sum of the empty list, rather than undef. (Of course, if you wished to distinguish the sum of an empty list from the sum of, say, (3, -5, 2), returning undef would be the right thing to do.)

If you don't want a possibly undefined return value, though, it's easy to remedy: simply initialize $sum to zero rather than using the default of undef:

```
my $sum = 0;
```

Now the subroutine will always return a number, even if the parameter list were empty.

2. Here's one way to do it:

```
# Remember to include &total from previous exercise!
print "The numbers from 1 to 1000 add up to ", &total(1..1000), ".\n";
```

Note that we can't call the subroutine from inside the double-quoted string,* so the subroutine call is another separate item being passed to print. The total should be 500500, a nice round number. And it shouldn't take any noticeable time at all to run this program; passing a parameter list of 1000 values is an everyday task for Perl.

Answers to Chapter 5 Exercises

1. Here's one way to do it:

```
my %last_name = qw{
   fred flintstone
   barney rubble
   wilma flintstone
};
print "Please enter a first name: ";
chomp(my $name = <STDIN>);
print "That's $name $last_name{$name}.\n";
```

In this one, we used a qw// list (with curly braces as the delimiter) to initialize the hash. That's fine for this simple data set, and it's easy to maintain because each data item is a simple given name and simple family name, with nothing tricky. But if your data might contain spaces—for example, if **robert de niro** or **mary kay place** were to visit Bedrock—this simple method wouldn't work so well.

You might have chosen to assign each key/value pair separately, something like this:

```
my %last_name;
$last_name{"fred"} = "flintstone";
$last_name{"barney"} = "rubble";
$last_name{"wilma"} = "flintstone";
```

Note that (if you chose to declare the hash with **my**, perhaps because **use strict** was in effect), you must declare the hash before assigning any elements. You can't use **my** on only part of a variable, like this:

```
my $last_name{"fred"} = "flintstone";   # Oops!
```

---

* We can't do this without advanced trickiness, that is. It's rare to find anything that you *absolutely* can't do in Perl.

The my operator works only with *entire* variables, never with just one element of an array or hash. Speaking of lexical variables, you may have noticed that the lexical variable $name is being declared inside of the chomp function call; it is fairly common to declare each my variable as it is needed, like this.

This is another case where chomp is vital. If someone enters the five-character string "fred\n" and we fail to chomp it, we'll be looking for "fred\n" as an element of the hash—and it's not there. Of course, chomp alone won't make this bulletproof; if someone enters "fred \n" (with a trailing space), we don't have a way with what we've seen so far to tell that they meant fred.

If you added a check whether the given key exists in the hash, so that you'll give the user an explanatory message when they misspell a name, give yourself extra points for that.

2. Here's one way to do it:

```perl
my(@words, %count, $word);      # (optionally) declare our variables
chomp(@words = <STDIN>);

foreach $word (@words) {
  $count{$word} += 1;           # or $count{$word} = $count{$word} + 1;
}

foreach $word (keys %count) {   # or sort keys %count
  print "$word was seen $count{$word} times.\n";
}
```

In this one, we declared all of the variables at the top. People who come to Perl from a background in languages like Pascal (where variables are always declared "at the top") may find that way more familiar than declaring variables as they are needed. Of course, we're declaring these because we're pretending that use strict may be in effect; by default, Perl won't require such declarations.

Next, we use the line-input operator, <STDIN>, in a list context to read all of the input lines into @words, and then we chomp those all at once. So @words is our list of words from the input (if the words were all on separate lines, as they should have been, of course).

Now, the first foreach loop goes through all of the words. That loop contains the most important statement of the entire program, the statement that says to add one to $count{$word}, and put the result back into $count{$word}. Although you could write it either the short way (with the += operator) or the long way, the short way is just a little bit more efficient, since Perl has to look up $word in the hash just once.*

For each word in the first foreach loop, we add one to $count{$word}. So, if the first word is fred, we add one to $count{"fred"}. Of course, since this is the first time we've seen $count{"fred"}, it's **undef**. But since we're treating it as a number (with the numeric += operator, or with +, if you wrote it the long way), Perl converts **undef** to 0 for us, automatically. The total is 1, which is then stored back into $count{"fred"}.

The next time through that **foreach** loop, let's say the word is **barney**. So, we add one to $count{"barney"}, bumping it up from **undef** to 1, as well.

Now let's say the next word is **fred** again. When we add one to $count{"fred"}, which is already 1, we get 2. This goes back into $count{"fred"}, meaning that we've now seen **fred** twice.

When we finish the first **foreach** loop, then, we've counted how many times each word has appeared. The hash has a key for each (unique) word from the input, and the corresponding value is the number of times that word appeared.

So now, the second **foreach** loop goes through the keys of the hash, which are the unique words from the input. In this loop, we'll see each *different* word once. For each one, it says something like "**fred was seen 3 times.**"

If you want the extra credit on this problem, you could put **sort** before **keys** to print out the keys in order. If there will be more than a dozen items in an output list, it's generally a good idea for them to be sorted, so that a human being who is trying to debug the program will fairly quickly be able to find the item he or she wants.

Answers to Chapter 6 Exercises

1. Here's one way to do it:

```
print reverse <>;
```

Well, that's pretty simple! But it works because **print** is looking for a list of strings to print, which it gets by calling **reverse** in a list context. And **reverse** is looking for a list of strings to reverse, which it gets by using the diamond operator in list context. So, the diamond returns a list of all of the lines from all of the files of the user's choice. That list of lines is just what *cat* would print out. Now **reverse** reverses the list of lines, and **print** prints them out.

2. Here's one way to do it:

```
print "Enter some lines, then press Ctrl-D:\n";  # or Ctrl-Z
chomp(my @lines = <STDIN>);
```

---

* Also, at least in some versions of Perl, the shorter way will avoid a warning about using an undefined value that may crop up with the longer one. The warning may also be avoided by using the ++ operator to increment the variable, although we haven't shown you that operator yet.

```
print "1234567890" x 7, "12345\n";  # ruler line to column 75

foreach (@lines) {
  printf "%20s\n", $_;
}
```

Here, we start by reading in and chomping all of the lines of text. Then we print the ruler line. Since that's a debugging aid, we'd generally comment-out that line when the program is done. We could have typed "1234567890" again and again, or even used copy-and-paste to make a ruler line as long as we needed, but we chose to do it this way because it's kind of cool.

Now, the **foreach** loop iterates over the list of lines, printing each one with the %20s conversion. If you chose to do so, you could have created a format to print the list all at once, without the loop:

```
my $format = "%20s\n" x @lines;
printf $format, @lines;
```

It's a common mistake to get 19-character columns. That happens when you say to yourself,* "Hey, why do we **chomp** the input if we're only going to add the newlines back on later?" So you leave out the **chomp** and use a format of "%20s" (without a newline).† And now, mysteriously, the output is off by one space. So, what went wrong?

The problem happens when Perl tries to count the spaces needed to make the right number of columns. If the user enters **hello** and a newline, Perl sees *six* characters, not five, since newline is a character. So it prints fourteen spaces and a six-character string, sure that it gives the twenty characters you asked for in "%20s". Oops.

Of course, Perl isn't looking at the contents of the string to determine the width; it merely checks the raw number of characters. A newline (or another special character, such as a tab or a null character) will throw things off.‡

3. Here's one way to do it:

```
print "What column width would you like? ";
chomp(my $width = <STDIN>);

print "Enter some lines, then press Ctrl-D:\n";  # or Ctrl-Z
chomp(my @lines = <STDIN>);

print "1234567890" x (($width+9)/10), "\n";      # ruler line as needed

foreach (@lines) {
  printf "%${width}s\n", $_;
}
```

---

* Or to Larry, if he's standing nearby.

† Unless Larry told you not to do that.

‡ As Larry should have explained to you by now.

This is much like the previous one, but we ask for a column width first. We ask for that first because we can't ask for more input *after* the end-of-file indicator, at least on some systems. Of course, in the real world, you'll generally have a better end-of-input indicator when getting input from the user, as we'll see in later chapters.

Another change from the previous exercise's answer is the ruler line. We used some math to cook up a ruler line that's at least as long as we need, as suggested as an "extra credit" part of the exercise. Proving that our math is correct is an additional challenge. (Hint: Consider possible widths of 50 and 51, and remember that the right side operand to x is truncated, not rounded.)

To generate the format this time, we used the expression `"%${width}s\n"`, which interpolates `$width`. The curly braces are required to "insulate" the name from the following s; without the curly braces, we'd be interpolating `$widths`, the wrong variable. If you forgot how to use curly braces to do this, though, you could have written an expression like `'%' . $width . "s\n"` to get the same format string.

The value of `$width` brings up another case where `chomp` is vital. If the width isn't chomped, the resulting format string would resemble `"%30\ns\n"`. That's not useful.

People who have seen `printf` before may have thought of another solution. Because `printf` comes to us from C, which doesn't have string interpolation, we can use the same trick that C programmers use. If an asterisk ("`*`") appears in place of a numeric field width in a conversion, a value from the list of parameters will be used:

```
printf "%*s\n", $width, $_;
```

Answers to Chapter 7 Exercises

1. Here's one way to do it:

    ```
    /fred/
    ```

    Of course, you have to put that into the test program! This is pretty simple. The more important part of this exercise is trying it out on the sample strings. It doesn't match `Fred`, showing that regular expressions are case-sensitive. (We'll see how to change that later.) It does match `frederick` and `Alfred`, since both of those strings contain the four-letter string `fred`.. (Matching whole words only, so that `frederick` and `Alfred` wouldn't match, is another feature we'll see later.)

If the test program is working correctly,* it should show those two matches as something like `|<fred>erick|` and `|Al<fred>|`, using the angle brackets to show where `fred` was found inside each string.

2. Here's one way to do it:

```
/a+b*/
```

That matches the letter `a` one or more times (that's the plus), followed by `b` zero or more times (that's the star). Well, that's what the exercise asked for, but you may have come up with something different. After all, if you're looking for *any* number of `b`'s, you know you'll always find what you're looking for. So you could have written `/a+/` instead, and matched the same strings.†

For that matter, when you want to match one or more `a`'s, you know that the match will succeed when you find even the first one. So, `/a/` will match the same set of strings as the first two. The description "any string containing at least one `a` followed by any number of `b`'s" means the exact same thing as "any string containing `a`." Of the sample strings, this matches all of them except `fred`.

There are even more ways to make this pattern than we show here. Often, in trying to write a pattern, you will need to decide which one of many possible patterns best suits your needs.

3. Here's one way to do it:

```
/\\*\**/
```

That's what the text asked for: a backslash (typed twice, since we mean a *real* backslash‡) zero or more times (that's the first star), followed by an asterisk (backslashed, since star is a metacharacter) zero or more times (that's the last star). Whew!

And what about the sample strings? Did it match any of them? You bet: it matches all of them! It's because the backslashes and asterisks aren't required in the pattern; that is, this pattern can match the empty string. Here's a rule you can rely upon: when a pattern *may* freely match the empty string, it'll *always* match, since the empty string can be found in any string. In fact, it'll always match in the *first* place that you look.

---

* If the test program didn't work correctly, you probably didn't download it as we suggested. And you probably didn't test what you typed, as we also suggested. But in that case, you probably didn't do the exercises either; you're just reading these answers in the back of the book, and so the test program (which you didn't actually run) performed flawlessly. In that case, this footnote is pointless.

† To be sure, you'll match different parts of the strings. But any string that matches `/a+b*/` will also match `/a+/`, and vice versa.

‡ Whenever you mean a real backslash in Perl, type two of them. A lone backslash may try to do something magical, but two of them will always mean a real backslash.

So, this pattern matches all four characters in **, as you'd expect. It matches the empty string at the beginning of fred, which you may not have expected. In the string barney ***, it matches the empty string at the beginning. You might wish it would hunt down the backslashes and stars at the end of that string, but it doesn't bother. It looks at the beginning, sees zero backslashes followed by zero asterisks, declares the match a success, and goes home to watch television. And in *wilma\, it matches just the star at the beginning; as you see, this pattern never gets away from the beginning of the string, since it always matches at the first opportunity.

Now, if someone asked you for a pattern to match any number of back-slashes followed by any number of asterisks, you'd be technically correct to give them this one. But chances are, that's not what they really wanted. Spoken languages like English may be ambiguous and not say exactly what they mean, but regular expressions always mean exactly what they say they mean.

In this case, maybe the person who asked for the pattern forgot to say that he or she always wants to match at least one character, when the pattern matches at all. We can do that. If there's at least one backslash, /\\+**/ will match. (That's just like what we had before, but there's a plus in place of the first star, meaning one or more backslashes.) If there's not at least one backslash, then in order to match at least one character, we'll need at least one asterisk, so we want /*+/. When you put those two possibilities together, you get:

```
/\\+\**|\*+/
```

Ugly, isn't it? Regular expressions are powerful but not beautiful. And they've contributed to Perl being maligned as a "write-only language." To be sure that no one criticizes your code in that way, though, it's kind to put an explanatory comment near any pattern that's not obvious. On the other hand, when you've been using these for a year, you will have a different definition of "obvious" than you have today.

How does this new pattern work with the sample strings? With **, it matches all four characters, just like the last one. It won't match fred, which is probably the right behavior given the problem description. For barney ***, it matches the six characters at the end, as you hoped. And for *wilma\, it matches the asterisk at the beginning.

4. Here's one way to do it:

```
while (<>) {
  if (/wilma/) {
    print;
  }
}
```

This is a *grep*-like program. For each line of text (contained in $_), we check to see whether the pattern matches. If it matches, we print it. This program uses **print**'s default: if you don't tell it to print something else, it prints $_. So we have written a program that uses $_ all the way through, but never mentions it anywhere. Perl folks love to use the defaults and save time typing, so you'll see a lot of programs that do this.

And if, for extra credit, you wanted to match a capitalized **Wilma** as well, /wilma|Wilma/ would do the job. Or, more simply, you could have written /(w|W)ilma/. People who have used other regular expression implementations and already know about character classes, which we'll discuss in the next chapter, could make that last one even shorter (and more efficient).*

5. Here's one way to do it:

```
while (<>) {
  if (/wilma/) {
    if (/fred/) {
      print;
    }
  }
}
```

This tests /fred/ only after we find /wilma/ matches, but **fred** could appear before or after **wilma** in the line; each test is independent of the other.

If you wanted to avoid the extra nested **if** test, you might have written something like this:†

```
while (<>) {
  if (/wilma.*fred|fred.*wilma/) {
    print;
  }
}
```

This works because we'll either have **wilma** before **fred**, or **fred** before **wilma**. If we had written just /wilma.*fred/, that wouldn't have matched a line like **fred and wilma flintstone**, even though that line mentions both of them.

---

* If you made the whole pattern case-insensitive, shame on you. We haven't learned that yet. Besides, that would match **WILMA**, which shouldn't match, according to the exercise description.

† Folks who know about the logical-and operator, which we saw in Chapter 10, could do both tests /fred/ and /wilma/ in the same **if** conditional. That's more efficient, more scalable, and an all-around better way than the ones given here. But we haven't seen logical-and yet.

We made this an extra-credit exercise because many folks have a mental block here. We showed you an "or" operation (with the vertical bar, "|"), but we never showed you an "and" operation. That's because there isn't one in regular expressions.* If you want to know whether one pattern and another are both successful, just test both of them.

Answers to Chapter 8 Exercises

1. Here's one way to do it:

    ```
    /\b(fred|wilma)\s+flintstone\b/
    ```

    If you forgot to use the \b word-boundary anchors, take off half a point; without those, this would mistakenly match strings like **alfred flintstones**. The exercise description said to match *words*.

2. The point of this exercise may not be obvious, but in the real world, you'll often have to do something similar. Someday, you'll be unlucky enough to have a confusing program to maintain, and you'll wonder what the author was trying to accomplish.†

    /"([^"]*)"/ matches a simple string in double quotes. By a "simple" string, we don't mean one like Perl's double-quoted strings, which could contain a backslashed double-quote mark or other backslash magic. This matches just a double-quote mark, the contents of the string (which can't contain a double quote), and a closing quote mark. The contents may be empty. The parentheses aren't needed for grouping, so they seem to be memory parentheses; as we'll see in the next chapter, this regular expression memory, which holds the quoted substring, is probably being saved for some later use. Perhaps this pattern would be used in reading a configuration file with quoted strings, although in that case it should probably use anchors.

    /^0?[0-3]?[0-7]{1,2}$/ matches if the string has nothing but an octal number (perhaps with a leading zero) in the range from 0 through 0377. Note that this one is anchored at both ends, so it doesn't allow anything else in the string before or after the number. (The previous pattern wasn't anchored; it could match anywhere in the string.)

    /^\b[\w.]{1,12}\b$/ matches strings made up of nothing but letters, digits, underscores, and dots, but never starting or ending with a dot. Also, the strings are limited to a maximum of 12 characters.

---

* But there are some tricky and advanced ways of doing what some folks would call an "and" operation. These are generally less efficient than using Perl's logical-and, though, depending upon what optimizations Perl and its regular expression engine can make.

† If you're especially unlucky, this happens when you look at your own code ten minutes after writing it.

You may have noticed that the dot inside the character class is not special, so it doesn't need to be backslashed. That makes the character class match ordinary letters, digits, and underscores, and also dots.

The way we can be sure that this one won't allow a string to start or end with a dot is that it has both a word-boundary anchor and a start-of-string or end-of-string anchor at each end of the string. The word-boundary anchor can match only if there's a "word" starting or ending there, and a dot can't be part of a word.

So, this would match strings like `perl.tar.gz`, but not `some_excessively_long_filename` or `perl.tar.` or `.profile` or `...`.[*] This pattern could be useful for validating user-chosen filenames.

3. Here's one way to do it:

    ```
    /^\$[A-Za-z_]\w*$/
    ```

   The dollar sign at the start has to be backslashed to mean a real dollar sign. What follows must be a letter or underscore, then zero or more letters, digits, or underscores.

4. This pattern is surprisingly tricky to get right. Here's how we construct it, step by step.

   We start out by needing to match a word, so that's `/\w+/`. Of course, we want to remember that word for later, so we add parentheses: `/(\w+)/`. And we want to match it when it occurs two or more times, so that's `/(\w+)\1+/`. (The plus sign at the end means *one* or more times—but that's in addition to the one time that the word occurred originally.)

   But we're not done yet. Now we need to allow for the whitespace which may come between the words. We don't want to memorize the whitespace (since it may vary), so we'll put it outside the parentheses: `/(\w+)\s\1+/`. Oh, but there could be any number of whitespace characters, so long as there's at least one, so we'll add a plus sign. So now we have `/(\w+)\s+\1+/`.

   But that's not right; the final plus sign is modifying the backreference alone. We need it to apply to both the backreference (that is, our repeated word) and the whitespace in front of it: `/(\w+)(\s+\1)+/`. So, now we can match a triple word. First, the part in the first parenthesis pair matches the first occurrence, then the part in the second parenthesis pair can twice match some whitespace followed by that same word. When we try it out, it matches all of our sentences with doubled words, so we happily put it into our program and move on to the next project.

---

[*] You may know that file and directory names beginning with a dot are not displayed by default on Unix systems, and that the special directory name `..` always means the directory one level higher in the hierarchy.

Then, the next week, we get a bug report! The pattern reports a match on the sentence `This is a test`, even though there's clearly no doubled word there. In moments, we've fired up the pattern test program* to see what part of the string is matching: `|Th<is is> a test|`. There it is, a doubled word `is`, hidden in an ordinary string.

Clearly, this is a job for a word boundary anchor; we can't have our word start in the middle of another word. So we fix the program to use `/\b(\w+)(\s+\1)+/`, and sit back, confident that we've got it right this time.

And then, just when you got started on another project, *another* bug report comes in. This time, we've matched the doubled word `the` in the phrase `the theory`. Yes, we need a word boundary at the *end* of the pattern to keep from matching a partial word there: `/\b(\w+)(\s+\1)+\b/`. Now we've finally gotten it right.

What you've just read is a true story. The regular expression has been changed, but the bug reports are real. It does happen, more often than we'd like to admit, that even after you've been writing these patterns for years, you can make a pattern which has a bug, you can test it with a number of test cases, you can put it into a long-running program, the Perl documentation, or even a best-selling Perl book, and not realize that the bug is there until much later.

The moral of the story is that regular expressions can be challenging. If you're serious about learning about regular expressions, though (and all Perl programmers should be), we highly recommend the book *Mastering Regular Expressions*, by Jeffry Friedl (O'Reilly & Associates, Inc.).

Answers to Chapter 9 Exercises

1. Here's one way to do it:

   ```
   /($what){3}/
   ```

   Once `$what` has been interpolated, this gives a pattern resembling `/(fred|barney){3}/`. Without the parentheses, the pattern would be something like `/fred|barney{3}/`, which is the same as `/fred|barneyyy/`. So, the parentheses are required.

2. Here's one way to do it:

   ```
   @ARGV = '/path/to/perlfunc.pod';   # or mentioned on the command line

   while (<>) {
     if (/^=item\s+([a-z_]\w*)/i) {
   ```

---

* We told you that it would come in handy, and we weren't kidding.

```
        print "$1\n";                    # print out that identifier name
    }
}
```

With what we've shown you so far, the only way to open an arbitrary file for input is to use the diamond operator (or to use input redirection, perhaps). So we put the path to `perlfunc.pod` into @ARGV.

The heart of this program is the pattern, which looks for an identifier name on an =item line. The exercise description was ambiguous, in that it didn't say whether =item had to be in lower case; the author of this pattern seems to have decided that it should be a case-insensitive pattern. If you interpreted it otherwise, you could have used the pattern /^=item\s+([a-zA-Z_]\w*)/.

3. Here's one way to do it:

```
@ARGV = '/path/to/perlfunc.pod';  # or mentioned on the command line

my %seen;                          # (optionally) declaring the hash

while (<>) {
  if (/^=item\s+([a-z_]\w*)/i) {
    $seen{$1} += 1;                # a tally for each item
  }
}

foreach (sort keys %seen) {
  if ($seen{$_} > 2) {             # more than twice
    print "$_ was seen $seen{$_} times.\n";
  }
}
```

This one starts out much like the previous one, but declares the hash %seen (in case use strict might be in effect). This is called %seen because it tells us which identifier names we've seen so far in the program, and how many times. This is a common use of a hash. The first loop now counts each identifier name, as an entry in %seen, instead of printing it out.

The second loop goes through the keys of %seen, which are the different identifier names we've seen. It sorts the list, which (although not specified in the exercise description) is a courtesy to the user, who might otherwise have to search for the desired item in a long list.

Although it may not be obvious, this program is pretty close to a real-world problem that most of us are likely to see. Imagine that your webserver's 400-megabyte logfile has some information you need. There's no way you're going to read that file on your own; you'll want a program to match the information you need (with a pattern) and then print it out in some nice report format. Perl is good for putting together quick programs to do that sort of thing.

Answer to Chapter 10 Exercise

1. Here's one way to do it:

```
my $secret = int(1 + rand 100);
# This next line may be un-commented during debugging
# print "Don't tell anyone, but the secret number is $secret.\n";

while (1) {
  print "Please enter a guess from 1 to 100: ";
  chomp(my $guess = <STDIN>);
  if ($guess =~ /quit|exit|^\s*$/i) {
    print "Sorry you gave up. The number was $secret.\n";
    last;
  } elsif ($guess < $secret) {
    print "Too small. Try again!\n";
  } elsif ($guess == $secret) {
    print "That was it!\n";
    last;
  } else {
    print "Too large. Try again!\n";
  }
}
```

The first line picks out our secret number from 1 to 100. Here's how it works. First, **rand** is Perl's random number function, so **rand** 100 gives us a random number in the range from zero up to (but not including) 100. That is, the largest possible value of that expression is something like 99.999.* Adding one gives a number from 1 to 100.999, then the **int** function truncates that, giving a result from 1 to 100, as we needed.

The commented-out line can be helpful during development and debugging, or if you like to cheat. The main body of this program is the infinite **while** loop. That will keep asking for guesses until we execute **last**.

It's important that we test the possible strings before the numbers. If we didn't, do you see what would happen when the user types **quit**? That would be interpreted as a number (probably giving a warning message, if warnings were turned on), and since the value as a number would be zero, the poor user would get the message that their guess was too small. We might never get to the string tests, in that case.

Another way to make the infinite loop here would be to use a naked block with **redo**. It's no more or less efficient; merely another way to write it. Generally, if you expect to mostly loop, it's good to write **while**, since that loops by default. If looping will be the exception, a naked block may be a better choice.

---

* The actual largest possible value depends upon your system; see *http://www.cpan.org/doc/ FMTEYEWTK/random* if you really need to know.

Answers to Chapter 11 Exercises

1. Here's one way to do it:

```
sub get_line {
  # prompts for, reads, chomps, and returns a line of input
  print $_[0];
  chomp(my $line = <STDIN>);
  $line;
}

my $source = &get_line("Which source file? ");
open IN, $source
  or die "Can't open '$source' for input: $!";

my $dest = &get_line("What destination file? ");
die "Won't overwrite existing file"
  if -e $dest;  # optional safety test
open OUT, ">$dest"
  or die "Can't open '$dest' for output: $!";

my $pattern = &get_line("What search pattern: ");
my $replace = &get_line("What replacement string: ");

while (<IN>) {
  s/$pattern/$replace/g;
  print OUT $_;
}
```

This one needs to ask the user for several things, so we decided to make a subroutine to take care of some of the work. The subroutine prints out the prompt, which is the first (and only) parameter to the subroutine. Then it reads a line of input, chomps it, and returns it. That makes it easy to ask for each parameter, one after the other.

Once we know what the user wants for the source file, we try opening it. An earlier version of this program asked for all of the parameters first, but if the source file name is incorrect, there's no point in having the user type more parameters. This way can save the user some time and trouble. Note that the die message reports the file name inside quote marks; this can be helpful in diagnosing a problem when a string has whitespace characters. If you opened "<$source" instead of just plain $source, that's fine, too. (There's no reason to worry that the user of this program will do something nefarious, since anything they can do with this program, they could accomplish just as well without it. If this program were made to run over the web, to give one example, we'd need to be *much* more cautious about opening the user's choice of file.)

As we hope you discovered when you tried it, it's easy to overwrite an existing file simply by opening it for output. So we put in a safety test using the -e file test. The corresponding die message doesn't include $! because we're not reporting a failed request of the system. By the way, this test for overwrite is fine here, but it would be insufficient in an environment where many copies of the same program (or different programs all working with the same files) might be running at once. This typically happens with programs on the web: Two processes check the same filename for existence at approximately the same time, and both see that it doesn't exist. So one of them creates the file, and an instant later the other one overwrites it with a file of its own. This kind of concurrency problem can't be solved with the -e file test; some kind of file locking (which is beyond the scope of this book) is needed.

With that safety test, the user won't accidentally overwrite an existing file. Is that test a good idea? Well, if the user comes to see you next week and says, "Golly, I'm glad you put in that safety test. It kept me from accidentally overwriting my file!", then you know that it was the right thing to do. But if the user says, "Dagnabit, your program is hard to use! I told it what filename I wanted to use for output, and it wouldn't let me use it until I first deleted that file!", then it was the wrong thing to do. Making decisions like this is often the toughest part of a programmer's job. Perhaps we should make the program ask something like, "Are you sure you want to overwrite the existing file 'barney'?" by default, but have a command-line option for the power user that says to overwrite without asking. Next version.

Once we've asked for everything and opened the files, the rest of the program is pretty simple. The heart of the program is the loop at the end, which reads lines, updates them, and prints them out. Note that the substitution uses the /g option—if you left that out, your program is broken, since the exercise asked that the program replace *every* occurrence of the search pattern, not just the first one on each line.

Were you able to use regular expression metacharacters in the search pattern? Sure; the substitution interpolates $pattern to make the search pattern. Were you able to use memory variables and backslash escapes in the replacement string? Nope; $replace is interpolated to make the replacement string, but it's not *re*-interpolated to interpret any magical characters. If $replace holds $1, that's a dollar sign and a numeral one in the replacement string. If Perl always kept re-interpolating, you could never put a dollar sign or backslash into the replacement string, since they'd always make something magical happen. (Actually, though, if you need one additional level of interpolation, it is possible. See the perlfaq manpages for some suggestions on how to do this.)

2. Here's one way to do it:

```
foreach my $file (@ARGV) {
  my $attribs = &attributes($file);
  print "'$file' $attribs.\n";
}

sub attributes {
  # report the attributes of a given file
  my $file = shift @_;
  return "does not exist" unless -e $file;

  my @attrib;
  push @attrib, "readable" if -r $file;
  push @attrib, "writable" if -w $file;
  push @attrib, "executable" if -x $file;
  return "exists" unless @attrib;
  'is ' . join " and ", @attrib;  # return value
}
```

In this one, once again it's convenient to use a subroutine. The main loop prints one line of attributes for each file, perhaps telling us that `'cereal-killer'` is executable or that `'sasquatch'` does not exist.

The subroutine tells us the attributes of the given filename. Of course, if the file doesn't even exist, there's no need for the other tests, so we test for that first. If there's no file, we'll return early.

If the file does exist, we'll build a list of attributes. (Give yourself extra credit points if you used the special _ filehandle instead of `$file` on these tests, to keep from calling the system separately for each new attribute.) It would be easy to add additional tests like the three we show here. But what happens if none of the attributes is true? Well, if we can't say anything else, at least we can say that the file exists, so we do. The **unless** clause uses the fact that `@attrib` will be true (in a Boolean context, which is a special case of a scalar context) if it's got any elements.

But if we've got some attributes, we'll join them with " **and** " and put `"is "` in front, to make a description like is **readable and writable**. This isn't perfect however; if there are three attributes, it says that the file is **readable and writable and executable**, which has too many **and**s, but we can get away with it. If you wanted to add more attributes to the ones this program checks for, you should probably fix it to say something like is **readable, writable, executable, and nonempty**. If that matters to you.

Note that if you somehow didn't put any filenames on the command line, this produces no output. This makes sense; if you ask for information on zero files, you should get zero lines of output. But let's compare that to what the next program does in a similar case, in the discussion below.

3. Here's one way to do it:

```
die "No file names supplied!\n" unless @ARGV;
my $oldest_name = shift @ARGV;
my $oldest_age = -M $oldest_name;

foreach (@ARGV) {
  my $age = -M;
  ($oldest_name, $oldest_age) = ($_, $age)
    if $age > $oldest_age;
}

printf "The oldest file was %s, and it was %.1f days old.\n",
  $oldest_name, $oldest_age;
```

This one starts right out by complaining if it didn't get any filenames on the command line. That's because it's supposed to tell us the oldest filename—and there ain't one if there aren't any files to check.

Once again, we're using the "high-water-mark" algorithm. The first file is certainly the oldest one seen so far. We have to keep track of its age as well, so that's in $oldest_age.

For each of the remaining files, we'll determine the age with the –M file test, just as we did for the first one (except that here, we'll use the default argument of $_ for the file test). The last-modified time is generally what people mean by the "age" of a file, although you could make a case for using a different one. If the age is more than $oldest_age, we'll use a list assignment to update both the name and age. We didn't have to use a list assignment, but it's a convenient way to update several variables at once.

We stored the age from –M into the temporary variable $age. What would have happened if we had simply used –M each time, rather than using a variable? Well, first, unless we used the special _ filehandle, we would have been asking the operating system for the age of the file each time, a potentially slow operation (not that you'd notice unless you have hundreds or thousands of files, and maybe not even then). More importantly, though, we should consider what would happen if someone updated a file while we're checking it. That is, first we see the age of some file, and it's the oldest one seen so far. But before we can get back to use –M a second time, someone modifies the file and resets the timestamp to the current time. Now the age that we save into $oldest_age is actually the *youngest* age possible. The result would be that we'd get the oldest file among the files tested from that point on, rather than the oldest overall; this would be a tough problem to debug!

Finally, at the end of the program, we use `printf` to print out the name and age, with the age rounded off to the nearest tenth of a day. Give yourself extra credit if you went to the trouble to convert the age to a number of days, hours, and minutes.

Answers to Chapter 12 Exercises

1. Here's one way to do it, with a glob:

```
print "Which directory? (Default is your home directory) ";
chomp(my $dir = <STDIN>);
if ($dir =~ /^\s*$/) {          # A blank line
  chdir or die "Can't chdir to your home directory: $!";
} else {
  chdir $dir or die "Can't chdir to '$dir': $!";
}

my @files = <*>;
foreach (@files) {
  print "$_\n";
}
```

First, we show a simple prompt, and read the desired directory, chomping it as needed. (Without a chomp, we'd be trying to head for a directory that ends in a newline—legal in Unix, and therefore cannot be presumed to simply be extraneous by the chdir function.)

Then, if the directory name is nonempty, we'll change to that directory, aborting on a failure. If empty, the home directory is selected instead.

Finally, a glob on "star" pulls up all the names in the (new) working directory, automatically sorted to alphabetical order, and they're printed one at a time.

2. Here's one way to do it:

```
print "Which directory? (Default is your home directory) ";
chomp(my $dir = <STDIN>);
if ($dir =~ /^\s*$/) {          # A blank line
  chdir or die "Can't chdir to your home directory: $!";
} else {
  chdir $dir or die "Can't chdir to '$dir': $!";
}
my @files = <.* *>;          ## now includes .*
foreach (sort @files) {      ## now sorts
  print "$_\n";
}
```

Two differences from previous one: first, the glob now includes "dot star", which matches all the names that *do* begin with a dot. And second, we now must sort the resulting list, because some of the names that begin with a dot must be interleaved appropriately either before or after the list of things without a beginning dot.

3. Here's one way to do it:

```
print "Which directory? (Default is your home directory) ";
chomp(my $dir = <STDIN>);
if ($dir =~ /^\s*$/) {          # A blank line
```

```
          chdir or die "Can't chdir to your home directory: $!";
        } else {
          chdir $dir or die "Can't chdir to '$dir': $!";
        }

        opendir DOT, "." or die "Can't opendir dot: $!";
        foreach (sort readdir DOT) {
          # next if /^\./; ##   if we were skipping dot files
          print "$_\n";
        }
```

Again, same structure as the previous two programs, but now we've chosen to open a directory handle. Once we've changed the working directory, we want to open the current directory, and we've shown that as the DOT directory handle.

Why DOT? Well, if the user asks for an absolute directory name, like /etc, there's no problem opening it. But if the name is relative, like fred, let's see what would happen. First, we **chdir** to **fred**, and then we want to use **opendir** to open it. But that would open **fred** in the new directory, not **fred** in the original directory. The only name we can be sure will mean "the current directory" is ".", which always has that meaning (on Unix and similar systems, at least).

The **readdir** function pulls up all the names of the directory, which are then sorted, and displayed. If we had done the first exercise this way, we would have skipped over the dot files, and that's handled by the uncommenting the commented-out line in the **foreach** loop.

You may find yourself asking, "Why did we **chdir** first? You can use **readdir** and friends on any directory, not merely on the current directory." Primarily, we wanted to give the user the convenience of being able to get to their home directory with a single keystroke. But this could be the start of a general file-management utility program; maybe the next step would be to ask the user which of the files in this directory should be moved to offline tape storage, say.

Answers to Chapter 13 Exercises

1. Here's one way to do it:

```
          unlink @ARGV;
```

...or, if you want to warn the user of any problems:

```
        foreach (@ARGV) {
          unlink $_ or warn "Can't unlink '$_': $!, continuing...\n";
        }
```

Here, each item from the command-invocation line is placed individually into $_, which is then used as the argument to **unlink**. If something goes wrong, the warning gives the clue about why.

2. Here's one way to do it:

```
use File::Basename;
use File::Spec;

my($source, $dest) = @ARGV;

if (-d $dest) {
  my $basename = basename $source;
  $dest = File::Spec->catfile($dest, $basename);
}

rename $source, $dest
    or die "Can't rename '$source' to '$dest': $!\n";
```

The workhorse in this program is the last statement, but the remainder of the program is necessary when we are renaming into a directory. First, after declaring the modules we're using, we name the command-line arguments sensibly. If $dest is a directory, we need to extract the basename from the $source name and append it to the directory ($dest). Finally, once $dest is patched up if needed, the **rename** does the deed.

3. Here's one way to do it:

```
use File::Basename;
use File::Spec;

my($source, $dest) = @ARGV;

if (-d $dest) {
  my $basename = basename $source;
  $dest = File::Spec->catfile($dest, $basename);
}

link $source, $dest
    or die "Can't link '$source' to '$dest': $!\n";
```

As the hint in the exercise description said, this program is much like the previous one. The difference is that we'll **link** rather than **rename**. If your system doesn't support hard links, you might have written this as the last line:

```
print "Would link '$source' to '$dest'.\n";
```

4. Here's one way to do it:

```
use File::Basename;
use File::Spec;

my $symlink = $ARGV[0] eq '-s';
shift @ARGV if $symlink;

my($source, $dest) = @ARGV;
```

```
if (-d $dest) {
  my $basename = basename $source;
  $dest = File::Spec->catfile($dest, $basename);
}

if ($symlink) {
  symlink $source, $dest
    or die "Can't make soft link from '$source' to '$dest': $!\n";
} else {
  link $source, $dest
    or die "Can't make hard link from '$source' to '$dest': $!\n";
}
```

The first few lines of code (after the two **use** declarations) look at the first command-line argument, and if it's "**-s**", we're making a symbolic link, so we note that as a true value for **$symlink**. If we saw that "**-s**", we then need to get rid of it (in the next line). The next few lines are cut-and-pasted from the previous exercise answers. Finally, based on the truth of **$symlink**, we'll choose either to create a symbolic link or a hard link. We also updated the dying words to make it clear which kind of link we were attempting.

5. Here's one way to do it:

```
foreach (<.* *>) {
  my $dest = readlink $_;
  print "$_ -> $dest\n" if defined $dest;
}
```

Each item resulting from the glob ends up in **$_** one by one. If the item is a symbolic link, then **readlink** returns a defined value, and the location is displayed. If not, then the condition fails, and we skip over it.

Answers to Chapter 14 Exercises

1. Here's one way to do it:

```
chdir "/" or die "Can't chdir to root directory: $!";
exec "ls", "-l" or die "Can't exec ls: $!";
```

The first line changes the current working directory to the root directory, as our particular hard-coded directory. The second line uses the multiple-argument **exec** function to send the result to standard output. We could have used the single-argument form just as well, but it doesn't hurt to do it this way.

2. Here's one way to do it:

```
open STDOUT, ">ls.out" or die "Can't write to ls.out: $!";
open STDERR, ">ls.err" or die "Can't write to ls.err: $!";
chdir "/" or die "Can't chdir to root directory: $!";
exec "ls", "-l" or die "Can't exec ls: $!";
```

The first and second lines reopen STDOUT and STDERR to a file in the current directory (before we change directories). Then, after the directory change, the directory listing command executes, sending the data back to the files opened in the original directory.

Where would the message from the last die go? Why, it would go into *ls.err*, of course, since that's where STDERR is going at that point. The die from chdir would go there, too. But where would the message go if we can't re-open STDERR on the second line? It goes to the old STDERR. For the three standard filehandles, STDIN, STDOUT, and STDERR, if re-opening them fails, the old filehandle is still open.

3. Here's one way to do it:

```
if (`date` =~ /^S/) {
  print "go play!\n";
} else {
  print "get to work!\n";
}
```

Well, since both Saturday and Sunday start with an S, and the day of the week is the first part of the output of the *date* command, this is pretty simple. Just check the output of the *date* command to see if it starts with S. There are many harder ways to do this program, and we've seen most of them in our classes.

If we had to use this in a real-world program, though, we'd probably use the pattern /^(Sat|Sun)/. It's a tiny bit less efficient, but that hardly matters; besides, it's so much easier for the maintenance programmer to understand.

Answers to Chapter 15 Exercises

1. Here's one way to do it:

```
my @numbers;
push @numbers, split while <>;
foreach (sort { $a <=> $b } @numbers) {
  printf "%20g\n", $_;
}
```

That second line of code is too confusing, isn't it? Well, we did that on purpose. Although we recommend that you write clear code, some people like writing code that's as hard to understand as possible,* so we want you to be prepared for the worst. Someday, you'll need to maintain confusing code like this.

---

* Well, we don't recommend it for *normal* coding purposes, but it can be a fun game to write confusing code, and it can be educational to take someone else's obfuscated code examples and spend a weekend or two figuring out just what they do. If you want to see some fun snippets of such code and maybe get a little help with decoding them, ask around at the next Perl Mongers' meeting. Or search for JAPHs on the Web, or see how well you can decipher the example obfuscated code block near the end of this chapter's answers.

Since that line uses the `while` modifier, it's the same as if it were written in a loop like this:

```
while (<>) {
  push @numbers, split;
}
```

That's better, but maybe it's still a little unclear. (Nevertheless, we don't have a quibble about writing it this way. This one is on the correct side of the "too hard to understand at a glance" line.) The `while` loop is reading the input a line at a time (from the user's choice of input sources, as shown by the diamond operator), and `split` is, by default, splitting that on whitespace to make a list of words—or, in this case, a list of numbers. The input is just a stream of numbers separated by whitespace, after all. Either way that you write it, then, that `while` loop will put all of the numbers from the input into `@numbers`.

The `foreach` loop takes the sorted list and prints each one on its own line, using the `%20g` numeric format to put them in a right-justified column. You could have used `%20s` instead. What difference would that make? Well, that's a string format, so it would have left the strings untouched in the output. Did you notice that our sample data included both `1.50` and `1.5`, and both `04` and `4`? If you printed those as strings, the extra zero characters will still be in the output; but `%20g` is a numeric format, so equal numbers will appear identically in the output. Either format could potentially be correct, depending upon what you're trying to do.

2. Here's one way to do it:

```
# don't forget to incorporate the hash %last_name,
# either from the exercise text or the downloaded file

my @keys = sort {
  "\L$last_name{$a}" cmp "\L$last_name{$b}"  # by last name
    or
  "\L$a" cmp "\L$b"                          # by first name
} keys %last_name;

foreach (@keys) {
  print "$last_name{$_}, $_\n";              # Rubble, Bamm-Bamm
}
```

There's not much to say about this one; we put the keys in order as needed, then print them out. We chose to print them in last-name-comma-first-name order just for fun; the exercise description left that up to you.

3. Here's one way to do it:

```
print "Please enter a string: ";
chomp(my $string = <STDIN>);
```

```
    print "Please enter a substring: ";
    chomp(my $sub = <STDIN>);

my @places;

    for (my $pos = -1; ; ) {                    # tricky use of three-part for loop
      $pos = index($string, $sub, $pos + 1);   # find next position
      last if $pos == -1;
      push @places, $pos;
    }

    print "Locations of '$sub' in '$string' were: @places\n";
```

This one starts out simply enough, asking the user for the strings and declaring an array to hold the list of substring positions. But once again, as we see in the `for` loop, the code seems to have been "optimized for cleverness", which should be done only for fun, never in production code. But this actually shows a valid technique which could be useful in some cases, so let's see how it works.

The `my` variable `$pos` is declared private to the scope of the `for` loop, and it starts with a value of −1. So as not to keep you in suspense about this variable, we'll tell you right now that it's going to hold a position of the substring in the larger string. The test and increment sections of the `for` loop are empty, so this is an infinite loop. (Of course, we'll eventually break out of it, in this case with `last`).

The first statement of the loop body looks for the first occurrence of the substring at or after position `$pos + 1`. That means that on the first iteration, when `$pos` is still −1, the search will start at position 0, the start of the string. The location of the substring is stored back into `$pos`. Now, if that was −1, we're done with the `for` loop, so `last` breaks out of the loop in that case. If it wasn't −1, then we save the position into `@places` and go around the loop again. This time, `$pos + 1` means that we'll start looking for the substring just after the previous place where we found it. And so we get the answers we wanted and the world is once again a happy place.

If you didn't want that tricky use of the `for` loop, you could accomplish the same result as shown here:

```
    {
      my $pos = -1;
      while (1) {
        ... # Same loop body as the for loop used above
      }
    }
```

The naked block on the outside restricts the scope of `$pos`. You don't have to do that, but it's often a good idea to declare each variable in the smallest possible scope. This means we have fewer variables "alive" at any given point in the program, making it less likely that we'll accidentally reuse the name $pos for some new purpose. For the same reason, if you don't declare a variable in a small scope, you should generally give it a longer name that's thereby less likely to be reused by accident. Maybe something like $substring_position would be appropriate in this case.

On the other hand, if you were *trying* to obfuscate your code (shame on you!), you could create a monster like this (shame on us!):

```
for (my $pos = -1; -1 !=
  ($pos = index
    +$string,
    +$sub,
    +$pos
    +1
  );
push @places, (((((+$pos))))) {
    'for ($pos != 1; # ;$pos++) {
      print "position $pos\n";#;';#' } pop @places;
}
```

That even trickier code works in place of the original tricky for loop. By now, you should know enough to be able to decipher that one on your own, or to obfuscate code in order to amaze your friends and confound your enemies. Be sure to use these powers only for good, never for evil.

Oh, and what did you get when you searched for t in This is a test.? It's at positions 10 and 13. It's not at position 0; since the capitalization doesn't match, the substring doesn't match.

Answers to Chapter 16 Exercises

1. Here's one way to do it:

```
open PF, '/path/to/perlfunc.pod' or die "Can't open perlfunc.pod: $!";
dbmopen my %DB, "pf_data", 0644 or die "Can't create dbm file: $!";

%DB = ();  # wipe existing data, if any

while (<PF>) {
  if (/^=item\s+([a-z_]\w*)/i) {
    $DB{$1} = $DB{$1} || $.;
  }
}

print "Done!\n";
```

This one is similar to the previous ones with *perlfunc.pod*. Here, though, we open a DBM file called *pf_data* as the DBM hash %DB. In case that file had any leftover data, we set the hash to an empty list. That's normally a rare thing to do, but we want to wipe out the entire database, in case a previous run of this program left incorrect or out-of-date data in the file. (After all, there's a new *perlfunc.pod* with each new release of Perl.)

When we find an identifier, we need to store its line number (from $.) into the database. The statement that does that uses the high-precedence short-circuit || operator. If the database entry already has a value, that value is true, so the old value is used. If the database entry is empty, that's false, so the value on the right ($.) is used instead. We could have written that line in a shorter way, like this:

```
$DB{$1} ||= $.;
```

When the program is done, it says so. That's not required by the exercise description, but it lets us know that the program did something; without that line, there would be no output at all. But how can we tell that it worked correctly? That's the next exercise.

2. Here's one way to do it:

```
dbmopen my %DB, "pf_data", undef or die "Can't open dbm file: $!";
my $line = $DB{$ARGV[0]} || "not found";

print "$ARGV[0]: $line\n";
```

Once we have the database, it's simple to look something up in it. Note that in this program, the third argument to dbmopen is undef, since that file must already exist for this program to work.

If the entry for $ARGV[0] (the first command-line parameter) isn't found in the database, we'll say it's **not found**, using the high-precedence short-circuit ||.

3. Here's one way to do it:

```
dbmopen my %DB, "pf_data", undef or die "Can't open dbm file: $!";

if (my $line = $DB{$ARGV[0]}) {
  exec 'less', "+$line", '/path/to/perlfunc.pod'
    or die "Can't exec pager: $!";
} else {
  die "Entry unknown: '$ARGV[0]'.\n";
}
```

This starts out like the previous one, but uses **exec** to start up a pager program if it can, and dies if it can't.

Answer to Chapter 17 Exercise

1. Here's one way to do it:

```
my $filename = 'path/to/sample_text';
open FILE, $filename
  or die "Can't open '$filename': $!";
chomp(my @strings = <FILE>);
```

```
while (1) {
  print "Please enter a pattern: ";
  chomp(my $pattern = <STDIN>);
  last if $pattern =~ /^\s*$/;
  my @matches = eval {
    grep /$pattern/, @strings;
  };
  if ($@) {
    print "Error: $@";
  } else {
    my $count = @matches;
    print "There were $count matching strings:\n",
      map "$_\n", @matches;
  }
  print "\n";
}
```

This one uses an **eval** block to trap any failure that might occur when using the regular expression. Inside that block, a **grep** pulls the matching strings from the list of strings.

Once the **eval** is finished, we can report either the error message or the matching strings. Note that we "unchomped" the strings for output by using **map** to add a newline to each string.

B

Beyond the Llama

We've covered a lot in this book, but there's even more. In this appendix, we'll tell about a little more of what Perl can do, and give some references on where to learn the details. Some of what we mention here is on the bleeding edge and may have changed by the time that you're reading this book, which is one reason why we frequently send you to the documentation for the full story. We don't expect many readers to read every word of this appendix, but we hope you'll at least skim the headings so that you'll be prepared to fight back when someone tells you "You just can't use Perl for project X, because Perl can't do Y."

Further Documentation

The documentation that comes with Perl may seem overwhelming at first. Fortunately, you can use your computer to search for keywords in the documentation. When searching for a particular topic, it's often good to start with the *perltoc* (table of contents) and *perlfaq* (frequently asked questions) sections. On most systems, the *perldoc* command should be able to track down the documentation for Perl, installed modules, and related programs (including *perldoc* itself).

Regular expressions

Yes, there's even more about regular expressions than we mentioned. *Mastering Regular Expressions* by Jeffrey Friedl is one of the best technical books we've ever read.* It's half about regular expressions in general, and half about Perl's regular expressions. It goes into good detail about how the regular expression engine

---

* And we're not just saying that because it's also published by O'Reilly & Associates, Inc. It's really a great book.

works internally, and why one way of writing a pattern may be much more efficient than another. Anyone who is serious about Perl should read this book. Also see the *perlre* manpage (and its companion *perlretut* and *perlrequick* manpages in newer versions of Perl).

Packages

Packages* allow you to compartmentalize the namespaces. Imagine that you have ten programmers all working on one big project. If you use the global names $fred, @barney, %betty, and &wilma in your part of the project, what happens when I accidentally use one of those same names in my part? Packages let us keep these separate; I can access your $fred, and you can access mine, but not by accident. Packages are needed to make Perl scalable, so that we can manage large programs.

Extending Perl's Functionality

One of the most common pieces of good advice heard in the Perl discussion forums is that you shouldn't reinvent the wheel. Other folks have written code that you can put to use. The most frequent way to add to what Perl can do is by using a library or module. Many of these come with Perl, while others are available from CPAN. Of course, you can even write your own libraries and modules.

Libraries

Many programming languages offer support for libraries much as Perl does. Libraries are collections of (mostly) subroutines for a given purpose. In modern Perl, though, it's more common to use modules than libraries.

Modules

A module is a "smart library". A module will typically offer a collection of subroutines that act as if they were built in functions, for the most part. Modules are smart in that they keep their details in a separate package, only importing what you request. This keeps a module from stomping on your code's symbols.

Although many useful modules are written in pure Perl, others are written using a language like C. For example, the MD5 algorithm is sort of like a high-powered

---

* The name "package" is perhaps an unfortunate choice, in that it makes many people think of a packaged-up chunk of code (in Perl, that's a module or a library). All that a package does is define a namespace (a collection of global symbol names, like $fred or &wilma). A namespace is *not* a chunk of code.

checksum.* It uses a lot of low-level bit-twiddling that could be done in Perl, but hundreds of times more slowly;† it's an algorithm that was designed to be efficiently implemented in C. So, the `Digest::MD5` module is made to use the compiled C code. When you use that module, it's as if your Perl had a built in function to calculate MD5 digests.

Finding and Installing Modules

Maybe your system already has the module you need. But how can you find out which modules are installed? You can use the program *inside*, which should be available for download from CPAN in the directory *http://www.cpan.org/authors/id/P/PH/PHOENIX/*.

If none of the modules already available on your system suits your needs, you can search for Perl modules on CPAN at *http://search.cpan.org/*. To install a module on your system, see the `perlmodinstall` manpage.

When using a module, you'll generally put the required **use** directives at the top of your program. That makes it easy for someone who is installing your program on a new system to see at a glance which modules it needs.

Writing Your Own Modules

In the rare case that there's no module to do what you need, an advanced programmer can write a new one, either in Perl or in another language (often C). See the `perlmod` and `perlmodlib` manpages for more information.

Some Important Modules

We describe some of the most important features‡ of the most important modules§ in this section. These modules that we discuss here should generally be found on every machine that has Perl, except where mentioned. You can always get the latest ones from CPAN.

---

* It's not really a checksum, but that's good enough for this explanation.

† The module `Digest::Perl::MD5` is a pure Perl implementation of the MD5 algorithm. Although your mileage may vary, we found it to be about 280 times slower than the `Digest::MD5` module on one sample dataset. Remember that many of the bit-twiddling operations in the C algorithm compile down to a *single* machine instruction; thus, entire lines of code can take a mere handful of clock cycles to run. Perl is fast, but let's not be unrealistic.

‡ We're including here merely the most important features of each module; see the module's own documentation to learn more.

§ To be sure, there are other important modules whose use is too complex for most readers of this book, typically because using the module requires understanding Perl's references or objects.

The CGI and CGI_Lite Modules

Many people use Perl to write programs that a web server will run, generally called *CGI programs*. The CGI module comes with Perl, while the CGI_Lite module is available separately from CPAN. See "The Common Gateway Interface (CGI)" later in this appendix.

The Cwd Module

Sometimes you need to know what the current working directory's name is. (Well, you could often use ".", but maybe you need to save the name so that you can change back to this directory later.) The Cwd module, which comes with Perl, provides the cwd function, which you can use to determine the current working directory.

```
use Cwd;

my $directory = cwd;
```

The Fatal Module

If you get tired of writing "or die" after every invocation of open or chdir, then maybe the Fatal module is for you. Just tell it which functions to work with, and those will be automatically checked for failure, as if you'd written "or die" and a suitable message after each one. This won't affect such calls in someone else's package (that is, code contained within a module you're using, for example), so don't use this to fix up poorly written code. It's just a timesaver, mostly for simple programs in which you don't need direct control over the error message itself. For example:

```
use Fatal qw/ open chdir /;

chdir '/home/merlyn';  # "or die" is now supplied automatically
```

The File::Basename Module

We covered this module in Chapter 13. It's primary uses are to portably pull the basename or directory name from a full filename:

```
use File::Basename;

for (@ARGV) {
  my $basename = basename $_;
  my $dirname = dirname $_;
  print "That's file $basename in directory $dirname.\n";
}
```

The File::Copy Module

When you need to copy or move files, the `File::Copy` module is for you. (It's often tempting to simply call a system program to do these things, but that's not portable.) This module provides the functions **move** and **copy**, which may be used much as the corresponding system programs would be used:

```
use File::Copy;

copy("source", "destination")
  or die "Can't copy 'source' to 'destination': $!";
```

The File::Spec Module

When you need to manipulate a filename (more formally called a "file specification"), it's generally more portable and reliable to use the `File::Spec` module than to do the work yourself from Perl. For example, you can use the `catfile` function to put together a directory name and a filename to produce a long filename (as we saw in Chapter 13), but you don't have to know whether the system your program is running on uses a forward slash or some other character to separate those. Or you could use the `curdir` function to get the name of the current directory (".", on Unix systems).

The `File::Spec` module is object-oriented, but you don't need to understand objects to use it. Just call each function ("method", really) by using `File::Spec` and a small arrow before the function's name, like this:

```
use File::Spec;

my $current_directory = File::Spec->curdir;
opendir DOT, $current_directory
  or die "Can't open current directory '$current_directory': $!";
```

The Image::Size Module

When you have an image file, you'll often want to know what its height and width are. (This is handy for making programs that write HTML, if you wish for an IMG tag to indicate the image's dimensions.) The `Image::Size` module, which is available from CPAN, understands the common GIF, JFIF (JPEG), and PNG image types, and some others. For example:

```
use Image::Size;

# Get the size of fred.png
my($fred_height, $fred_width) = imgsize("fred.png");
die "Couldn't get the size of the image"
  unless defined $fred_height;
```

The Net::SMTP Module

If you want your program to be able to send email through an SMTP server
(which is the way most of us send email these days, whether you knew that or
not), you may use the Net::SMTP module to do the work.[*] This module, which is
available from CPAN, is object-oriented, but you may simply follow the syntax to
use it. You will need to change the name of your SMTP host and the other items
to make this work on your system. Your system administrator or local expert can
tell you what to use. For example:

```
use Net::SMTP;

my $from = 'YOUR_ADDRESS_GOES_HERE';         # maybe fred@bedrock.edu
my $site = 'YOUR_SITE_NAME_GOES_HERE';       # maybe bedrock.edu
my $smtp_host = 'YOUR_SMTP_HOST_GOES_HERE';  # maybe mail or mailhost
my $to = 'president@whitehouse.gov';

my $smtp = Net::SMTP->new($smtp_host, Hello => $site);

$smtp->mail($from);
$smtp->to($to);
$smtp->data();

$smtp->datasend("To: $to\n");
$smtp->datasend("Subject: A message from my Perl program.\n");
$smtp->datasend("\n");
$smtp->datasend("This is just to let you know,\n");
$smtp->datasend("I don't care what those other people say about you,\n");
$smtp->datasend("I still think you're doing a great job.\n");
$smtp->datasend("\n");
$smtp->datasend("Have you considered enacting a law naming Perl \n");
$smtp->datasend("the national programming language?\n");

$smtp->dataend();                            # Not datasend!
$smtp->quit;
```

The POSIX Module

If you need access to the POSIX (IEEE Std 1003.1) functions, the POSIX module is
for you. It provides many functions that C programmers may be used to, such as
trigonometric functions (asin, cosh), general mathematical functions (floor,
frexp), character-identification functions (isupper, isalpha), low-level IO functions (creat, open), and some others (asctime, clock). You'll probably want to
call each of these with its "full" name; that is, with POSIX and a pair of colons as a
prefix to the function's name:

```
use POSIX;
```

---

[*] Yes, this means that you are now able to use Perl to send spam. Please don't.

```
print "Please enter a number: ";
chomp(my $str = <STDIN>);

$! = 0;  # Clear out the error indicator
my($num, $leftover) = POSIX::strtod($str);

if ($str eq '') {
  print "That string was empty!\n";
} elsif ($leftover) {
  my $remainder = substr $str, -$leftover;
  print "The string '$remainder' was left after the number $num.\n";
} elsif ($!) {
  print "The conversion function complained: $!\n";
} else {
  print "The seemingly-valid number was $num.\n";
}
```

The Sys::Hostname Module

The `Sys::Hostname` module provides the `hostname` function, which will be the network name of your machine, if that can be determined. (If it can't be determined, perhaps because your machine is not on the Internet or not properly configured, the function will die automatically; there's no point in using **or die** here.) For example:

```
use Sys::Hostname;
my $host = hostname;
print "This machine is known as '$host'.\n";
```

The Text::Wrap Module

The `Text::Wrap` module supplies the `wrap` function, which lets you implement simple word-wrapping. The first two parameters specify the indentation of the first line and the others, respectively; the remaining parameters make up the paragraph's text:

```
use Text::Wrap;

my $message = "This is some sample text which may be longer " .
  "than the width of your output device, so it needs to " .
  "be wrapped to fit properly as a paragraph. ";
$message x= 5;

print wrap("\t", "", "$message\n");
```

The Time::Local Module

If you have a time (for example, from the `time` function) that needs to be converted to a list of year, month, day, hour, minute, and second values, you can do that with Perl's built-in `localtime` function in a list context.* (In a scalar context, that gives a nicely formatted string representing the time, which is more often what you'd want.) But if you need to go in the other direction, you may use the `timelocal` function from the `Time::Local` module instead. It's important to note that the value of `$mon` and `$year` for January 2004 are not 1 and 2004 as you might expect, so be sure to read the documentation before you use this module. For example:

```
use Time::Local;

my $time = timelocal($sec, $min, $hr, $day, $mon, $year);
```

Pragmas

Pragmas are special modules that come with each release of Perl and tell Perl's internal compiler something about your code. You've already used the **strict** pragma. The pragmas available for your release of Perl should be listed in the `perlmodlib` manpage.

You use pragmas much like you'd use ordinary modules, with a **use** directive. Some pragmas are lexically scoped, like lexical ("my") variables are, and they therefore apply to the smallest enclosing block or file. Others may apply to the entire program or to the current package. (If you don't use any packages, the pragmas apply to your entire program.) Pragmas should generally appear near the top of your source code. The documentation for each pragma should tell you how it's scoped.

The constant Pragma

If you've used other languages, you've probably seen the ability to declare constants in one way or another. Constants are handy for making a setting just once, near the beginning of a program, but that can be easily updated if the need arises. Perl can do this with the package-scoped **constant** pragma, which tells the compiler that a given identifier has a constant value, which may thus be optimized wherever it appears. For example:

```
use constant DEBUGGING => 0;
use constant ONE_YEAR => 365.2425 * 24 * 60 * 60;

if (DEBUGGING) {
  # This code will be optimized away unless DEBUGGING is turned on
  ...
}
```

---

* The actual return value of `localtime` in a list context is a little different than you might expect; see the documentation.

The diagnostics Pragma

Perl's diagnostic messages often seem somewhat cryptic, at least the first time you see them. But you can always look them up in the `perldiag` manpage to find out what they mean, and often a little about what's likely to be the problem and how to fix it. But you can save yourself the trouble of searching that manpage if you use the `diagnostics` pragma, which tells Perl to track down and print out the related information for any message. Unlike most pragmas, though, this one is *not* intended for everyday use, as it makes your program read the entire `perldiag` manpage just to get started. (This is potentially a significant amount of overhead, both in terms of time and memory.) Use this pragma only when you're debugging *and* expecting to get error message you don't yet understand. It affects your entire program. The syntax is:

```
use diagnostics;
```

The lib Pragma

It's nearly always best to install modules in the standard directories, so that they're available for everyone, but only the system administrator can do that. If you install your own modules, you'll have to store them in your own directories—so, how will Perl know where to find them? That's what the `lib` pragma is all about. It tells Perl that the given directory is the first place to look for modules. (That means that it's also useful for trying out a new release of a given module.) It affects all modules loaded from this point on. The syntax is:

```
use lib '/home/rootbeer/experimental';
```

Be sure to use a nonrelative pathname as the argument, since there's no telling what will be the current working directory when your program is run. This is especially important for CGI programs (that is, programs run by a web server).

The strict Pragma

You've been using `use strict` for a while already without having to understand that it's a pragma. It's lexically scoped, and it enforces some good programming rules. See its documentation to learn what restrictions are available in your release of Perl.

The vars Pragma

In the rare case that you truly need a global variable while **use strict** is in effect, you may declare it with the **vars** pragma.* This package-scoped pragma tells Perl that you are intentionally using one or more global variables:

```
use strict;
use vars qw/ $fred $barney /;

$fred = "This is a global variable, but that's all right.\n";
```

The warnings Pragma

Starting in Perl version 5.6, you may choose to have lexically scoped warnings with the **warnings** pragma.† That is, rather than using the −w option crudely to turn warnings on or off for the entire program at once, you may specify that you want no warnings about undefined values in just one section of code, while other warnings should be available. This also serves as a signal to the maintenance programmer that says, "I know that this code would produce warnings, but I know what I'm doing anyway." See the documentation for this pragma to learn about the categories of warnings available in your release of Perl.

Databases

If you've got a database, Perl can work with it. This section describes some of the common types of databases.

Direct System Database Access

Perl can directly access some system databases, sometimes with the help of a module. These are databases like the Windows Registry (which holds machine-level settings), or the Unix password database (which lists which username corresponds to which number, and related information), as well as the domain-name database (which lets you translate an IP number into a machine name, and vice versa).

Flat-file Database Access

If you'd like to access your own flat-file databases from Perl, there are modules to help you with doing that (seemingly a new one every month or two, so any list here would be out of date). You can even do quite a bit without a module, with what we give in Chapter 16.

---

* If your program will never be used with a version of Perl prior to 5.6, you should use the **our** keyword instead of the **vars** pragma.

† If your program may be used with a version of Perl prior to 5.6, you should not use the **warnings** pragma.

Relational Database Access

Relational databases include Sybase, Oracle, Informix, mysql, and others. These are complex enough that you generally do need to know about modules to use them. But if you use the DBI module, whose name stands for "database-independent," you can minimize your dependence upon any one type of database—then, if you have to move from mysql to Oracle, say, you might not even need to change anything at all in your program.

Other Operators and Functions

Yes, there are more operators and functions than we can fit here, from the scalar `..` operator to the scalar `,` operator, from `wantarray` to `goto`(!), from `caller` to `chr`. See the *perlop* and *perlfunc* manpages.

Transliteration with tr///

The `tr///` operator looks like a regular expression, but it's really for transliterating one group of characters into another. It can also efficiently count selected characters. See the *perlop* manpage.

Here documents

Here documents are a useful form of multiline string quoting; see the *perldata* manpage.

Mathematics

Perl can do just about any kind of mathematics you can dream up.

Advanced Math Functions

All of the basic mathematical functions (square root, cosine, logarithm, absolute value, and many others) are available as built in functions; see the *perlfunc* manpage for details. Some others (like tangent or base-10 logarithm) are omitted, but those may be easily created from the basic ones, or loaded from a simple module that does so. (See the `POSIX` module for many common math functions.)

Imaginary and Complex Numbers

Although the core of Perl doesn't directly support them, there are modules available for working with complex numbers. These overload the normal operators and functions, so that you can still multiply with * and get a square root with `sqrt`, even when using complex numbers. See the `Math::Complex` module.

Large and High-Precision Numbers

You can do math with arbitrarily large numbers with an arbitrary number of digits of accuracy. For example, you could calculate the factorial of two thousand, or determine π to ten-thousand digits. See the `Math::BigInt` and `Math::BigFloat` modules.

Lists and Arrays

Perl has a number of features that make it easy to manipulate an entire list or array.

map and grep

We mentioned (in Chapter 17) the `map` and `grep` list-processing operators. They can do more than we could include here; see the *perlfunc* manpage for more information and examples.

The splice Operator

With the `splice` operator, you can add items to the middle of an array, or remove them, letting the array grow or shrink as needed. (Roughly, this is like what `substr` lets you do with strings.) This effectively eliminates the need for linked lists in Perl. See the *perlfunc* manpage.

Bits and Pieces

You can work with an array of bits (a *bitstring*) with the **vec** operator, setting bit number 123, clearing bit number 456, and checking to see the state of bit 789. Bitstrings may be of arbitrary size. The **vec** operator can also work with chunks of other sizes, as long as the size is a small power of two, so it's useful if you need to view a string as a compact array of nybbles, say. See the *perlfunc* manpage.

Formats

Perl's formats are an easy way to make fixed-format template-driven reports with automatic page headers. In fact, they are one of the main reasons Larry developed Perl in the first place, as a Practical Extraction and *Report* Language. But, alas, they're limited. The heartbreak of formats happens when someone discovers that he or she needs a little more than what formats provide. This usually means ripping out the program's entire output section and replacing it with code that doesn't use formats. Still, if you're sure that formats do what you need, *all* that you'll need, and all that you'll *ever* need, they are pretty cool. See the *perlform* manpage.

Networking and IPC

If there's a way that programs on your machine can talk with others, Perl can probably do it. This section shows some common ways.

System V IPC

The standard functions for System V IPC (interprocess communication) are all supported by Perl, so you can use message queues, semaphores, and shared memory. Of course, an array in Perl isn't stored in a chunk of memory in the same way* that an array is stored in C, so shared memory can't 'share Perl data as-is. But there are modules that will translate data, so that you can pretend that your Perl data is in shared memory. See the *perlfunc* manpage and the *perlipc* module.

Sockets

Perl has full support for TCP/IP sockets, which means that you could write a web server in Perl, or a web browser, Usenet news server or client, finger daemon or client, FTP daemon or client, SMTP or POP or SOAP server or client, or either end of pretty much any other kind of protocol in use on the Internet. Of course, there's no need to get into the low-level details yourself; there are modules available for all of the common protocols. For example, you can make a web server or client with the LWP module and one or two lines of additional code.† The LWP module (actually, a tightly integrated set of modules, which together implement nearly everything that happens on the Web) is also a great example of high-quality Perl code, if you'd like to copy from the best. For other protocols, search for a module with the protocol's name.

---

* In fact, it would generally be a lie to say that a Perl array is stored in "a chunk of memory" at all, as it's almost certainly spread among many separate chunks.

† Although LWP makes it easy to make a simple "web browser" that pulls down a page or image, actually rendering that to the user is another problem. You can drive an X11 display with Tk or Gtk widgets though, or use curses to draw on a character terminal. It's all a matter of downloading and installing the right modules from CPAN.

Security

Perl has a number of strong security-related features that can make a program written in Perl more secure than the corresponding program written in C. Probably the most important of these is data-flow analysis, better known as *taint checking*. When this is enabled, Perl keeps track of which pieces of data seem to have come from the user or environment (and are therefore untrustworthy). Generally, if any such piece of so-called "tainted" data is used to affect another process, file, or directory, Perl will prohibit the operation and abort the program. It's not perfect, but it's a powerful way to prevent some security-related mistakes. There's more to the story; see the *perlsec* manpage.

Debugging

There's a very good debugger that comes with Perl and supports breakpoints, watchpoints, single-stepping, and generally everything you'd want in a command-line Perl debugger. It's actually written in Perl (so, if there are bugs in the debugger, we're not sure how they get those out). But that means that, in addition to all of the usual debugger commands, you can actually run Perl code from the debugger—calling your subroutines, changing variables, even redefining subroutines—while your program is running. See the *perldebug* manpage for the latest details.

Another debugging tactic is to use the `B::Lint` module, which is still preliminary as of this writing.

The Common Gateway Interface (CGI)

One of the most popular uses for Perl on the Web is in writing CGI programs. These run on a web server to process the results of a form, perform a search, produce dynamic web content, or count the number of accesses to a web page.

The `CGI` module, which comes with Perl, provides an easy way to access the form parameters and to generate some HTML in responses. (If you don't want the overhead of the full `CGI` module, the `CGI_Lite` module provides access to the form parameters without all the rest.) It may be tempting to skip the module and simply copy-and-paste one of the snippets of code that purport to give access to the form parameters, but nearly all of these are buggy.[*]

---

[*] There are some details of the interface that these snippets don't support. Trust us; it's better to use a module.

When writing CGI programs, though, there are several big issues to keep in mind. These make this topic one too broad to fully include in this book:[*]

Security, security, security

We can't overemphasize security. Somewhere around half of the successful attacks on computers around the world involve a security-related bug in a CGI program.

Concurrency issues

It's easy to have several processes that are concurrently trying to access a single file or resource.

Standards compliance

No matter how hard you try, you probably won't be able to test your program thoroughly with more than about 1 or 2% of the web browsers and servers that are in use today.[†] That's because there are literally thousands of different programs available, with new ones popping up every week. The solution is to follow the standards, so your program will work with all of them.[‡]

Troubleshooting and debugging

Since the CGI program runs in a different environment than you're likely to be able to access directly, you'll have to learn new techniques for troubleshooting and debugging.

Security, security, security!

There, we've said it again. Don't forget security—it's the first and last thing to think about when your program is going to be available to everyone in the world who wants to try breaking it.

And that list didn't even mention URI-encoding, HTML entities, HTTP and response codes, Secure Sockets Layer (SSL), Server-side Includes (SSI), here documents, creating graphics on the fly, programmatically generating HTML tables, forms, and widgets, hidden form elements, getting and setting cookies, path info, error trapping, redirection, taint checking, internationalization and localization,

---

[*] Several of the reviewers who looked over a draft of this book for us wished we could cover more about CGI programming. We agree, but it wouldn't be fair to the reader to give just enough knowledge to be dangerous. A proper discussion of the problems inherent in CGI programming would probably add at least 50% to the size (and cost) of this book.

[†] Remember that every new release of each brand of browser on each different platform counts as a new one that you're probably not going to be able to test. We really chuckle when we hear someone tested a web site with "both browsers" or when they say "I don't know if it works with the other one."

[‡] At the very least, following the standards lets you put the blame squarely on the other programmer, who didn't.

embedding Perl into HTML (or the other way around), working with Apache and
`mod_perl`, and using the `LWP` module.* Most or all of those topics should be
covered in any good book on using Perl with the Web. *CGI Programming with
Perl* by Scott Guelich, et al. (O'Reilly & Associates, Inc.) is mighty nice here, as is
Lincoln Stein's *Network Programming with Perl* (Addison-Wesley).

Command-Line Options

There are many different command-line options available in Perl; many let you
write useful programs directly from the command line. See the *perlrun* manpage.

Built in Variables

Perl has dozens of built-in variables (like `@ARGV` and `$0`), which provide useful
information or control the operation of Perl itself. See the *perlvar* manpage.

Syntax Extensions

There are more tricks you could do with Perl syntax, including the `continue`
block and the `BEGIN` block. See the *perlsyn* and *perlmod* manpages.

References

Perl's references are similar to C's pointers, but in operation, they're more like
what you have in Pascal or Ada. A reference "points" to a memory location, but
because there's no pointer arithmetic or direct memory allocation and dealloca-
tion, you can be sure that any reference you have is a valid one. References allow
object-oriented programming and complex data structures, among other nifty
tricks. See the *perlreftut* and *perlref* manpages.

Complex Data Structures

References allow us to make complex data structures in Perl. For example, suppose you want a two-dimensional array? You can do that,† or you can do something much more interesting, like have an array of hashes, a hash of hashes, or a
hash of arrays of hashes.‡ See the *perldsc* (data-structures cookbook) and *perllol*
(lists of lists) manpages.

---

* Do you see why we didn't try to fit all of that into this book?

† Well, not really, but you can fake it so well that you'll hardly remember that there's a difference.

‡ Actually, you can't make any of these things; these are just verbal shorthands for what's really happening. What we call "an array of arrays" in Perl is really an array of *references to* arrays.

Object-Oriented Programming

Yes, Perl has objects; it's buzzword-compatible with all of those other languages. Object-oriented (OO) programming lets you create your own user-defined datatypes with associated abilities, using inheritance, overriding, and dynamic method lookup.*

Unlike some object-oriented languages, though, Perl doesn't force you to use objects. (Even many object-oriented modules can be used without understanding objects.) But if your program is going to be larger than N lines of code, it may be more efficient for the programmer (if a tiny bit slower at runtime) to make it object-oriented. No one knows the precise value of N, but we estimate it's around a few thousand or so. See the `perlobj` and `perlboot` manpages for a start, and Damian Conway's excellent *Object-Oriented Perl* (Manning Press) for more advanced information.

Anonymous Subroutines and Closures

Odd as it may sound at first, it can be useful to have a subroutine without a name. Such subroutines can be passed as parameters to other subroutines, or they can be accessed via arrays or hashes to make jump tables.

Closures are a powerful concept that comes to Perl from the world of Lisp. A closure is (roughly speaking) an anonymous subroutine with its own private data.

Tied Variables

Do you remember how the DBM hash (in Chapter 16) is "magically" connected to a file, so that accesses to the hash are really working with the corresponding DBM file? You can actually make any variable magical in that way. A tied variable may be accessed like any other, but using your own code behind the scenes. So you could make a scalar that is really stored on a remote machine, or an array that always stays sorted. See the *perltie* manpage.

Operator Overloading

You can redefine operators like addition, concatenation, comparison, or even the implicit string-to-number conversion with the `overload` module. This is how a module implementing complex numbers (for example) can let you multiply a complex number by 8 to get a complex number as a result.

---

* OO has its own set of jargon words. In fact, the terms used in any one OO language aren't even the same ones that are typically used in another.

Dynamic Loading

The basic idea of dynamic loading is that your program decides at runtime that it needs more functionality than what's currently available, so it loads it up and keeps running. You can always dynamically load Perl code, but it's even more interesting to dynamically load a binary extension.* This is how non-Perl modules are made.

Embedding

The reverse of dynamic loading (in a sense) is embedding.

Suppose you want to make a really cool word processor, and you start writing it in (say) C++.† Now, you decide you want the users to be able to use Perl's regular expressions for an extra-powerful search-and-replace feature, so you embed Perl into your program. Then you realize that you could open up some of the power of Perl to your users. A power user could write a subroutine in Perl that could become a menu item in your program. Users can customize the operation of your word processor by writing a little Perl. Now you open up a little space on your website where users can share and exchange these Perl snippets, and you've got thousands of new programmers extending what your program can do at no extra cost to your company. And how much do you have to pay Larry for all this? Nothing—see the licenses that come with Perl. Larry is a really nice guy. You should at least send him a thank-you note.

Although we don't know of such a word processor, some folks have already used this technique to make other powerful programs. One such example is Apache's `mod_perl`, which embeds Perl into an already-powerful web server. If you're thinking about embedding Perl, you should check out `mod_perl`; since it's all open source, you can see just how it works.

Converting Other Languages to Perl

If you've got old *sed* and *awk* programs that you wish were written in Perl, you're in luck. Not only can Perl do everything that those can do, there's also a conversion program available, and it's probably already installed on your system. Check the documentation for *s2p* (for converting from *sed*) or *a2p* (for converting from

---

* Dynamic loading of binary extensions is generally available if your system supports that. If it doesn't, you can compile the extensions statically—that is, you can make a Perl binary with the extension built in, ready for use.

† That's probably the language we'd use for writing a word processor. Hey, we love Perl, but we didn't swear an oath in blood to use no other language. When language X is the best choice, use language X. But often, X equals Perl.

awk).[*] Since programs don't write programs as well as people do, the results won't necessarily be the best Perl—but it's a start, and it's easy to tweak. The translated program may be faster or slower than the original, too. But after you've fixed up any gross inefficiencies in the machine-written Perl code, it should be comparable.

Do you have C algorithms you want to use from Perl? Well, you've still got some luck on your side; it's not too hard to put C code into a compiled module that can be used from Perl. In fact, any language that compiles to make object code can generally be used to make a module. See the *perlxs* manpage, and the `Inline` module, as well as the SWIG system.

Do you have a shell script that you want to convert to Perl? Your luck just ran out. There's no automatic way to convert shell to Perl. That's because the shell hardly does anything by itself; it spends all of its time running other programs. Sure, we could make a program that would mostly just call `system` for each line of the shell, but that would be much slower than just letting the shell do things in the first place. It really takes a human-level of intelligence to see how the shell's use of *cut*, *rm*, *sed*, *awk*, and *grep* can be turned into efficient Perl code. It's better to rewrite the shell script from scratch.

Converting find Command Lines to Perl

A common task for a system administrator is to recursively search the directory tree for certain items. On Unix, this is typically done with the *find* command. We can do that directly from Perl, too.

The *find2perl* command, which comes with Perl, takes the same arguments that *find* does. Instead of finding the requested items, however, the output of *find2perl* is a Perl program that finds them. Since it's a program, you can edit it for your own needs. (The program is written in a somewhat odd style.)

One useful argument that's available in *find2perl* but not in the standard *find* is the `-eval` option. This says that what follows it is actual Perl code that should be run each time that a file is found. When it's run, the current directory will be the directory in which some item is found, and `$_` will contain the item's name.

Here's an example of how you might use *find2perl*. Suppose that you're a system administrator on a Unix machine, and you want to find and remove all of the old files in the */tmp* directory.[†] Here's the command that writes the program to do that:

---

[*] If you're using *gawk* or *nawk* or some other variant, *a2p* may not be able to convert it. Both of these conversion programs were written long ago and have had few updates except when needed to keep working with new releases of Perl.

[†] This is a task typically done by a *cron* job at some early-morning hour each day.

```
$ find2perl /tmp -atime +14 -eval unlink >Perl-program
```

That command says to search in */tmp* (and recursively in subdirectories) for items whose atime (last access time) is at least 14 days ago. For each item, the program should run the Perl code `unlink`, which will use `$_` by default as the name of a file to remove. The output (redirected to go into the file *Perl-program*) is the program that does all of this. Now you merely need to arrange for it to be run as needed.

Command-line Options in Your Programs

If you'd like to make programs that take command-line options (like Perl's own **-w** for warnings, for example), there are modules that let you do this in a standard way. See the documentation for the `Getopt::Long` and `Getopt::Std` modules.

Embedded Documentation

Perl's own documentation is written in *pod* (plain-old documentation) format. You can embed this documentation in your own programs, and it can then be translated to text, HTML, or many other formats as needed. See the *perlpod* manpage.

More Ways to Open Filehandles

There are other modes to use in opening a filehandle; see the *perlopentut* manpage.

Locales and Unicode

It's a small world, after all. In order to work properly in places where even the alphabet is different, Perl has support for locales and Unicode.

Locales tell Perl how things are done locally. For example, does the character æ sort at the end of the alphabet, or between ä and å? And what's the local name for the third month? See the *perllocale* manpage (not to be confused with the *perllocal* manpage).

See the *perlunicode* manpage for the latest on how your version of Perl deals with Unicode. As of this writing, each new release of Perl has many new Unicode-related changes, but we hope things will settle down soon.

Threads and Forking

Perl now has support for threads. Although this is experimental (as of this writing), it can be a useful tool for some applications. Using `fork` (where it's available) is better supported; see the *perlfork* and *perlthrtut* manpages.

Graphical User Interfaces (GUIs)

A large and powerful module set is `Tk`, which lets you make on screen interfaces that work on more than one platform. See *Learning Perl/Tk* by Nancy Walsh or the upcoming *Mastering Perl/Tk* by Nancy Walsh and Steve Lidie (O'Reilly & Associates, Inc.).

And More...

If you check out the module list on CPAN, you'll find modules for even more purposes, from generating graphs and other images to downloading email, from figuring the amortization of a loan to figuring the time of sunset. New modules are added all the time, so Perl is even more powerful today than it was when we wrote this book. We can't keep up with it all, so we'll stop here.

Larry himself says he no longer keeps up with all of the development of Perl, because the Perl universe is big and keeps expanding. And he can't get bored with Perl, because he can always find another corner of this ever-expanding universe. And we suspect, neither will we. Thank you, Larry!

Index

Symbols

+ addition operator, 22
& ampersand, 57, 70
< > angle brackets, 18, 170
.= append operator, 29
@_ array variable, 60–62
= assignment operator, 28
@ at-sign, 45
-- autodecrement operator, 133
++ autoincrement operator, 133–135
` ` backquotes/backticks, 17, 197–201
\ backslash, 23, 110
=> big arrow, 79, 238
=~ binding operator, 117
^ caret anchor, 108
, comma, 80
{ } curly braces (see curly braces)
$_ default variable (see default variable)
< > diamond operator (see diamond operator)
/ division operator, 22
$ dollar sign (see dollar sign)
./ dot and slash, 14
. dot (see dot)
.. dot-dot, 177
" " double quotes (see double quotes)
_ _END_ _ marker, 138
** exponentiation operator, 22
_ _FILE_ _ and _ _LINE_ _ tokens, 154

_ filehandle, 166
// forward slashes, 100, 115
> greater-than sign, 150
- hyphen, 88, 105
< less-than sign, 150
#! line, 15, 17
-> little arrow, 80, 190
% modulus operator, 22, 236
* multiplication operator, 22
! negation operator (see negation operator)
&& operator, 142, 146
. operator, 24
| | operator (see OR operator)
( ) parentheses (see parentheses)
% percent sign (see percent sign)
| pipe, 149, 201
+ plus sign, 101
# pound sign, 14
? question mark, 101
**= raise to the power of operator, 29
.. range operator, 43
; semicolon (see semicolon)
' ' single quotes, 23
<=> spaceship operator, 215
[ ] square brackets, 103, 105
* star, 101
. string concatenate operator, 29
- subtraction operator, 22
?: ternary operator, 144

We'd like to hear your suggestions for improving our indexes. Send email to *index@oreilly.com*.

About the Author

Randal L. Schwartz is a two-decade veteran of the software industry. He is skilled in software design, system administration, security, technical writing, and training. Randal has coauthored the "must-have" standards: *Programming Perl, Learning Perl, Learning Perl for Win32 Systems,* and *Effective Perl Programming,* and is a regular columnist for *WebTechniques, PerformanceComputing, SysAdmin,* and *Linux* magazines. He is also a frequent contributor to the Perl newsgroups, and has moderated *comp.lang.perl.announce* since its inception. His offbeat humor and technical mastery have reached legendary proportions worldwide (but he probably started some of those legends himself). Randal's desire to give back to the Perl community inspired him to help create and provide initial funding for The Perl Institute. He is also a founding board member of the Perl Mongers (*perl.org*), the worldwide Perl grassroots advocacy organization. Since 1985, Randal has owned and operated Stonehenge Consulting Services, Inc. Randal can be reached for comment at *merlyn@stonehenge.com* or (503) 777-0095, and welcomes questions on Perl and other related topics.

Tom Phoenix has been working in the field of education since 1982. After more than thirteen years of dissections, explosions, work with interesting animals, and high-voltage sparks during his work at a science museum, he started teaching Perl classes for Stonehenge Consulting Services, where he's worked since 1996. Since then, he has traveled to many interesting locations, so you might see him soon at a Perl Mongers' meeting. When he has time, he answers questions on Usenet's *comp.lang.perl.misc* and *comp.lang.perl.moderated* newsgroups, and contributes to the development and usefulness of Perl. Besides his work with Perl, Perl hackers, and related topics, Tom spends his time on amateur cryptography and speaking Esperanto. His home is in Portland, Oregon.

Colophon

Our look is the result of reader comments, our own experimentation, and feedback from distribution channels. Distinctive covers complement our distinctive approach to technical topics, breathing personality and life into potentially dry subjects.

The animal featured on the cover of *Learning Perl,* Third Edition, is the llama, a relation of the camel native to the Andean range. Also included in this llamoid group is the domestic alpaca and their wild ancestors, the guanaco and the vicuna. Bones found in ancient human settlements suggest that domestication of the alpaca and llama dates back 4,500 years. In 1531, when Spanish conquistadors overran the Inca Empire in the high Andes, they found both animals present in great numbers. These llamas are suited for high mountain life; their hemoglobin can take in more oxygen than that of other mammals.

Llamas can weigh up to 300 pounds and are mainly used as beasts of burden. A packtrain may contain several hundred animals and can travel up to twenty miles per day. Llamas will carry loads up to fifty pounds, but have a tendency to be short-tempered and resort to spitting and biting to demonstrate displeasure. To the people of the Andes, llamas also provide meat, wool for clothing, hides for leather, and fat for candles. Their wool can also be braided into rope and rugs, and their dried dung is used for fuel.

Sarah Jane Shangraw and Ann Schirmer were the production editors for *Learning Perl,* Third Edition. Nicole Arigo copyedited the text. Sarah Jane Shangraw, Ann Schirmer, and Claire Cloutier provided quality control. Kimo Carter, Claire Cloutier, Ann Schirmer, and Sarah Jane Shangraw did interior page composition. Brenda Miller wrote the index.

Edie Freedman designed the cover of this book. The cover image is a 19th-century engraving from the Dover Pictorial Archive. Emma Colby produced the cover layout with QuarkXPress 4.1 using Adobe's ITC Garamond font.

Melanie Wang designed the interior layout based on a series design by Nancy Priest. The text and heading fonts are ITC Garamond Light and Garamond Book; the code font is Constant Willison. The illustrations that appear in the book were produced by Robert Romano and Jessamyn Read using Macromedia FreeHand 9 and Adobe Photoshop 6.

Whenever possible, our books use a durable and flexible lay-flat binding. If the page count exceeds this binding's limit, perfect binding is used.

How to stay in touch with O'Reilly

1. Visit Our Award-Winning Web Site

http://www.oreilly.com/

★ "Top 100 Sites on the Web" —*PC Magazine*
★ "Top 5% Web sites" —*Point Communications*
★ "3-Star site" —*The McKinley Group*

Our web site contains a library of comprehensive product information (including book excerpts and tables of contents), downloadable software, background articles, interviews with technology leaders, links to relevant sites, book cover art, and more. File us in your Bookmarks or Hotlist!

2. Join Our Email Mailing Lists

New Product Releases

To receive automatic email with brief descriptions of all new O'Reilly products as they are released, send email to:
ora-news-subscribe@lists.oreilly.com
Put the following information in the first line of your message (*not* in the Subject field):
subscribe ora-news

O'Reilly Events

If you'd also like us to send information about trade show events, special promotions, and other O'Reilly events, send email to:
ora-news-subscribe@lists.oreilly.com
Put the following information in the first line of your message (*not* in the Subject field):
subscribe ora-events

3. Get Examples from Our Books via FTP

There are two ways to access an archive of example files from our books:

Regular FTP

- ftp to:
  ftp.oreilly.com
  (login: anonymous
  password: your email address)
- Point your web browser to:
  ftp://ftp.oreilly.com/

FTPMAIL

- Send an email message to:
  ftpmail@online.oreilly.com
  (Write "help" in the message body)

4. Contact Us via Email

order@oreilly.com
To place a book or software order online. Good for North American and international customers.

subscriptions@oreilly.com
To place an order for any of our newsletters or periodicals.

books@oreilly.com
General questions about any of our books.

software@oreilly.com
For general questions and product information about our software. Check out O'Reilly Software Online at **http://software.oreilly.com/** for software and technical support information. Registered O'Reilly software users send your questions to: **website-support@oreilly.com**

cs@oreilly.com
For answers to problems regarding your order or our products.

booktech@oreilly.com
For book content technical questions or corrections.

proposals@oreilly.com
To submit new book or software proposals to our editors and product managers.

international@oreilly.com
For information about our international distributors or translation queries. For a list of our distributors outside of North America check out:
http://www.oreilly.com/distributors.html

5. Work with Us

Check out our website for current employment opportunites:
http://jobs.oreilly.com/

O'Reilly & Associates, Inc.
101 Morris Street, Sebastopol, CA 95472 USA
TEL   707-829-0515 or 800-998-9938
       (6am to 5pm PST)
FAX   707-829-0104

O'REILLY®

TO ORDER: **800-998-9938** • **order@oreilly.com** • **http://www.oreilly.com/**
OUR PRODUCTS ARE AVAILABLE AT A BOOKSTORE OR SOFTWARE STORE NEAR YOU.
FOR INFORMATION: **800-998-9938** • **707-829-0515** • **info@oreilly.com**

International Distributors

UK, EUROPE, MIDDLE EAST AND AFRICA (EXCEPT FRANCE, GERMANY, AUSTRIA, SWITZERLAND, LUXEMBOURG, AND LIECHTENSTEIN)

INQUIRIES
O'Reilly UK Limited
4 Castle Street
Farnham
Surrey, GU9 7HS
United Kingdom
Telephone: 44-1252-711776
Fax: 44-1252-734211
Email: information@oreilly.co.uk

ORDERS
Wiley Distribution Services Ltd.
1 Oldlands Way
Bognor Regis
West Sussex PO22 9SA
United Kingdom
Telephone: 44-1243-843294
UK Freephone: 0800-243207
Fax: 44-1243-843302 (Europe/EU orders)
or 44-1243-843274 (Middle East/Africa)
Email: cs-books@wiley.co.uk

FRANCE

INQUIRIES & ORDERS
Éditions O'Reilly
18 rue Séguier
75006 Paris, France
Tel: 1-40-51-71-89
Fax: 1-40-51-72-26
Email: france@oreilly.fr

GERMANY, SWITZERLAND, AUSTRIA, LUXEMBOURG, AND LIECHTENSTEIN

INQUIRIES & ORDERS
O'Reilly Verlag
Balthasarstr. 81
D-50670 Köln, Germany
Telephone: 49-221-973160-91
Fax: 49-221-973160-8
Email: anfragen@oreilly.de (inquiries)
Email: order@oreilly.de (orders)

CANADA (FRENCH LANGUAGE BOOKS)
Les Éditions Flammarion ltée
375, Avenue Laurier Ouest
Montréal (Québec) H2V 2K3
Tel: 00-1-514-277-8807
Fax: 00-1-514-278-2085
Email: info@flammarion.qc.ca

HONG KONG
City Discount Subscription Service, Ltd.
Unit A, 6th Floor, Yan's Tower
27 Wong Chuk Hang Road
Aberdeen, Hong Kong
Tel: 852-2580-3539
Fax: 852-2580-6463
Email: citydis@ppn.com.hk

KOREA
Hanbit Media, Inc.
Chungmu Bldg. 210
Yonnam-dong 568-33
Mapo-gu
Seoul, Korea
Tel: 822-325-0397
Fax: 822-325-9697
Email: hant93@chollian.dacom.co.kr

PHILIPPINES
Global Publishing
G/F Benavides Garden
1186 Benavides Street
Manila, Philippines
Tel: 632-254-8949/632-252-2582
Fax: 632-734-5060/632-252-2733
Email: globalp@pacific.net.ph

TAIWAN
O'Reilly Taiwan
1st Floor, No. 21, Lane 295
Section 1, Fu-Shing South Road
Taipei, 106 Taiwan
Tel: 886-2-27099669
Fax: 886-2-27038802
Email: mori@oreilly.com

INDIA
Shroff Publishers & Distributors Pvt. Ltd.
12, "Roseland", 2nd Floor
180, Waterfield Road, Bandra (West)
Mumbai 400 050
Tel: 91-22-641-1800/643-9910
Fax: 91-22-643-2422
Email: spd@vsnl.com

CHINA
O'Reilly Beijing
SIGMA Building, Suite B809
No. 49 Zhichun Road
Haidian District
Beijing, China PR 100080
Tel: 86-10-8809-7475
Fax: 86-10-8809-7463
Email: beijing@oreilly.com

JAPAN
O'Reilly Japan, Inc.
Yotsuya Y's Building
7 Banch 6, Honshio-cho
Shinjuku-ku
Tokyo 160-0003 Japan
Tel: 81-3-3356-5227
Fax: 81-3-3356-5261
Email: japan@oreilly.com

SINGAPORE, INDONESIA, MALAYSIA AND THAILAND
TransQuest Publishers Pte Ltd
30 Old Toh Tuck Road #05-02
Sembawang Kimtrans Logistics Centre
Singapore 597654
Tel: 65-4623112
Fax: 65-4625761
Email: wendiw@transquest.com.sg

ALL OTHER ASIAN COUNTRIES
O'Reilly & Associates, Inc.
101 Morris Street
Sebastopol, CA 95472 USA
Tel: 707-829-0515
Fax: 707-829-0104
Email: order@oreilly.com

AUSTRALIA
Woodslane Pty., Ltd.
7/5 Vuko Place
Warriewood NSW 2102
Australia
Tel: 61-2-9970-5111
Fax: 61-2-9970-5002
Email: info@woodslane.com.au

NEW ZEALAND
Woodslane New Zealand, Ltd.
21 Cooks Street (P.O. Box 575)
Waganui, New Zealand
Tel: 64-6-347-6543
Fax: 64-6-345-4840
Email: info@woodslane.com.au

ARGENTINA
Distribuidora Cuspide
Suipacha 764
1008 Buenos Aires
Argentina
Phone: 5411-4322-8868
Fax: 5411-4322-3456
Email: libros@cuspide.com

O'REILLY®